Globe Law
and Business

Business Families and Family Businesses

The STEP Handbook for Advisers,
Third Edition

Consulting Editor **Clare Stirzaker**

Consulting editor
Clare Stirzaker

Managing director
Sian O'Neill

Business Families and Family Businesses: The STEP Handbook for Advisers, Third Edition **is published by**

Globe Law and Business Ltd
3 Mylor Close
Horsell
Woking
Surrey GU21 4DD
United Kingdom
Tel: +44 20 3745 4770
www.globelawandbusiness.com

Printed and bound by CPI Group (UK) Ltd, Croydon CR0 4YY, United Kingdom

Business Families and Family Businesses: The STEP Handbook for Advisers, Third Edition

ISBN 9781837230679
EPUB ISBN 9781837230686
Adobe PDF ISBN 9781837230693

Table of contents

Part III. Succession

About STEP

STEP is a global professional body, with more than 22,000 members comprising lawyers, accountants, trustees and other practitioners that help families plan for their futures.

Its mission is to inspire confidence in families planning their assets across generations by setting and upholding high professional standards, informing public policy, promoting education and connecting practitioners globally to share knowledge and best practice.

STEP members help families plan for their futures, from drafting a will to advising on issues concerning international families, protection of the vulnerable, family businesses and philanthropic giving. Full STEP members, identified by the letters 'TEP' (Trust and Estate Practitioner) after their name, are internationally recognised as experts in their field, with proven qualifications and experience.

STEP's Business Families Special Interest Group provides an international forum of debate, education and support on issues related to family businesses and business families. It focuses on what makes business families distinct, their particular challenges and how best to address them. The Group serves as a platform for education, training, thought leadership and connecting with others who specialise in this area. The group is open to both STEP members and non-members with an interest in this area.

Find out more at www.step.org

Foreword

Clare Stirzaker
Boodle Hatfield LLP

Since the second edition of this book was published in 2018, the world has experienced some seismic changes – COVID-19, wars, economic downturn and a more urgent focus on climate change are just some of the key events that have created far greater geopolitical risk.

Family businesses are having to grapple with such challenges not just from a business perspective but also in the context of their succession planning. For many this has sharpened their focus on preserving their wealth to provide for future generations, but for others it has caused them to reflect on how their wealth can best help others in society with a growth of interest in philanthropy and impact investment.

In preparing this third edition, we have aimed to look at developments within the approach to family-business advising, particularly taking account of the current geopolitical backdrop of change and the shift in attitude in a growing number of clients towards succession, philanthropy and investments.

However, for those new to the field we have ensured that there remains ongoing guidance on:

- how to understand the unique nature of family businesses;
- typical family dynamics that impact succession;
- the power of governance in supporting good ownership and management;
- the typical stages of the family business and the key structuring, commercial and finance issues that need to be borne in mind; and
- the key non-succession risk issues that will invariably arise and the different legal and non-legal approaches to tackling such problems.

Supporting families in developing a clear succession plan in respect of their business and wealth, and designing the right governance and legal framework for them is critical to helping families manage both their own internal and external risk factors. This book should help you identify how you best adapt and develop your personal approach to advising on these topics, and support families in thinking more deeply and communicating more effectively on wealth transition and distribution.

Understanding the family business mindset: an evolutionary approach

Justin B Craig
Tecnológico de Monterrey; Kellogg School of Management; Bond University
Catharina C Jecklin
Bond University

"There is nothing more practical than a good theory" – Kurt Lewin[1]

1. Introduction

Family businesses are so defined because of family. It seems obvious. But the scholarly debate over a universally accepted definition of this term has occupied pundits for decades. Relatedly, the field remains devoid of an accepted way to capture the generational transition mindset synonymous with family and the business transformation required of long-lived organisations. It is these concurrent evolving *foci* that drive our introduction of an evolutionary approach to understanding the family business mindset.

In the sections that follow, after a brief discussion of paradigm development, we distinguish between orthodox versus heterodox economics approaches and competence-based versus contractual theories. Our comparative reasoning enables us to establish that heterodox economics provides an approach to answer the quandary at hand, as it delivers a practical, largely overlooked, way to understand the family business mindset. We then position evolutionary theories at our epicentre and adopt Nelson and Winter's[2] seminal Lamarckian-inspired evolutionary arguments.[3] We complement this with the notion that the trust literature offers us a way to integrate the role of trust and loyalty to better understand how families transition and businesses transform successfully. Next, we bring our conversation to life by sharing firsthand knowledge of a generational family firm that is mid-process in both its transition and transformation, and describe several of its novel, idiosyncratic approaches. We conclude with an invitation to stakeholders to consider jettisoning, or at least

1 A Marrow, *The Practical Theorist* (Knopf, 1969).
2 R Nelson and S Winter, *An Evolutionary Theory of Economic Change* (Harvard University Press, 1985).
3 Lamarckian and Darwinian evolutionary theories are different because Lamarck thought that organisms changed out of need and after a change in the environment, and Darwin believed organisms changed by random chance when they were born and before there was a change in the environment.

complementing, their current worldview of the family business mindset and to add some of their intellectual bandwidth to this conversation.

2. Previous literature

2.1 Paradigm development

The quest for legitimacy for family business as a credible research pursuit has followed predictable pathways[4] and benefited from adapting accepted theoretical approaches.[5] For instance, research camps formed around pioneering scholars who were able to elbow their way into the 'better' journals. Notable among these figures were Mike Lubatkin and Bill Schulze (agency), Ian McMillan and contemporaries (resource-based view) and Jim Davis and colleagues (stewardship). Arguably, this was the catalyst for inquiry into this space from researchers in multiple disciplines; it was not that the publication flood gates opened, but that others became intrigued. Consequently, established 'names' contributed tentatively to what was increasingly identified as a fertile research pursuit. For example, Danny Miller and Shaker Zahra, 'influencers' before the term was popularised, were converts who brought with them serious strike power. Similarly, Mike Hitt and Duane Ireland hitched their management discipline ponies to this figurative post at about the same time, and Howard Aldrich brought with him a new flock of disciples from sociology. But, despite the considerable influence and publications pedigree of these scholars, the opportunity to deliver a practical approach to the family business mindset was overlooked. Socio-emotional wealth (SEW) proponents, with their behavioural agency angle, temporarily filled the void but, given the ongoing debate and confusion, and despite the initial enthusiasm, many remain unconvinced that SEW delivers as hoped.[6] This chapter delivers a timely, and overdue, solution.

It is an important time for this development. Family business as a research pursuit is criticised for lacking a defendable paradigm.[7] Moreover, ongoing disagreement regarding the definition of what constitutes a family business is an indicator that family business is a field of inquiry with relatively low

---

4 TS Kuhn, "Second Thoughts on Paradigms" in *The Structure of Scientific Theories*, ed F Suppe (University of Illinois Press, 1974); Ken Moores, "Paradigms and Theory Building in the Domain of Business Families", *Family Business Review* 22, no 2 (2009).

5 Justin B Craig, Ken Moores, Carole Howorth and Panikkos Poutziouris, "Family Business Research at a Tipping Point Threshold", *Journal of Management & Organization* 15, no 3 (2009).

6 Justin B Craig and Scott Newbert, "Reconsidering socioemotional wealth: A Smithian-inspired socio-economic theory of decision-making in the family firm", *Journal of Family Business Strategy* 11, no 4 (2020), www.sciencedirect.com/science/article/abs/pii/S1877858520300802?via%3Dihub.

7 R Duane Ireland, Christopher R Reutzel and Justin W Webb, "Entrepreneurship Research in *AMJ*: What Has Been Published, and What Might the Future Hold?", *Academy of Management Journal* 48, no 4 (2005); Pramodita Sharma, Frank Hoy, Joseph H Astrachan and Matti Koiranen, "The Practice-Driven Evolution of Family Business Education", *Journal of Business Research* 60, no 10 (2007).

paradigmatic development.[8] Further, divergent opinions as to the type of research scholars should complete to examine important questions, including the question of how a construct should be defined, are also symptomatic of low paradigm development.[9] This is not an abnormal problem in itself. Rather, it is affirmation of a necessary rite of passage in the quest for academic legitimacy.[10] Our proposal of a competence-based approach rooted in heterodox economics addresses many of the above issues.

2.2 Heterodox economics

Heterodox economics is defined primarily in terms of opposition to orthodox economics; the latter is guided by the prevailing assumptions of utility maximisation in a static equilibrium.[11] Although heterodoxy in economics remains a widely debated term, its origins can be traced back to Adam Smith's seminal reflections from his 1776 work *Wealth of Nations*.[12] Smith proposed that specialisation enabled labourers to improve their skills through learning-by-doing, which cumulated in a "virtuous circle of economic growth and prosperity".[13] With that assertion, Smith built the bedrock for generations of heterodox thinkers. The quest to theorise dynamic, ever-changing internal production processes, however, fell behind with the rise of the neoclassical focus on static, external markets.[14] Orthodox neoclassical theorists are more concerned with a firm's cost and revenue structure than with the firm as an organisation. Yet the main constraint of this focus on financial equilibrium is its inability to acknowledge and consider the role of time and, relatedly, how to deal with uncertainty, change and growth. Orthodox theories, therefore, operate solely on calculable risk assumptions, and ignore uncertainty beyond numeric probability. Heterodox approaches, in contrast, place the things that make up the firm in a dynamic environment where a continuously evolving complex of individuals with idiosyncratic yet mouldable needs, capabilities and perceptions are the very reason for the firm's existence.[15] Accordingly, orthodox and heterodox inference bring forth two fundamentally different theories of the firm.

---

8 Jess H Chua, James J Chrisman and Pramodita Sharma, "Defining the Family Business by Behavior", *Entrepreneurship Theory and Practice* 23, no 4 (1999). Their definition is often cited: "[F]amily business is defined as a business governed and/or managed with the intention to shape and pursue the vision of the business held by a dominant coalition controlled by members of the same family or a small number of families in a manner that is potentially sustainable across generations of the family or families" (p25).

9 Ireland, Reutzel and Webb, see note 7.

10 Kuhn, see note 4.

11 Geoffrey M Hodgson, "Debating the Future of Heterodox Economics", *Journal of Economic Issues* 55, no 3 (2021), https://doi.org/10.1080/00213624.2021.1945874.

12 Adam Smith, *An Inquiry into the Nature and Causes of the Wealth of Nations*, ed E Cannan (Modern Library, 1994).

13 Geoffrey M Hodgson, "Evolutionary and competence-based theories of the firm", *Journal of Economic Studies* 25, no 1 (1998), p36.

14 *Ibid.*

15 FH Knight, *Risk, Uncertainty, and Profit* (Houghton Mifflin, 1921).

2.3 Competence versus contractual theories

From the orthodox camp of economics emerged contractual-based theories of the firm; the heterodox school of thought, in contrast, operates predominantly on competence-based theories (also termed resource-based or capabilities theories). Orthodox contractarian theories, with transaction cost-based theories from the Coase-Williamson tradition among the most prominent,[16] reduce their analysis of the firm to assessing static costs related to complete or incomplete "formulating, enforcing, and monitoring contracts".[17] From a heterodox perspective, this limited view of the firm poses severe problems.[18] A focus on cost minimisation in a static environment, for example, ignores the seizing of opportunities through dynamic capabilities in a long-term perspective. Particularly when examining the unique mindset of long-term-oriented family firms,[19] this limitation creates significant challenges. Specifically, contractual theories disregard disequilibrium situations, and with it the capabilities of long-term-oriented companies to use foresight and planning to take advantage of such disequilibria.[20] Relatedly, contractual theories assess corporate governance structures detached from production and innovation processes.

Most of these problems hinge on the contractarian theorist's belief that firms differ but individuals do not.[21] The tradition's main flaw, then, is that individuals are not only assumed to be a given, but they are also believed to all be "the same, representative rational individual",[22] not influenced by the environment and with perpetual access to knowledge of how to solve problems. Consequently, contractual theories overlook completely the existence and necessity of non-contractual elements, such as trust and loyalty, along with the existence and necessity of continual learning.[23]

Competence-based theories, on the other hand, see "the existence, structure and boundaries of the firm as explained in some way by the associated existence of individual or team competences – such as skills and tacit knowledge".[24] We claim that both non-contractual elements and the capacity to learn are key concepts in understanding the mindset required to consider how families

---

16 RH Coase, "The nature of the firm", *Economica* IV (1937); Oliver E Williamson, *Markets and hierarchies: Analysis and Anti-Trust Implications: A Study in the Economics of Internal Organization* (Free Press, 1975); Oliver E Williamson, *The Economic Institutions of Capitalism: Firms, Markets, Relational Contracting* (Macmillan, 1985).

17 Hodgson, see note 13, p26.

18 *Ibid.*

19 Justin B Craig and Ken Moores, *Leading a Family Business: Best Practices for Long-term Stewardship* (Praeger, 2017); GT Lumpkin, Keith H Brigham and Todd W Moss, "Long-Term Orientation: Implications for the Entrepreneurial Orientation and Performance of Family Businesses", *Entrepreneurship and Regional Development* 22, no 3–4 (2010); Danny Miller and Isabelle Le Breton-Miller, *Managing for the Long Run: Lessons in Competitive Advantage from Great Family Businesses* (Harvard Business Press, 2005).

20 Hodgson, see note 13.

21 M Douglas, "Converging on autonomy: Antropoloty and institutional economics", in *Organization Theory: from Chester Barnard to the Present and Beyond* (Oxford University Press, 1990).

22 *Ibid*, p102.

23 Hodgson, see note 13.

24 *Ibid*, p25.

transition and businesses transform. Hence, drawing from competence-based theories enables us to build our conceptual model, which recognises that stewards with different viewpoints and capabilities steer the ship.

We suggest that a key feature of the competence-based view of the firm is its attempt to grasp theoretically the notion of organisational learning, and with it the notion of growth. The common denominator for embarking on this endeavour, again, is the acknowledgement that individuals differ. Challenges to theories of the firm can therefore not be reduced to information asymmetry in the narrow sense of imperfect information flow, as contractarians do, but ought to account for interpretative ambiguity that surfaces only through shared experience.[25] Through shared experience, mental models can be put to the test, indicating that learning is destruction as much as it is construction.[26] In her *The Theory of the Growth of the Firm,* Edith Penrose saw tacit knowledge as a cornerstone of organisational growth, and alluded to the fact that experience cannot be separated from individuals.[27] Despite this inseparability, organisational learning through shared experiences manifests in a firm having a memory that is larger than its individuals' memory components.[28] Organisational knowledge and change, therefore, "emerges as a property of the learning system and is shaped by the interaction among the various learning processes that constitute the organization".[29] This concept of learning is incompatible with rational optimisation and equilibrium in traditional contractarian theories of the firm.[30] Importantly, contrary to orthodox counter-arguments that knowledge can be acquired on the market, purchasing the required knowledge requires prior, interpretative knowledge of *what* to buy. Put differently, gaining the right externally contracted knowledge requires internal judgement based on imperfect information. Thus, in our search for a practical approach of family firm mindset, the integration of (un)learning through interorganisational exchange is critical. To develop our argument, we draw from Nelson and Winter's evolutionary theory of the firm.

2.4 Evolutionary theory of the firm

Nelson and Winter's evolutionary theory of the firm is a hybrid theory resulting from the integration of two theoretical approaches.[31] The first theoretical foundation is rooted in evolutionary principles and sees the firm evolving as it:

---

25 *Ibid.*

26 Chris Argyris and Donald A Schön, *Organizational Learning: A Theory of Action Perspective* (Addison-Wesley, 1978).

27 Edith T Penrose, "The firm in theory" in *The Theory of the Growth of the Firm* (ME Sharpe, 1959).

28 Nelson and Winter, see note 2.

29 Giovanni Dosi and Luigi Marengo, "Some Elements of an Evolutionary Theory of Organizational Competences" in *Evolutionary Concepts in Contemporary Economics*, ed RW England (University of Michigan Press, 1994), p162.

30 Hodgson, see note 13.

31 Nelson and Winter, see note 2.

(i) develops routines or repetitive activities that ensure the coherence between individual and collective behaviour; and (ii) mutates and is involved in continually searching behaviours that consist of exploring and testing new routines and thus introducing new characteristics into the firm. The second theoretical premise relies on the existence of cognitive (and behavioural) mechanisms of individuals and "the development of a collective knowledge base that encompasses the establishment of rules, habits, norms and codes".[32]

This approach offers the advantage of providing an explanation of three key issues crucial to a theoretical understanding of the firm: (i) how the firm can be defined (ie, in terms of the set of competences that it controls); (ii) why the firm differs from other firms (ie, because of the reliance on different routines and competences that are specific and that cannot be transferred); and (iii) the dynamics of the firm (ie, through the combined mechanisms of selection and variation that work on the body of existing routines).[33] The Nelson-Winter approach thus stresses dynamic transformation and change.[34] In Figure 1, we share our conceptual model. Noteworthy is how Nelson and Winter's approach is integrated with accepted stewardship concepts[35] and long-term orientation,[36] which position individuals, family, owners and managers as stewards[37] in the well-established family business three-circle paradigm.[38]

Figure 1: Conceptual model

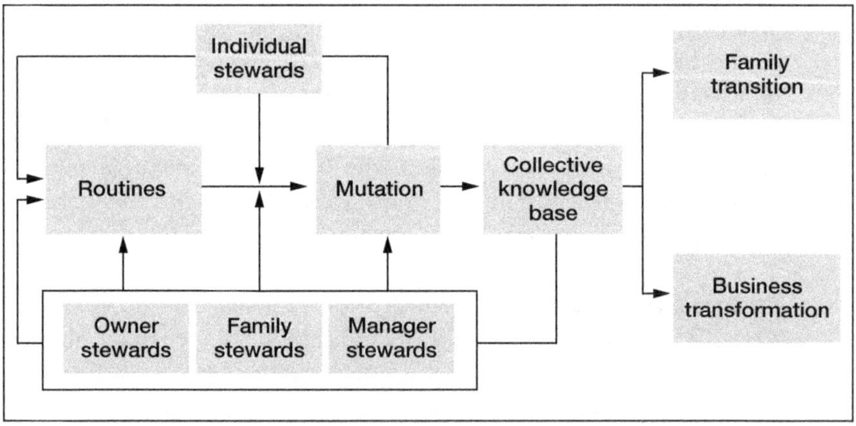

32 NJ Foss *et al*, "Is There a Pilot in the Evolutionary Firm?", *Competence, Governance, and Entrepreneurship* (Oxford University Press, 2000): p96.
33 B Coriat and O Weinstein, *Les Nouvelles Théories de L'entreprise* (Le Livre de Poche, 1995); Foss *et al*, *ibid.*
34 Hodgson, see note 11.
35 Donald O Neubaum, Christopher H Thomas, Clay Dibrell and Justin B Craig, "Stewardship Climate Scale: An Assessment of Reliability and Validity", *Family Business Review* 30, no 1 (2016).
36 Lumpkin, Brigham and Moss, see note 19.
37 Craig and Moores, see note 19.
38 Moores, see note 4.

2.5 The integral role of trust and loyalty

We argue that the interplay among (i) defining components of the firm; (ii) why the firm differs from others; and (iii) how it operates depends on trust and loyalty.[39] Although we acknowledge that explicit, written agreements are necessary for any contractual exchange, these are always complemented by non-contractual elements.[40] In the context of employment contracts, for instance, non-explicit contractual elements are often explained through the psychological contract, referring to an "individual's belief in mutual obligations between that person and another party".[41] Psychological contracts are formed by two parties' beliefs about promises made that result in obligations in a two-way exchange relationship.[42] Consequently, each party feels bound to the other by their own perceived obligations, formed on promises and expectations as rooted in the trust literature. Therefore, without trust as a relational governance component of the firm,[43] the organisation's operational intricacies and its *façade* change. Indeed, in our research projects focused on better understanding the family business mindset, trust was omnipresent as a key ingredient.[44] Among the reasons are the close-knit social ties of family firm leaders, as these individuals "are emotionally committed to the long-run survival and reputation of their firms as their fortunes, careers, and their personal honour".[45] Therefore, adopting our evolutionary approach, we claim that family firms operate on a trust-centred approach to idiosyncratically: (i) build a collective knowledge base among family and non-family members; and (ii) orchestrate the evolutionary principles of routine optimisation and mutation exploration among the incumbent and new generations.

Moreover, the collective family members' "willingness to be vulnerable",[46] we argue, is a fundamental ingredient that lubricates business-owning families' ability to *transition* from one generation to the next by simultaneously *transforming* the firm through either expansion or consolidation and integration that is uniquely tailored to inclusion of the new generation.

---

39 J David Lewis and Andrew Weigert, "Trust as a Social Reality" *Social Forces* 63, no 4 (1985), https://doi.org/10.2307/2578601; Niklas Luhmann, *Trust and power*, ed Michael King and Christian Morgner (Polity Press, 2017), https://content.e-bookshelf.de/media/reading/L-10880467-29bef71368.pdf.

40 E Durkheim, *The Division of Labour in Society*, translated from the French edition of 1893 by WD Halls with an introduction by Lewis Coser (Macmillan, 1984).

41 Denise M Rousseau, "Psychological Contract Inventory Technical Report", 2000, Heinz School of Public Policy and Graduate School of Industrial Administration, p1.

42 Carol Atkinson, "Trust and the Psychological Contract", *Employee Relations* 29, no 3 (2007); David E Guest and Neil Conway, "Communicating the Psychological Contract: An Employer Perspective", *Human Resource Management Journal* 12, no 2 (2002).

43 Zhi Cao and Fabrice Lumineau, "Revisiting the Interplay Between Contractual and Relational Governance: A Qualitative and Meta-Analytic Investigation", *Journal of Operations Management* 33–34, no 1 (January 2015), https://doi.org/10.1016/j.jom.2014.09.009.

44 Lloyd Steier and Miriam Muethel, "Trust and family businesses" in *The Sage Handbook of Family Business*, ed Leif Melin, Mattias Nordqvist and Pramodita Sharma (Sage, 2014).

45 Isabelle Le Breton-Miller and Danny Miller, "Agency vs. Stewardship in Public Family Firms: A Social Embeddedness Reconciliation", *Entrepreneurship Theory and Practice* 33, no 6 (2009), p1171.

46 Roger C Mayer, James H Davis and F David Schoorman, "An Integrative Model of Organizational Trust", *Academy of Management Review* 20, no 3 (July 1995), p712, https://doi.org/10.2307/258792.

3. Living case example

To illustrate and provide preliminary application of our thesis, we adopt a single-case study embedded in a longitudinal, participatory-action research project.[47] A case study is considered best practice for exploring emergent theoretical frameworks and complex phenomena.[48] Still, given our ambition to bring the constructs of our evolutionary theory to life, the living case-family example had to meet certain conditions. More specifically, the business operations needed to be sufficiently complex and mature, ideally with a multinational focus and omni-channel selling. Further, the family needed to have successfully navigated at least one generational transition and be large enough to provide an adequately rich context for our arguments. The vertically integrated multi-generation business we introduce below adequately fits these business and family criteria.

3.1 Case family business

Our case family business is in the textile and apparel industry, has more than 1,000 employees, and is currently transitioning from the second to the third generation. The incumbent second generation numbers 11 siblings, with all but one still living. Five of the remaining 10 have leadership roles in the business. The 29 third-generation members, meanwhile, are between 12 and 44 years of age; four of them have full-time roles in the business. Others have part-time or contributing roles, and some have shadow family governance roles and/or are studying or pursuing careers outside the family business. One of the incumbent generation's motivations to take a proactive stance regarding transition and continuity is to provide opportunities after the incumbent generation's departure to engage in the family legacy and the current and future operating business(es), as we outline in more detail below. The vertically integrated operation manufactures most of the business's products, which are sold in multiple countries through a variety of channels including catalogue sales, physical presence (company-owned and through select major retail chains) and web portals.

3.2 Drawing a line between family and business

To efficiently and effectively distinguish between family (ie, that which is *transitioning*) and business (ie, that which is *transforming*) in governance and structural terms, the family designed a comprehensive family and business organisational structure chart. In it, the family occupied the upper section, and

---

47 Robert K Yin, *Case Study Research: Design and Methods*, 4th ed (Sage, 2009); David L Brown and Rajesh Tandon, "Ideology and Political Economy in Inquiry: Action Research and Participatory Research", *The Journal of Applied Behavioral Science* 19, no 3 (1983).

48 Kathleen M Eisenhardt, "Building Theories from Case Study Research", *Academy of Management Review* 14, no 4 (1989).

the business occupied the lower section. A dotted line divided the two sections, with the family labelled 'Church' and the business 'State' (Figure 2).

Figure 2: Church and state model applied to living case

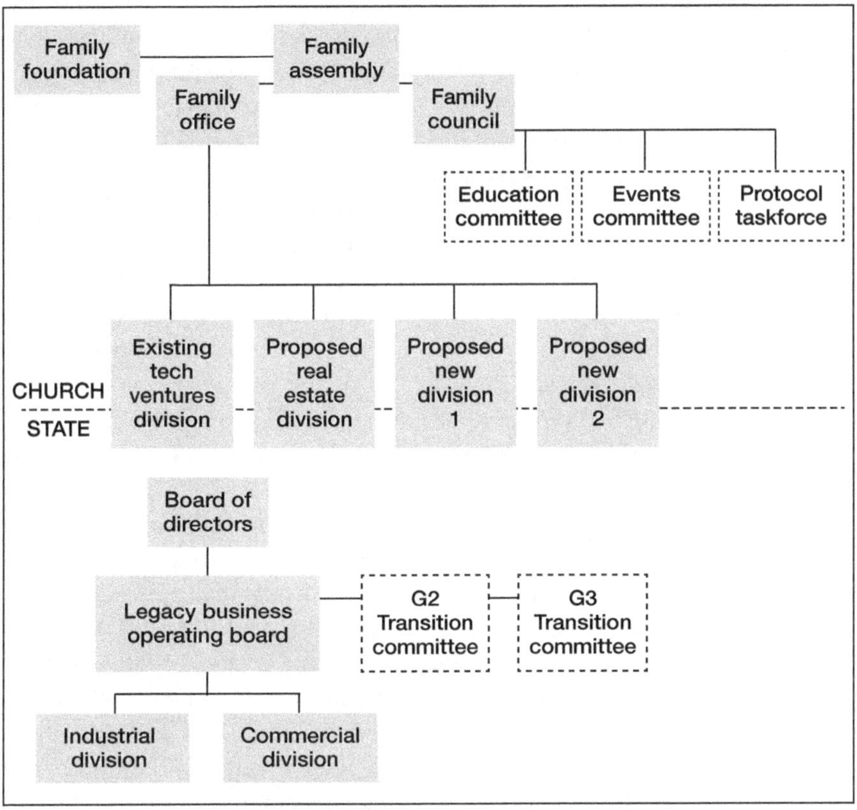

As can be seen in Figure 2, forums were designed to ensure next-generation members were offered participation opportunities. Importantly, the incumbent generation demonstrated their commitment to the *transition* and *transformation* process through their proactive stance and championship of the approach. Having a clear, accepted and easy-to-interpret model was necessary to build alignment within and between the 10 second-generation and 29 third-generation individuals, who had differing levels and types of exposure to the family forums and business operations. This also provided a way to transition the next generation into roles. A good example is the shadow role next-generation members can hold in the legacy business operating board, which led to development of the G3 Transition Committee and ultimately responsibility for a stand-alone division (details not included in the figure). The family signalled to other next-generation members that they would be considered for future opportunities by including the 'proposed new divisions' in the model.

This overall approach is consistent with how Nelson and Winter (1982) position the importance of routines and mutation in the development of a collective knowledge base. Recall that Nelson and Winter's evolutionary theory thesis considered how the firm: (i) develops routines or repetitive activities that ensure coherence between individual and collective behaviour; and (ii) mutates and continually engages in behaviours that consist of exploring and testing new routines and therefore introducing new characteristics into the firm. The scholars' second theoretical premise is the development of a collective knowledge base that encompasses establishment of rules, habits, norms and codes and is viewed as reliant on the existence of cognitive (and behavioural) mechanisms of individuals. In this example, a new coterie of individuals (G3) – with a mandate to search for, test and introduce new routines – is transitioning in as both groups (G2 and G3) respond to challenges and jointly work to transform the business.

As is evident from how G2 introduced structures and processes in their transition, they unknowingly addressed the three key issues crucial to a theoretical understanding of the firm. Specifically, they: (i) were cognisant to ensure alignment in how their firm is defined, inculcating the next-generation leadership in terms of the set of competences that they control, and how these needed to be reconfigured in the future; (ii) intentionally provided rising leaders meaningful understanding experiences and made clear why their firm differs from others, and this was particularly evident in the necessity to comprehend the intangible idiosyncratic resources rooted in the founder's values and beliefs, and the incumbents' interpretation of these; and (iii) had the advantage of having the next generation appreciate the dynamics of the firm because they were exposed to the challenges and responses to the drama associated with two rare events (ie, the COVID-19 pandemic and a national election, which challenged the familiar economic agenda significantly). This provided opportunity for next-generation individuals to extend their family business mindset and participate in shaping, and ultimately owning, the transformed business.

The Nelson-Winter approach stresses dynamic transformation and change.[49] The intention was that G3 members first thoroughly grasp how the routines and norms manifest in their various operational roles, which gave way to their being able to consider how these would need to evolve (ie, continue to mutate) on their watch. Their input and responsibility (ie, to the transition and transformation process) evolved (is evolving) over time, and with an intentional escalation of responsibility. The incumbent generation identified the need to

---

49 Hodgson, see note 11.

develop the next generation as strategic thinkers and orchestrated this through various formal and informal roles. This also facilitated throughout the family and the business systems the opportunity to build trust within and between groups of vested stakeholders.

To further facilitate clear understanding of the various roles and responsibilities for the broader family community, the family overhauled the existing Family Protocol and Shareholders' Agreement, both of which had been written by the second generation. The former was a multi-year process undertaken by an assigned third-generation taskforce that was diligent and, importantly, conscious of the need to collect detailed information from family and business stakeholders. Updates of the document were shared and family input included throughout the exhaustive process. The purpose, structure and process were ultimately detailed for each forum included in the Church and State model. Linkages back to the founder's philosophy were collected from multiple sources and the family included a letter from G2. The review of the Shareholders' Agreement was being undertaken at the time of writing with a taskforce of G2 and G3 assembled to work on what is, arguably, the most influential of all family and business documents.

As part of the evolving processes to align around a shared mindset, family members rallied behind a positioning statement: "One Family of Eleven Families – Aligned, United, Committed". Throughout, they adapted and applied proven frameworks to guide them. They are committed, moreover, to seek and share experiences from other families. This resulted in several anchor 'mindset' statements that serve as constant reminders. For example, the next generation are instructed that a role in the legacy business is an option but not the only option, and that pathways are being developed to enable meaningful contributions – with the caveat that individuals need to be ready, willing and capable to contribute in whatever capacity. To ensure that as a collective they are not thinking too short term, at one point they also committed to a '2121 Horizon'. That is, a 100-year orientation. Next-generation education programmes reinforce the importance of understanding the value of values, keeping the philosophies of previous and current generations but not the detail, in order to continue differently. Individuals are celebrated for their individual contributions and encouraged to *become a voice not an echo.*

Of course, this process has not been without challenges. However, we can report that there is current consensus within and between generations, and that trust is being developed through, among other aspects, the simple understanding of the importance of appreciating individual differences. That is very consistent with the theoretical arguments posed by competence-theory exponents, which ratifies our approach and gives us impetus to continue to fine-tune it.

4. Synthesis and conclusion

Our evolutionary framework, grounded in heterodox theoretical views of the firm, explains the mindset required by family firms as they *transition* across generations while they simultaneously *transform* the business. We propose that both transition and transformation processes occur based on a unique interplay between routine and mutation assessments characterised by trust, loyalty and a collective knowledge base. By offering a conceptual framework that operates on these non-contractual elements of trust, loyalty and organisational learning as prominent in heterodox theory, we aim to remind family firm practitioners, advisers and scholars that the field should look beyond current explanations of why family firms behave a certain way. We argue that Nelson and Winter's evolutionary principles offer a promising tool to help us better understand the family firm evolutionary mindset as they develop and mutate routines collectively to search behaviours that allow for continuous growth and ensure their legacy.

Our delve into heterodox economics and the linked competence-based evolutionary approach is seemingly consistent with other arguments (ie, resource-based view), with a practical twist that is passing muster in the field, as is exemplified in our living case study. We are hopeful that others will accept our invitation to join in the discussion. We are inspired by business-owning families like that in our case example, who are committed to continuity because they have made the decision to be *cathedral* builders rather than *church* builders. Why? *Because cathedrals take generations to build.*

Clarifying purpose and values: guiding families towards meaningful goals

Catherine Grum
Catherine Grum Consultancy Ltd

1. Introduction

In the complex ecosystem of business families, the concept of a shared purpose is often referred to as their North Star. It represents both a guiding light and a binding force. This is more than a mission statement or a strategic vision. It's not just what a business family aims to achieve, it's an expression of who they are and what they stand for.

The shared purpose arises from the family's history and culture, their collective values and their aspirations for the future. It should act as a compass for individual, family and business decisions. This will enable them to navigate the challenges of growth, succession and governance with a sense of intention and continuity. Done well, it provides a narrative that's compelling for generations to come.

You might think that a shared purpose is a noble idea but doubt its real benefits. Families (and advisers) can be reluctant to spend time on creating a statement of purpose or a set of family values. How will this make a difference? Hasn't the family done fine without them until now?

This chapter aims to show why a family in business together (as owners of a business, a portfolio of businesses or a family office) needs a shared purpose and values. It also gives some tools to help you or your clients identify your purpose and values. Finally, it shows how to apply them in practice to guide you, keep everyone on the same path and motivated for the journey.

2. The benefits of a shared purpose and common values

2.1 Alignment and cohesion

A family is not one homogenous unit but is made up of different people, each with their own needs and opinions. Imagine two siblings who want to buy a holiday property together and rent it out. They start searching for properties but can't agree on any. The reason is that they have different goals: one wants to earn enough rental income to change their career and looks for the most profitable options, while the other wants to use the property themselves and only rent it out sometimes to cover the costs. They want a place with a luxury finish and are willing to pay more for it.

This is a simple example, but many families have never really discussed why they keep going with a family business after the founder is no longer around. Saying "It's Dad's legacy" or "We'll make more money together than investing separately" does not give you very much to go on. What are you really trying to achieve? Are you trying to maximise profits to support the family's lifestyle? Are you trying to create opportunities for family members? Are you trying to grow the business to provide jobs for the local community?

Without a shared vision, people can be working towards very different objectives. This might be satisfactory in the short term but almost inevitably causes issues over time. Being clear on the real motivations makes sure everyone is on the same page, aligns expectations and reduces the potential for conflict.

Figure 1: Balancing activities versus truly aligning values

Families also need to feel that their actions, and those taken on their behalf within a business or family office, are aligned with their values. The old way of using philanthropy to offset wealth creation activities no longer works for many, especially the rising generation. Nowadays, with more information and awareness of issues and more empowerment of individuals, a mismatch between values and what's done in practice in any area of the family's ecosystem can have a significant negative impact.

2.2 Enhanced decision making

Having a clear shared purpose can help you make better choices because everyone knows what they are aiming for. In the example above, the siblings would have an easier time finding suitable properties to buy if they both understood and aimed to agree on an objective (are they more interested in the lifestyle or the investment returns). Shared values also help with this. For example, a value around community might mean they prefer to hire local workers instead of outsourcing to a big national company, even if the latter option was faster or cheaper.

Values can offer a consistent framework for decision making. The Rogers*[1] are successful entrepreneurs. They are both self-made and are trying to raise their children with a healthy attitude towards money. After selling one of their

---

1 All names marked * are fictional and used for illustrative purposes only.

businesses, they have more than enough money to last, not just their own lifetimes, but their children's lifetimes too. They have encouraged their teenage children to get Saturday jobs but, if asked for money, they know they can afford it so find it difficult to say no. After working with a trusted adviser on their legacy plans, they have identified hard work and responsibility as core values. Now, whenever they are asked for money, they think about their values and long-term goals and use these as a guide before making any decision. The children are given money each term and budget for the things they 'want' (but don't necessarily 'need'), such as new fashion trainers. For larger purchases, such as a trip or car, the Rogers provide 60% and the children work to pay off the rest.

2.3 Resilience and connection

For families, whose outlook may span generations, having a clear shared purpose can make them more resilient and help them cope with difficulties and changes. It usually goes beyond immediate financial gains and offers a long-term perspective that can help the family weather life's passing storms. The Singh* family's shared purpose involves supporting the family's well-being and celebrating and preserving their heritage through art, music and storytelling. The family organises a cultural festival every two years as part of their family assembly. They have also created an educational programme that teaches younger generations about their heritage and another one for spouses joining the family. When the COVID-19 pandemic struck, their strong sense of purpose and bond gave them support and emotional resilience. The family worked together and was able to act fast. Even the youngest family members got involved, helping them to adjust and adapt some of their traditions to fit an online world.

2.4 Authenticity and trust

One way to show authenticity and build trust among your family, customers and stakeholders is to repeatedly take actions that match your purpose and values. This is certainly the case for the Chouinard family and their business Patagonia. The leader of the business, Yvon Chouinard, always made decisions that followed his purpose and values around environmental conservation. As a result, there were many business initiatives that supported sustainable practices, perhaps most notably in 2011 when they asked customers to only buy what they need with the campaign slogan "Don't Buy This Jacket".[2] As part of their personal succession planning, the family continued to maintain their purpose and values and gave a proportion of their shares in Patagonia to a non-profit

2 See, Patagonia, "Don't Buy This Jacket", 25 November 2011, https://eu.patagonia.com/gb/en/stories/dont-buy-this-jacket-black-friday-and-the-new-york-times/story-18615.html?srsltid=AfmBOoqy6QbF1pk667mr3uTvrU4_-SNsbIQ5eyNTX5ByeG5M4iY3tjN_.

organisation that will use what it receives from the company to fight climate change. While not their prime motivation, their approach has reaped commercial rewards, with Patagonia ranked the most reputable brand in the United States in 2023,[3] and 91% of employees saying it is a great place to work.[4]

On a smaller scale, an example of this could be a family that wants to strengthen the relationships in their growing family and values transparency. As family members increase and not everyone has the same access to information, tensions begin to rise. Returning to their values, they develop a programme to share updates about their business and charity with family members regularly. This includes a monthly newsletter and quarterly calls. Over time, by doing what they say they are going to do and ensuring consistency, the family rebuilds trust. If at some point they forget to mention an important decision taken by the family business, by acknowledging this and correcting it as soon as they realise, they also demonstrate accountability.

If things start to go wrong, having a shared purpose and values can also help resolve conflicts. When disagreements happen, as they do in all families, having a strong common purpose can help prevent personal differences from getting in the way of their collective goals. The family's core values can help them find solutions that are acceptable to everyone even if they involve compromise.

2.5 Motivation and engagement

Finally, a meaningful shared purpose can help motivate and engage family members and employees. Many studies show that millennials value businesses that have a clear purpose[5] and they are not the only ones. Simon Sinek explains this in the book *Start with Why*.[6] The part of the brain that controls trust, loyalty and decision making responds better to the emotional appeal that a strong purpose or 'why' gives compared to the more practical 'what' (products and services) or 'how' (methods and processes). One example that Simon uses is Apple. Their 'what' are products like phones and computers. Their 'how' includes innovative designs and easy-to-use interfaces. Their 'why' is to challenge the *status quo*, think differently and empower individuals.

In the family setting, knowing that the family care about something more

---

3 The 2023 Axios Harris Poll 100 reputation rankings, 23 May 2023, www.axios.com/ 2023/05/23/ corporate-brands-reputation-america.

4 Great Place to Work, www.greatplacetowork.com/certified-company/1000745.

5 Deloitte's 2024 Gen Z and Millennial Survey found that nearly nine in 10 millennials say purpose is important to their job satisfaction, and they are increasingly likely to turn down work or employers that don't align with their values (www.deloitte.com/global/en/issues/work/content/genz-millennialsurvey.html). Kantar Consulting's Purpose 2020 Report found nearly two-thirds of millennials and Gen Z express a preference for brands that have a point of view and stand for something, (www.kantar.com/inspiration/brands/the-journey-towards-purpose-led-growth). McKinsey's Organisational Purpose Survey of 2019 found that 82% of respondents felt it was important for companies to have a purpose and 72% felt purpose should receive more weight than profit (www.mckinsey.com/capabilities/people-and-organizational-performance/our-insights/purpose-shifting-from-why-to-how#).

6 Simon Sinek, *Start with Why: How Great Leaders Inspire Everyone to Take Action* (Penguin Books, 2011).

than making widgets or making money has the same impact. Think about which of these sounds more attractive:

The Sheikh family have established a family office to invest their family's collective wealth in public and private markets and generate a return of at least 7%.*

The Sheikh family began their journey in a tiny flat. All the family members worked on the family's market stall as soon as they left school just to make ends meet. Through perseverance and hard work, this grew into a successful business. Now they have sold their business and created their family office, this gives them financial security, access to the best education for their descendants and the chance to follow their interests. In addition, it provides the resources to assist others in their community who find themselves struggling financially.

3. So why don't families all have purpose and value statements already?

One might wonder why not every family business has a well-defined purpose and set of values, given these advantages. Many families will have a sense of a higher purpose for their work, and often make choices based on subconscious values, so they don't see any need to go further. However, without a precise expression of what their values and purpose are, they miss out on the added benefits that focus and consistency bring – strengthening them just like working out a muscle at the gym.

Some families (and advisers) may find the concept of discussing purpose and values a little vague and abstract. The results of doing this work will not be immediate and there are always more urgent issues on the agenda like business expansions or new IT systems.

Finally, there are those that are put off by fear of difficult conversations that may be triggered. Not all families will have a clear purpose for staying together in a shared venture. Others may not share the same values. In these instances, they may all be better off apart. This is not a bad thing to admit, and it's better to do it sooner rather than later. Exiting a family business, making some money and keeping relationships intact should be seen as a success, not a failure. Staying together despite the warning signs will cause issues further down the line. A good question for a family that doesn't want to talk about purpose and values for this reason is: "What risks do you face if you choose to avoid this important conversation?"

4. Identifying purpose

So, we agree that purpose matters. But how do you identify what that purpose is? The best way to do that will vary depending on where you're starting from and what the family's like. It will usually involve some of these steps:

- *Listening:* What stories do individuals share about the family and business? Which events are significant to them? Understanding what has shaped them often tells you a lot about their why. Don't just rely on the past, however.

- *Individual conversations or structured interviews with relevant family members:* These provide an opportunity to understand each person's expectations, aspirations and concerns. If these are led by someone outside the family, it can enable people to be more candid. Often people are more at ease expressing their true views one on one rather than in a bigger group. Explain how the information will be used beforehand.
- *Facilitated group workshops:* It can help everyone join in when someone outside the family helps to plan, ask relevant questions and lead the conversations. Some families who find it hard to express their views may benefit from exercises like envisioning or picture cards that act as prompts. The creation of a family vision board can help to align everyone's goals and purpose and can also make the output more memorable.
- *Surveys:* These can work well with larger groups or families with a lot of introverts. Like individual conversations, this may encourage more forthcoming responses, especially if done anonymously. They are a bit harder to get more nuance from, however, and are only as good as the questions they include.

It is beneficial to have as many family stakeholders as possible involved in the process. This doesn't mean that the matriarch or patriarch must give full decision-making power to their 20-something-year-old children. However, ignoring the opinions of the rising generation misses a good opportunity to foster engagement. Moreover, if there are differences between what the older and younger family members want and these aren't taken into account, you are not creating an enduring common purpose that everyone will buy into.

4.1 Assimilating individual views to create a shared purpose

Pulling together everyone's different perspectives to establish some common ground requires careful thought, particularly if you have many stakeholders. The first step is to consider what common themes have emerged. For example, can you identify similar responses around their financial goals, legacy, family unity or community impact?

If you have lots of different and potentially competing ideas, involve the family in an exercise to rank these. They can either work individually or in small groups to identify which points are most important to them. Are there some areas where consensus comes easily and others where there is much more disparity? These may be signs that individuals need autonomy to pursue those aspects by themselves. Families do not have to be joined at the hip across all their affairs.

Another way to evaluate and improve different options is to do scenario planning. This means talking about various possible future situations (such as a significant economic downturn affecting the business or generating an unexpected windfall profit) and how the family would react. It can help the family understand different viewpoints and encourage younger family members to think more ahead. They may not have their own families yet but imagining how things might affect their future children may alter their responses.

Writing down the shared purpose may take several iterations. It's often harder to agree on the exact wording than on the main points verbally. Keep working at it until you reach a consensus where people feel it is good enough. Some trade-offs may be necessary, but if people have had the opportunity to participate, they are usually willing to accept some degree of compromise. At the same time, don't force everyone to agree. One of the benefits of going through this process can be to discover if some individuals do not feel a sufficient pull to want to remain part of the enterprise.

4.2 What does a 'good' purpose look like?

"We're in business together to provide financial security for our family's future." Is this sufficient to qualify as a shared purpose? As with all good questions, it depends. There is no magic formula, and statements can range from a brief paragraph to a page or more.

To test a family's statement of purpose, consider whether it is clear what the vision encapsulates. Does it reflect the collective views of everyone (or can everyone get behind it at least)? Will it help to guide future decision making? Is it actionable? Does it inspire commitment?

Instead of "providing financial security for our family", imagine something along the following lines:

Almost a century ago, our family came to the UK with nothing but a hope of giving future generations a better life. We have now built a thriving business that enables us to support each family member in achieving their educational and career aspirations and to get a foot on the property ladder. We want to encourage ongoing development and the ability to explore opportunities that were not open to the original founders. As stewards of the business, we are committed to sustainable practices that align with the family's values and support all stakeholders for the long term. As a family, we are committed to fostering an environment that encourages individuals to apply themselves and to use their privilege to give back to the family and wider community in some way.

4.3 Family or business purpose?

A common question that families may face at the beginning of this process is whether they should concentrate on their shared purpose as a family or more precisely their shared purpose for the family business. These are clearly related but have different functions and may include different participants. If you are uncertain which is required, start with the family's shared purpose.

A shared family purpose typically has a broad and holistic focus, encompassing the overall well-being, values and aspirations of the family. The family's financial health is often not the ultimate objective but the means to help achieve it. Goals can be quite intangible and relate to areas such as the family bond, personal growth, health and happiness. There is likely to be a strong emotional or relational component, promoting family harmony, shared traditions or cultural heritage. There's also likely to be a long time horizon, typically spanning multiple generations.

A shared purpose for the family business typically has a narrower focus. It concentrates on the mission for the business entity while considering the role that plays for a wider group of stakeholders (such as employees, suppliers, clients or the local community). Measures of success generally include more tangible outcomes such as financial performance or market share, among others. Depending on the family's views, there may be something more specific about the family's involvement in the future leadership of the business.

Environmental and social responsibility may feature in both family and business purpose. At a business level, these usually focus on topics relevant to the business or its employees. At a family level, they can be more wide-ranging and consider different ways in which the family may fulfil them.

The family's values and the business's values are often very similar, as the family usually shape the business culture. But this doesn't mean they are the same in every way. Even when the family and business are tightly linked, there may be some more personal values (such as love, joy or spirituality) that would fit better with a family than a business.

5. Exploring values

It can be an interesting and rewarding exercise to try to establish your own family's values before working on a client's. Many of the same techniques used to establish shared purpose also work here. If the business has values, don't take them for granted without checking how meaningful they are to the family. Ask how any existing values were identified – who was involved and how long ago it was.

Even if a family doesn't have a written statement of values, you aren't starting from scratch. The family will have shared values for generations, passing them down through interactions, behaviour modelling, family rituals and storytelling. These values are also likely to have changed over time with each generation, based on their experiences and the impact of new members of the family.

When trying to capture which values are most important, one method is to spend some time reflecting on family history. Notice which stories particularly stand out and consider what values they represent.

Another approach is to go through a list of common values and identify which resonate (you can also get packs of cards with different values written on each). Next, everyone can share their top values and why they chose those particular ones. You can do this by getting everyone to write on Post-it notes or using a digital tool like Slido that can produce a word-art image in real time as individuals enter their suggestions on their phones. Notice how much alignment there is. Are there clusters of words around similar themes? Continue the discussion until you reach consensus.

When you come to write out the values, include a clear meaning for each and/or an example of how it might be used in practice. Individual words can be interpreted so broadly and this helps to ensure there's a real shared understanding.

5.1 Culture eats value statements for breakfast

You might have heard the phrase "Culture eats strategy for breakfast".[7] It implies that no strategy can work unless the culture aligns and supports it in practice. The same is true for values. It doesn't make a difference what values you write down if they don't match how people actually behave. If it's unintended, a disconnect between what is being espoused and actual behaviour can have a negative impact. In some business situations, aspirational values might be used to try to change or improve the business culture (eg, wanting the business to be more innovative). In a family situation, what you usually want is to capture existing values. While it is not necessarily wrong to recognise some aspirational values as well (depending on the context), this needs to be acknowledged. If a family portrays themselves as having values of transparency and openness but decisions are actually made by only a few people behind closed doors, it is likely to face issues of trust and credibility, not improve them.

6. Aligning wealth with purpose and values

Once a family has invested their time and effort establishing their shared purpose and values, what's next? Are these just documented as part of a family constitution or do they have any practical use?

I would suggest that they have great practical significance across many areas of the family members' lives. These include how the plans and values influence the board or individuals running the family enterprise, how they shape the investment of the family's wealth, what charitable activities the family undertakes, and even the family's attitude to tax. At a family level, they can also help guide and develop younger family members and improve relationships more generally.

---

7 Widely attributed to management consultant Peter Drucker.

6.1 Family

Being conscious of the family's values and purpose enables everyone to apply them more consistently. You are more aware of what's important and you can develop practices accordingly. If family relationships are key, what is the family doing to foster them across generations or distant locations? If transparency is critical, how consistent is the information given to younger family members in different branches?

Awareness also encourages stories to be shared that help to pass on and reinforce these values. For example, telling young children how hard their grandparents worked to establish the family business, like the fact their grandmother got up before dawn every day to get to the market as it opened and secure the best produce. This way, children brought up in different households can already start to develop a shared identity.

Individual family members can also use their values to guide their own choices. For example, when thinking about buying a private plane, if the family has a shared purpose to teach the next generation to have a good relationship with money and values moderation or values around sustainability, they might ask themselves how this action aligns with each of these and what it teaches their children.

6.2 Business

Some people claim that family businesses are more likely to embrace environmental and social goals, or to treat employees well, because they think beyond quarterly results. This is not necessarily true. If any such areas are truly important to a family, 'how' they act as owners matters. This is particularly important when the family is less involved in daily operations.

Understanding the family's shared purpose and values can be very helpful for the board of any family enterprise. Only if they are aware of it, can they align their strategy with it. This is particularly important where they have a bearing on decisions that might be seen to go beyond, or even contrary to, profit maximisation. In an interview, Mark Preston, executive trustee and group CEO of Grosvenor Estate, said: "We have made some specific investments that we might not have made without our purpose being so clearly articulated."[8]

If you want a more robust approach, one thing to do is establish a decision-making framework for the board or family council to use which causes them to consider their purpose and values. Guiding questions might include:

- How does this decision align with our shared purpose?
- How does this action impact the environment (if one of their values is sustainability)?

---

8 RG Eccles, M Johnstone-Louis, C Mayer and JC Stroehle, "The Board's Role in Sustainability: A New Framework for Getting Directors Behind ESG Efforts", (2020) *Harvard Business Review*, 98(5), pp48–51.

6.3 Investing

The family should also share their purpose and values with the people who handle their investments (and even use them as a factor to choose who they work with). This can have a significant effect on their outcomes. Knowing the family's shared purpose for their wealth should help to shape their investment objectives. For example, think of a family that has very significant wealth. They want this to provide financial security and enable younger family members to have a great start in life. At the same time, they also want to encourage hard work and independence and expect individuals to be mostly self-sufficient. They don't necessarily need to maximise their returns to achieve this and it should be included in any discussions around their investment goals.

On a more detailed level, the family's values can also help inform specific investment choices. A family that values innovation might prefer an approach that uses some of their money to invest in and support cutting-edge start-ups or R&D-driven firms. Others that value sustainability might look to invest some of their wealth in businesses that create a positive environmental impact and avoid others that are heavy polluters. Values may also be relevant to how they set their risk tolerance and return expectations. If one of their values is community, they might accept higher risk or slower growth from an investment that supports local social enterprises.

6.4 Philanthropy

Similarly, values can inform and shape a family's approach to philanthropy. A family that particularly values gratitude might donate to a hospital that treated one of their relatives. Besides using purpose and values to help choose the causes they support, it can also help determine how they support them. For example, a family that values lifelong learning might see this it an opportunity to get different generations involved to understand more deeply about underlying issues. Another that values relationships might unite cousins to collaborate on a project or invest time building more of a partnership with an organisation they support.

7. Concluding thoughts

Values and purpose are powerful tools for families of wealth and are worth investing in. Across all their domains, values and purpose guide families towards an aligned and meaningful vision and support decision making and engagement along the way. By articulating and sharing their values, families can foster a sense of identity and belonging among their members, as well as create a positive impact in the world through their business, investments and philanthropy.

Theories and models in family enterprise advising

Patricia M Annino
Rimon Law
Judy Green
Family Firm Institute Inc.

In the late 1980s, the introduction of the family enterprise as a field separate from entrepreneurship marked a change in the way multi-generational family enterprises were looked at, from both science and social science perspectives. Since then, a field of practice and/or professional discipline for advisers and consultants has evolved in parallel with increased understanding and research on the family enterprises themselves. This new profession has identified, developed and espoused certain theories, models and terminologies to further articulate the skills and knowledge that professionals from related disciplines (eg, law, finance and behavioural and management science) should be aware of and conversant in, before they step out of or add to their profession of origin and engage with multi-generational family enterprise clients.

This chapter is intended both as a self-assessment tool and as a roadmap for ongoing education in the family enterprise advising field for those professionals who find themselves advising multi-generational family-owned companies or wish to extend their practices to family enterprise business – entities that generate somewhere between 50%–90% of the world's economy.[1]

The chapter[2] is divided into four sections:

1. *Foundational theories and models* identifies concepts that are basic knowledge for professionals working in the family enterprise field.
2. *Other theories and models* identifies theories and models that more seasoned advisers should be aware of and consider using when advising their clients.
3. *Emerging theories and concepts* includes newer theories that contribute to the understanding and the education of advisers currently practising in the family enterprise field.
4. A concluding section brings the chapter together.

1 Readers should note that there is no single source for this statistic since the percentages are tied to the definitions used for 'family business' and/or 'family enterprise'.

2 For the purposes of the chapter, we use the term 'family enterprise' to include multi-generational companies with operating businesses, holding companies, and family offices. The term 'advising' encompasses advising and consulting, terms which are sometimes used interchangeably or with specifically identified functions.

1. Foundational theories and models

The family enterprise field was founded on four theoretical models, which are described below, and should be familiar to – and engaged with by – individuals and organisations working with multi-generational family companies.

1.1 Three-circle Model

The model that jump-started the approach to advising family enterprises is the Three-circle Model[3] developed by John Davis and Renato Tagiuri while both were professors at Harvard Business School in 1982. It remains widely used because it is easy to understand and provides a clear graphic snapshot that families can relate to.

The Three-circle Model is a Venn diagram that clarifies three interdependent and overlapping groups (family, business and ownership) that comprise the family-based system. Each sector must be respected and integrated to set direction for the family business system. The goals of the three circles can overlap or be distinct.

Figure 1: Three-circle Model[4]

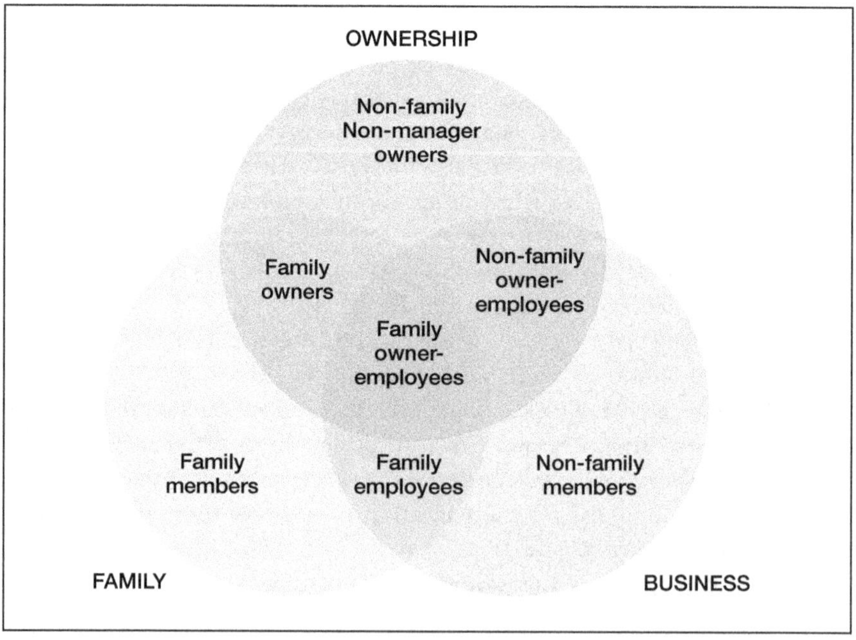

3 Renato Tagiuri and John Davis, "Bivalent Attributes of the Family Firm", *Family Business Review*, vol 9, issue 2 (1996), https://doi.org/10.1111/j.1741-6248.1996.00199.x.

4 John Davis and Renato Tagiuri, Three-circle Model, published with permission.

Each circle has a governance structure and plan. A family council would govern the family circle and create a family plan; a management team would lead the business circle and prepare a management succession plan; a board of directors would govern the owners or shareholders circle and be responsible for the strategic plan, continuity plan, contingency plan and succession plan.

Within the three circles there are seven potential positions that intersect and overlap and that various individuals can hold. People normally evolve and change position during their lifetimes as they exit or enter the business or ownership. However, their family membership remains constant, although their role in the family will change as they enter adulthood.

Advisers do not have a clear place in the model.

In Figure 1, the boundaries around each circle are solid. However, in real life the boundaries are elastic and must be resilient. If they are not resilient, they will snap and cause problems. A sustainable system is one that allows the boundaries among family, ownership and business to flex, bend and absorb the occasional shocks. The boundaries are where innovation, creativity, change and destruction lie.

The most common issues family businesses face at the intersection of the boundaries include competition, guilt, the need for a powerful legacy, jealousy, seeking approval (from living persons and the ghosts of past authority figures), sandbox secrets, generational dynamics, blended-family complexities and adviser blocks. Additional stressors that impact these boundaries include mental illness, substance abuse, dementia, narcissism, poor financial planning and an unrealistic sense of financial realities. These boundary issues flare up when there is an inability to look in the mirror and take personal responsibility and when there are control issues between parents and children, among siblings and step-parents, and step-parents and stepchildren.

Advisers should be aware of the boundaries and their resiliency. It is important to understand that the process takes time and observation to reach the point where the boundaries can be elastic and not snap. A resilient approach is one in which communication and expectations are improved. It introduces independent, non-emotionally charged data, such as compensation surveys, job performance metrics and financial expenditure ratios to relieve the pressure on the boundary. A foundation of a resilient boundary is to put estate planning and financial planning in place (and monitor them on an ongoing basis) so that there is financial stability across all three circles and the system is financially sound. When there is a resilient approach to boundaries, the members of each circle own the responsibility for their own actions; there is no sense of entitlement. A resilient approach to the boundaries enhances and empowers the system. A rigid approach to the boundaries weakens and jeopardises the system.

1.2 Developmental Model

In 1997, Gersick, Davis, Hampton and Lansberg, in their book, *Generation to Generation*,[5] noted that the Three-circle Model is a snapshot in time and understood that a more elaborate model was needed to examine how each circle may change as time evolves. Their Developmental Model draws on the Three-circle Model and offers dynamic perspectives by introducing development stages along the family, business and ownership axes. Their thesis is that each component of the three circles has a different development stage.

Figure 2: Developmental Model[6]

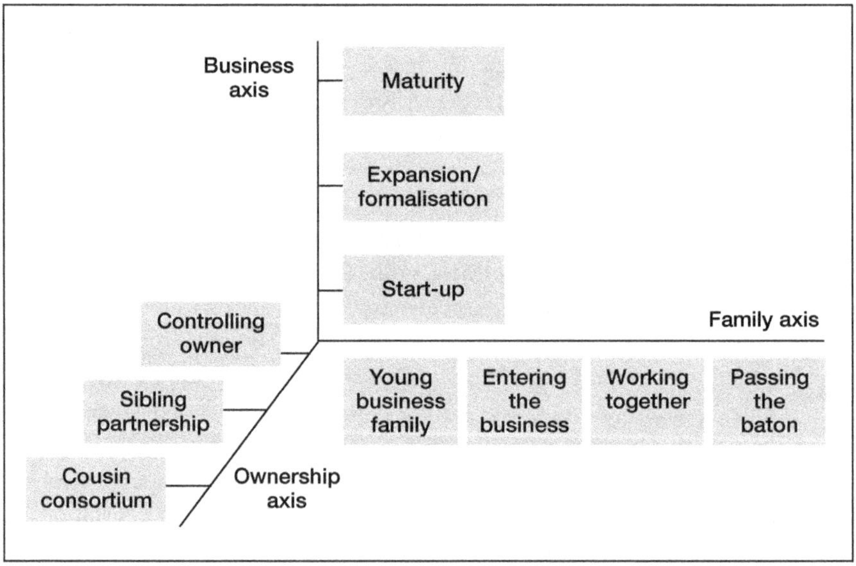

In the Developmental Model there are three development axes: the ownership development axis, the business development axis and the family development axis.

The entire system changes as individuals move across boundaries inside the system. A person's movement from one circle to another sector (eg, 'family member' to 'family member who is an employee') can cause a reaction to the entire system. Estate planning, transferring shares and retirement are also examples of changes that affect the entire system.

The ownership development axis assumes (but not always) a progression from controlling owner to a sibling partnership to a cousin consortium.

5 Kelin E Gersick, John A Davis, Marion McCollom Hampton and Ivan Lansberg, *Generation to Generation: Life Cycles of the Family Business, Harvard Business Review Press* (1997).
6 Adapted from Gersick, Davis, Hampton and Lansberg, *ibid.*

The business development axis progresses from start-up to expansion/formalisation to mature business over the passage of time. There are important variations in growth, product maturity, capitalisation and indebtedness, non-family manager development and institutionalisation that arise from the business stages. The business development stages have a powerful impact on decisions, such as transferring family shares to outsiders and succession planning.

The family development axis progresses from 'young' (one generation) to 'entering business' (two generations) to 'maturity' (three generations). It captures the structural and interpersonal development of the family through issues such as marriage, parenthood, adult sibling relationships, in-laws, communication patterns and family roles.

Structure is needed to guide the development along each axis. For the ownership dimension, it is important to have shareholder meetings and a board of directors, or at least a board of advisers.

For the family dimension, it is important to provide a forum in which family members can articulate their values, needs and expectations *vis-à-vis* the company, often defined as a 'family council', which we will continue to use for ease of reference. The family council can educate the family members about the rights and responsibilities that come with business ownership and management, help clarify the boundary between family and business, provide a forum for discussions (other than including business discussions on family holidays), and provide a structure to help the family create a shared vision and code of understanding. The family council can establish a family plan that includes a family history, a vision of the future, a family mission statement and an action plan.

The business dimension structure includes forming a management development team and a management development plan. It is very important to coordinate the structure and plans for all three axes.

Since the publication of this model, the authors have evolved their thinking to reflect that rather than focusing on what happens within a single generation, the family development axis should reflect the stages of what happens as the family evolves from a nuclear family to a multi-generational family and then, possibly, to networks of families.

1.3 Process consulting

In working with family businesses, the consultant must be able to provide information as well as manage the change process. Content and technical expertise and knowledge of change management are needed to work with family businesses. The adviser must know the difference between process and content, understand the importance of each and use not one but both as the situation indicates. For example, the consultant working with a business family must be able to answer specific questions about the estate plan, transfer of ownership and management issues in the succession process, as well as manage and guide the change process. Most change efforts in family businesses are not likely to succeed unless there is the right combination of both content and process, creating outcomes as well as process improvement.

Figure 3: Process Consulting Model[7]

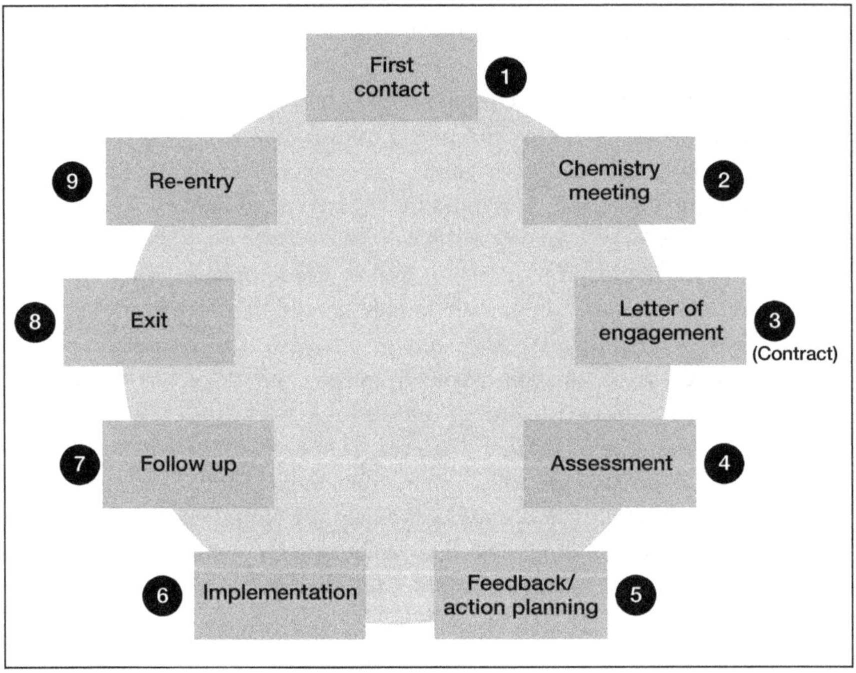

As soon as work starts with the client and the consultant has established trust and a set of ground rules for interaction between family members, the consultant continues to help the client by:

- *Clarifying communications:* For example, everyone speaks for themselves and differentiates between "what you think", "what you feel" and "what you know for a fact". The consultant may initially repeat what they have heard each individual say.
- *Encouraging a positive problem-solving approach:* For example, if there is a disagreement, the family decides at the first meeting how to make decisions, which could be by majority vote, consensus or that whoever is most affected decides. An agreed-to process for managing the conflicts can be the foundation for solving the larger issues of management transition and company ownership.

7 Jane Hilburt-Davis, Process Consulting Model, *FFI Practitioner*, 2021, published with permission.

- *Challenging the family's way of seeing the problems and proposing solutions,* which might include regular family council meetings and/or executive management meetings, involving:
  - learning how to conduct effective meetings and making fair decisions; and
  - establishing agreed-to ground rules for the interactions, meaning the family will begin to solve their own problems.
- *Creating structures:* Structures are an integral part of the consultation process. These structures can provide the safety and predictability to rebuild the trust necessary for agreements and consensus. Building and enforcing structures in each of the systems – family, ownership and business – generates healthier interactions, enforces healthy boundaries, and offers methods and mechanisms for planning, solving problems and managing conflict. The ongoing dialogue, negotiations, compromises, exchanges of ideas and collaboration between the families and the business should sustain both the firm and the family over the long run. These mechanisms may include an 'offline' conflict coaching session with the consultant, a 'fishbowl' during the meeting with coaching from the consultant, or stopping the conflict with a "deal with that outside the meeting" admonition. In the ownership system, the structures may include an outside board of directors; in the business system, performance reviews for family members and fair compensation mechanisms are other examples.

(a) Systems theory

Systems thinking is about creating structures to manage the interactions between the systems. It involves working with multiple levels of the client system and the complex web of relationships. The family's reality has been constructed over time by their interplay and interactions. As they learn how to build new ways of dealing with each other, they develop more effective methods of solving problems. Much of the work is building structures, processes and procedures, such as family councils, family employment policies, shareholder agreements and codes of conduct to manage and monitor the interaction between the systems. It involves creating healthy boundaries, not barriers, between the family and the business. It emphasises the need to focus on the issues at hand while at the same time taking into account the dynamics of the entire system.

An example of systems theory is the Bowen Family Systems Theory,[8] originated by Dr Murray Bowen, a psychiatrist, which is a theory of human

8 The Bowen Center for the Study of the Family, "Learn about Bowen Theory", www.thebowencenter.org/core-concepts-diagrams.

behaviour that views the family as an emotional unit and uses systems thinking to describe the unit's complicated interactions. Dr Bowen described the 'fusion force' – when people tend to agree or disagree with each other without having formulated their own ideas. Bowen's theory was to take a three-generational family diagram and then coach the stronger ones in the family. He wanted to convey that a family system is a multi-generational field with values and instincts, and contains various levels of awareness and sensitivity. The differentiation of self is the cornerstone of his theory. It assumes that if one person becomes better defined and in better contact with family members, the individuals will be more responsible for themselves.

2. Other theories and models

As the field grew after the Three-circle Model in the 1980s, other theories and models were created based on the foundational models. Four of these are described below.

2.1 Four-circle Model

In 1996, Dean Fowler's Four-circle Model[9] was presented in the Family Firm Institute's conference proceedings. Designed to enhance the Three-circle Model, the Four-circle Model focuses attention on the individual adult in relationship to their family of origin.

This model differs from the Three-circle Model in four ways:

- It adds an individual circle because family owners' business advisers often deal with a family of adults, and healthy adults typically individuate themselves from their family of origin. Healthy adult families are intentional.
- It focuses on competence, particularly the competencies that must be mastered at the four intersection points in the diagram.
- It highlights that individuals or individual beneficiaries within the family own the family business – not the family as one unit.
- Individuals serve as board members, and advisers who are not family members fit the model in section 8 of Fowler's diagram.

Fowler outlines 12 competencies that must be mastered by individuals and families for success: maturity, purpose, communication, roles, business competency, compensation, strategy, structure, leadership, succession, governance and estate planning.

9 Dean Fowler, "The Four-Circle Model", *FFI Practitioner*, 6 October 2021, https://ffipractitioner.org/the-four-circle-model/.

Figure 4: Four-circle Model[10]

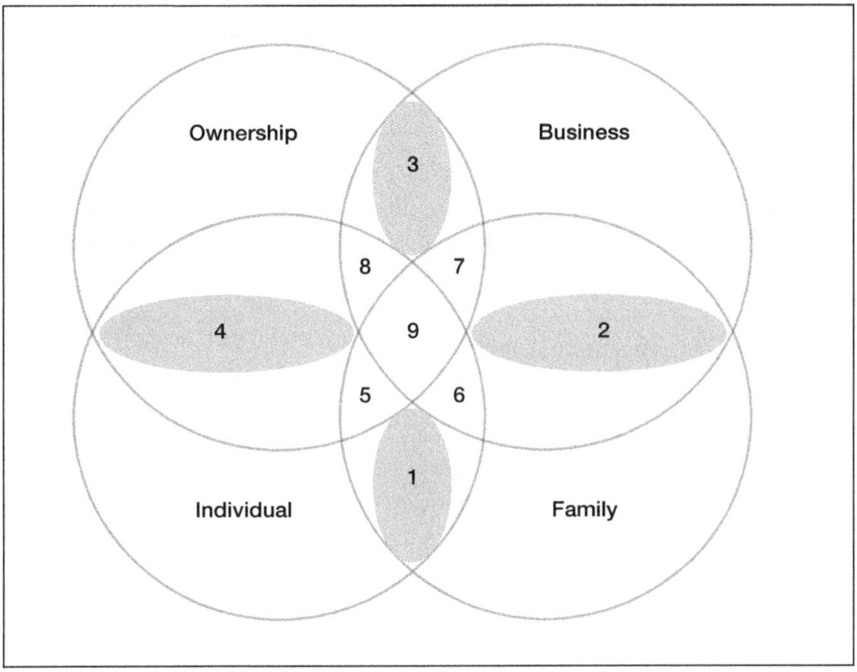

2.2 Cluster Model: an extension of the Three-circle Model

Nava Michael-Tsabari, Rania Labaki and Ramona Kay Zachary articulated an extension of the Three-circle Model in a 2014 *Family Business Review* article.[11] They regard the Three-circle Model as an oversimplification of the family enterprise, considered as consisting only of a single business entity. Although this may be true at the first stage of the business, in later stages, a family enterprise can control a portfolio of multiple firms. They propose a cluster model as an extension of the Three-circle Model to describe a family that owns more than one firm.

The Cluster Model describes a family that owns more than one firm and demonstrates the implications of the different constructs (eg, transgenerational wealth, transgenerational family effect and family entrepreneurial orientation) that are suggested at the family level to capture transgenerational survival. These constructs raise the understanding of how family businesses employ financial assets to create business continuity. In the Cluster Model, a family starts at the first generation with Firm A. In later stages, the basic structure of a family and a firm may evolve into a portfolio of assets.

10 *Ibid*, published with permission.

11 Nava Michael-Tsabari, Rania Labaki and Ramona Kay Zachary, "Toward the Cluster Model: The Family Firm's Entrepreneurial Behavior Over Generations", *Family Business Review*, vol 27, issue 2, https://doi.org/10.1177/0894486514525803.

A family that owns a firm is referred to as 'organic'. A family that owns several firms is referred to as a 'portfolio' family firm. With the portfolio, the family's entrepreneurial behaviour is a cluster model for the family that acts by founding, selling, merging and buying other firms.

2.3 Four-room Model

This model, developed by Banyan Global,[12] uses the analogy of a home. There are four key rooms: owner room, board room, management room and family room. There are two key governance components: setting the structure of each room and the process of integrating the rooms.

Figure 5: Four-room Model[13]

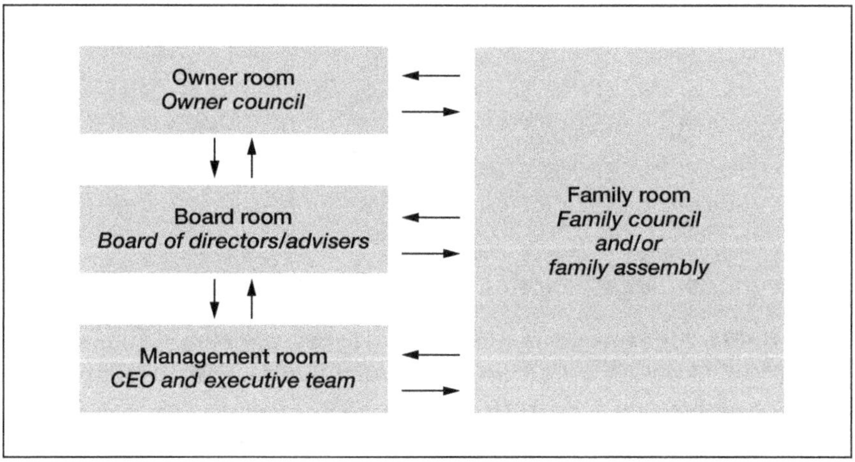

- Owner room: owner, beneficiaries and trustees (power and influence).
- Board room: directors and advisers (wisdom and judgement).
- Management room: CEO, management, employees (competence and execution).
- Family room: descendants, spouses and next gen (love, unity and development).

This model divides the work of the family business into groups most appropriate for certain decisions. The model focuses on who and which discussions occur in which room.

12 Josh Baron, "Understanding the Four-Room Model", Banyan Global, https://banyan.global/ideas/understanding-the-four-room-model/. See also *The Harvard Business Review Family Business Handbook: How to Build and Sustain a Successful, Enduring Enterprise* by Josh Baron and Rob Lachenauer, https://d2fahduf2624mg.cloudfront.net/pre_purchase_docs/BK_GDAN_004405/2021-03-03-02-31-19/bk_gdan_004405.pdf.

13 Banyan Global, Four-room Model, published with permission.

- In the owner room, the owners should decide key ideas to hold onto and delegate the rest to other rooms.
- Owners should build a governance structure by establishing forums to do the work of each room – even if some people are involved in each of the rooms.
- The rooms should work together. The governance of the system depends on each person knowing the rooms he or she is allowed to enter and understanding how the rooms work together. The decision making and information flow among the rooms is critical.
- The placement of each room in the model is deliberate. The family room runs along the side of the other rooms to underscore the influence and development of the family members. The family members can eventually enter different rooms. It indicates the importance of maintaining family influence and unity, and developing the talent of family members.
- The model identifies four common problem areas in family governance: (i) the loft (an informal decision-making approach with few boundaries between decision makers. The roles and responsibilities of the decision makers are unclear); (ii) the silo (which replicates the decision-making approach of a loft but within individual areas or silos. People avoid any important cross-business decisions); (iii) missing rooms (often the owner room is missing); and (iv) messy rooms (a room or two that has lost its original purpose and function).

It is important to be aware of the lofts, silos, missing rooms and messy rooms. When these are visible, families need to go back and renovate the governance structure and process.

2.4 ZOPA (Zone of Possible Agreements) Model: An approach for navigating emotional negotiations in family enterprises

Figure 6: ZOPA Model[14]

My non-negotiables	ZOPA (Zone of possible agreements)	Another's non-negotiables

14 Doug Gray, "The ZOPA Model: An approach for navigating emotional negotiations in family enterprises", *FFI Practitioner*, 14 March 2023, https://ffipractitioner.org/the-zopa-model-an-approach-for-navigating-emotional-negotiations-in-family-enterprises/.

In 2023, Doug Gray applied the ZOPA Model (2017)[15] to family business advising. With the ZOPA model, the adviser reduces the complexity of dealing with the emotionally charged issues of succession, continuity, conflict, communication and asset transfers.

In the column on the left is a list of the family's non-negotiables (what the family must hold true in the future). These are the family's core values and may include career clarity, ownership or asset management. If the 'important' is important and negotiable, it is added to the ZOPA column.

Each member of the family then lists possible non-negotiables for other family members who are involved in the negotiation. These are, of course, educated guesses. Examples may include specific assets and sunk costs in an investment. If the item is important and negotiable, it is added to the ZOPA column.

The ZOPAs should then be listed. Gray recommends listing at least 20 ZOPAs if possible. Examples may include:

- working together as a family enterprise;
- dividing assets for/among specific owners;
- distributing assets to the next generation;
- amending the shareholder agreement's buy/sell provisions regarding the transfer of assets within the family;
- distributing some assets outside the family ownership;
- defining phases of asset transfer; and
- gifting ownership from the current generation to the next generation.

3. Emerging theories and concepts in the family enterprise field

As the field of family enterprise consulting continues to evolve, there is a noticeable change. While earlier research and existing practice have frequently focused on financial, managerial or innovative topics, there is growing interest in exploring non-financial outcomes, or outcomes that take non-financial as well as financial, innovative and managerial behaviours into account.

What follows are brief descriptions of selected non-financial concepts that are currently under exploration and development both in research and in practice in the field of family enterprise.

3.1 Concepts of family

Concepts of the family are evolving. Although values and traditions may remain, more complicated family issues now exist. Second marriages, same-sex relationships, children with one parent, transgender and gender identity issues are increasingly prevalent, and advisers should be aware that these issues are perceived differently across generations. The ramifications and impacts of these

15 *Ibid.*

issues may not be front and centre, but they are present and have an impact on the system. Advisers must have eyes and ears open to bring the issues and discussion on the concept of the family forward.

3.2 Health and wellness

Evolving trends in society (eg, mental health, longevity, elder care, diversity, and drug and alcohol abuse) have a dramatic effect on the family enterprise and how the family and the enterprise are managed. Issues that were long buried or were not at the forefront of discussion are now commonplace conversations. Advisers to the enterprise need to be aware of these issues and the impact they have on the entire system.

3.3 Socioemotional Wealth (SEW)

SEW[16] is the family enterprise's intentional pursuit of non-economic goals and objectives that influence the enterprise's strategic decision making. It was pioneered by Luis Gómez-Mejía and colleagues in 2007. Objectives include control, transgenerational succession, social capital, emotional connection to the family enterprise and succession. SEW has been applied to social responsibility, CEO risk behaviour, non-family employment decisions, and research and development investments. While non-family firms may primarily aim to maximise financial value, a family enterprise may consider both financial values and SEW when making strategic decisions. A family enterprise may be willing to accept a level of risk and economic loss to prevent the reduction of its SEW.

3.4 Systemic investing

Jason Jay, professor at MIT Sloan, is a strong proponent of the evolving concept of systemic investing.[17] It drives the evolution of the impact of the investment on how it integrates and enhances the value of the broader world. It forces thinking past one investment to how that project, programme, asset or venture fits into a broader system that is shaped by thinking in broader terms. It is grounded in a systems view of the world and encourages a different mindset, which can be accomplished by:

- adopting a systems lens and an understanding that the world is interconnected, contingent and ever-changing;

---

16 Luis R Gómez-Mejía and Inés Herrero, "Back to square one: The measurement of Socioemotional Wealth (SEW)", *Journal of Family Business Strategy*, vol 13, issue 4, December 2022, www.sciencedirect.com/science/article/abs/pii/S1877858521000619?via%3Dihub.

17 Jason Jay and John Davis, "Systemic Investing: A year-end conversation with 2023 FFI Scholar-in-Residence Jason Jay and John Davis", *FFI Practitioner*, 6 December 2023, https://digital.ffi.org/editions/systemic-investing-a-year-end-conversation-with-2023-ffi-scholar-in-residence-jason-jay-and-john-davis/. See also Jess Daggers, Alex Hannant and Jason Jay, "Systemic Investing for Social Change", *Stanford Social Innovation Review*, 12 December 2023, https://ssir.org/articles/entry/systemic_investing_for_social_change.

- being open to different understandings of investment success (not just the conventional rate of return);
- having respect for complexity and understanding the power of collaboration;
- deprivileging finance by searching for ways to put capital to use and understanding how it is interdependent with other actors and inputs; and
- focusing on the real economy with a view to how finance can help and shift systems that meet wider needs.

3.5 Wingspan Legacy's Four-circle Model: understanding the role of family enterprise in society and philanthropy

Christina Wing of HBS and her colleagues at Wingspan[18] have developed an emerging model that addresses the family enterprise as an ecosystem where family dynamics intersect with business, wealth and philanthropy. The model identifies four areas that require governance: (i) the family; (ii) the family office; (iii) the operating company; and (iv) the family foundation/philanthropy. Merging investments with philanthropy with an eye to society at large creates a paradigm for marrying social impact with long-term interest.

4. Conclusion

In this chapter, the authors have identified and discussed:

- Foundational theories and models that shaped the field of family enterprise advising consulting in the early years. Readers will notice that these foundational models are often based on models developed in related fields, since in essence, family enterprise consulting is a multidisciplinary activity.
- Other theories and models that evolved in subsequent years, based on these foundational models or on other models from what are frequently called the core disciplines or professions of origin, that is, behavioural science, finance, law and management science.
- Emerging theories and models that, for the most part, are based on non-financial considerations or changing constructs in the larger society, for example, concepts of the family, philanthropy, or concepts that are occasioned by the burgeoning family office component to the traditional family business governance models.

These selections are based on the authors' experience and research with

18 Christina Wing, "Perspectives on Family Philanthropy and Social Impact Governance", *FFI Practitioner*, 19 March 2024, https://ffipractitioner.org/perspectives-on-family-philanthropy-and-social-impact-governance-an-interview-with-christina-wing/.

family enterprises and family enterprise advising, and are not intended to include all theories and models that have been created in the last 40 years. Nonetheless, we hope that these selections will be part of the ongoing corporate education and personal knowledge offered to multi-generational companies worldwide by advisers and consultants who work in and want to lead this new professional field.

Structuring the family business

Toby Crooks
Katharine Haggie
Hiral Kanzaria
Rawlinson & Hunter LLP

In this chapter, we set out a number of the fundamental considerations and decisions for family members entering business together. Addressing how to structure the business, considering many aspects including taxation and privacy, will be an early decision but an enduring one. Thereafter, funding and supporting the expansion of the business, and potential pitfalls around individuals and international exposure are crucial points for the business to consider.

1. Structure

Following the decision to establish a family business, one of the first things to decide on is the optimal structure of the business. This includes both the structure required to facilitate the operation of the business and the ownership.

1.1 Operating business

There are several commercial, practical and legal factors which will have a bearing on the structure of the operating business. The principal considerations will usually be liability, privacy and taxation. There are generally three commonly used structures in the United Kingdom for an operating business:

- a limited liability company;
- a partnership; and
- a limited liability partnership.

Most jurisdictions will have equivalent structures to those used in the United Kingdom, each with different benefits and potential drawbacks.

(a) Company limited by shares

A company limited by shares is a distinct legal entity (ie, separate from its owners) and responsible for its own liabilities. The liability of the owners is limited to the amount subscribed for shares in that company. The company's profits and losses are generally subject to a form of corporation tax. Further tax may be incurred by the owners of the company upon extraction of profits.

(b) ***Partnership***

A partnership is not a distinct legal entity but instead is a business carried on by the partners as a group. Each partner has joint and several liability for the debts of the partnership.

The profits or losses of the partnership are generally attributable to the partners (as determined by the partners or the partnership agreement), who are each responsible for the tax on their respective share of profits or losses.

(c) ***Limited Liability Partnership (LLP)***

An LLP is a hybrid of a company and a partnership. It is a separate legal entity with the partners' liability limited to the level of their capital contribution. However, subject to meeting the relevant criteria, an LLP is treated like a partnership with regard to the taxation of profits and losses.

Key aspects of the above are considered in the following paragraphs.

1.2 Limitation of liability

Business ventures can be inherently risky and uncertain, hence the ability to ring-fence risk and capital can be attractive for owners. The importance of this will depend on the business activities, associated risks, as well as the risk appetite of the owners.

In practice (as discussed in section 2 below), while limitation of liability can be achieved, this does not stop investors/lenders from seeking personal guarantees – in effect 'piercing the veil' of incorporation.

Directors, who may also be owners initially, have certain fiduciary duties and can be exposed to personal liability in particular circumstances.

Some risks around liability may be managed through ensuring that the business has robust insurance coverage in place.

1.3 Privacy

Given the changing landscape and the prevalence of social media through which privacy is voluntarily ceded, it may appear somewhat anachronistic that business owners expect privacy in order to undertake their business activities. However, privacy remains an important consideration for family businesses, in particular when funding derives from existing family wealth.

Key aspects of business information may be public, depending on the chosen legal structure. This can include a record of individuals (including directors and beneficial owners) and financial information (eg, annual financial statements), as follows:

- In the United Kingdom, both companies and LLPs are required to file annual financial statements and submit information, including director details, at Companies House; and

- Companies House maintains a Persons with Significant Control (PSC) register, which is designed to ensure disclosure of the actual controlling party rather than an intermediary or office holder such as a director or nominee trustee (ie, the ultimate beneficial owners).

There is a notable shift towards increasing transparency across a number of jurisdictions, but disclosure requirements will vary on a jurisdiction-by-jurisdiction basis.

In the United Kingdom, the partnership (as it does not provide limitation of liability to its partners) does not have any requirement to file control or financial information with Companies House. There are other less commonly used entities that require limited public disclosure such as unlimited companies and limited partnerships. Further detail around these entities is outside the scope of this chapter, but where privacy is of particular concern, they should be considered as a possible alternative to a partnership.

If privacy is a key consideration for the family business or one of the family members, then the partnership should be considered as a starting point. It should be noted that partnerships, in the United Kingdom, are still required to file tax returns with His Majesty's Revenue and Customs (HMRC) and provide copies of their annual financial statements to HMRC. However, these submissions are not publicly available.

As above, the disclosure requirements for partnerships vary between jurisdictions.

1.4 Taxation

With respect to family businesses, there are normally three key areas of taxation to consider, namely:

- the ongoing taxation of profits arising in the business;
- taxation of the owners; and
- taxation on the transfer of ownership of the business to the next generation or other family members.

While the taxation on setup of the family business is also relevant, unless an existing sole trade business is being incorporated, or significant capital assets are being transferred, there are unlikely to be significant tax implications arising. Therefore, it will usually be the longer-term tax treatment of the structures that will influence the choice.

1.5 Tax implications

(a) Ongoing taxation of the business

Partners in a partnership are each treated as taxed on their share of the taxable profits of the partnership, and are subject to income tax and social security contributions in a personal capacity on their share of partnership profits (and losses).

Members of an LLP are taxed in exactly the same way. Forming the business as a partnership (or an LLP) therefore means that all profits are taxed each year, even though the profits may be surplus to the personal spending requirements of the partners or are not drawn from the partnership.

Corporate tax rates tend to be lower than personal tax rates, so conducting the business through a company – either from the outset or at a later stage by incorporating the business – has the advantage of profits of the company being subject to corporation tax, with a retention of profits within a company allowing for a deferral of taxes on the owners.

A corporate structure may, however, result in a second layer of taxation as profits would still need to be extracted from the company in order to be used personally by the shareholders.

The flexibility of being able to utilise any tax losses should also be considered. In the United Kingdom, utilising losses which have arisen within a company would typically be more restrictive as they can only be utilised against other profits of the company, while an individual might be able to offset losses arising to them individually against other taxable income. One would hope that this is only a relevant consideration in the early days of the business.

(b) Taxation of the owners

If a partnership or LLP structure is chosen, then as the profits are subject to tax each year, there are no further tax considerations when profit is actually extracted from the partnership by the owners.

For a company, consideration will need to be given to how owners can extract profits, as follows:

- For a family member employed by the company and seeking to extract a regular income from the company, the family member will typically negotiate a salary (and certain benefits), which will usually be subject to income tax and social security contributions for both the employee and employer. The cost of salaries and social security contributions should generally be tax deductible against the company's taxes.
- If a family member is also a shareholder, then dividends may supplement any salary payment or, indeed, may be paid instead of salary or a bonus. Although dividends may be paid without the burden of social security contributions and may also attract a lower rate of income

tax, dividends are generally paid out of profits that have already been taxed at the company level.

In order for dividends to be paid, the company will need to have distributable reserves (ie, retained earnings) and the directors of the company will need to agree to any dividend distributions. It is possible to differentiate the dividends received by different shareholders or groups of shareholders by using 'alphabet shares'.[1] However, where there is any differentiation in dividends being drawn, care needs to be taken that this is implemented in an equitable manner and shareholders are not left disaffected.

Neither extracting as salary or dividends is likely to be markedly more tax efficient in the United Kingdom, but benefits may be notable elsewhere.

Because of the tax implications of extracting profits, family members may be inclined to leave profits in the business. The strategy may be, therefore, to extract value on exiting the business, if they sell or IPO (initial public offering) the company, as the tax rates for capital gains tend to be lower than income. However, individuals should be aware that where tax rates favour capital gains over income, there are often anti-avoidance rules to consider.

(c) Taxes on succession

It will be important to plan early and understand the impact of the chosen structure on the tax consequences of passing on the business to family members, although succession may be many years hence.

The principal relevant taxes are inheritance or estate taxes and capital taxes. Business interests may pass on death as an inheritance or be gifted during lifetime; and different rules may apply to each. On a non-tax related point, some jurisdictions also have forced heirship rules, which may be relevant when planning for the future of the business.

The applicable tax rules will vary significantly from jurisdiction to jurisdiction, but usually there will be a favourable tax treatment for interests in trading rather than investment businesses, which can be very helpful in avoiding tax attrition on the succession of family businesses. This is a policy lever aimed at encouraging entrepreneurship and investment into business.

While ostensibly trading, caution should be exercised where profits are directed to investing in property or other investment assets, albeit that the main trade continues and remains the dominant activity. In such circumstances, the trading status may be jeopardised and the opportunity to benefit from favourable tax treatments may be lost.

---

1 'Alphabet shares' refer to different shareholders, each holding shares in separate share classes, which are usually named A shares, B shares, C shares, and so on. This allows for different dividends to be declared on different share classes.

1.6 Ownership structure

As detailed above, the form of the operating structure needs to be considered, but so too does the ownership of that operating structure.

The trading business may be owned directly by the family, though the family may wish to consider other holding structures to ease the transition on succession and support the shared objectives of the family.

The choice of holding structure can be complex, with multiple jurisdictions and specific tax treatments to be taken into account. It may also be that the most suitable holding structure changes with time. Therefore, it is essential that professional advice is taken to ensure that the chosen holding structure meets the objectives of the family and does not result in any unforeseen tax, or administrative or operational consequences.

(a) Direct ownership

The family members could own a family business directly, as partners of shareholders. This is a simple ownership structure that minimises administration and is clear in its purpose. It will often be the case that direct ownership will be the most suitable in the early stages of trading, with alternative structures perhaps becoming more suitable as the business and family grows.

(b) Family Investment Company (FIC)

Interests in the family business could be owned through a FIC, which is a label for a company used to hold family investments. FICs can be used flexibly and allow, for example, for the segregation of future economic rights (usually held by younger generations), from the voting rights (usually held by older generations).

In addition to the trading family business, a FIC would typically hold other family investment assets. However, the ownership of investment and trading assets should be carefully considered, as entities holding mainly trading assets tend to receive more favourable tax treatment; and mixing the two could taint this.

(c) Trusts

Holding the family business through a trust structure can be an attractive option, as it would allow for family members to enjoy economic benefits on a discretionary basis, while allowing for voting and control to be retained by the trustees.

Other structures, such as foundations, may fulfil a similar purpose in other jurisdictions, particularly those with a civil law framework. They allow for a balance between taking a long-term view to ensure the enduring success of the business and the short-term economic needs of family members. Decision making can be considered by the trustees and prevents the fragmentation of voting rights as families expand, which may help prevent the dilution of a family interest.

Trusts can also be used to defer decision making in connection with succession plans for a family business. This latter point can be beneficial if the next generation are not yet ready to take on full responsibility for the family business, or, indeed, if it is not clear who among them may be best suited.

However, trusts require a certain amount of administration and will incur running costs. Most notably, alongside more senior family members, it may be preferred to have professional trustees in place.

The settlement of value into trusts and the ongoing taxation of trusts and their recognition can be complex and vary from jurisdiction to jurisdiction. Therefore, it is essential that jurisdiction-specific advice is sought in connection with any proposed trust structure.

(d) Limited partnership

Family members could be members of a limited partnership which owns the interest in the family business. A partnership in this context would allow for flexibility around the allocation of profit share (according to a partnership agreement) and a smooth change in owners (partners). However, interposing a limited partnership between the shareholders and the underlying trading company is not without its complexities – and potential tax pitfalls – and jurisdiction-specific advice should be sought as to its suitability.

2. Finance

Businesses can require financing for a number of reasons. Often it will be to commence trading or fund the next stage of growth. However, finance may also be required to navigate through periods of economic difficulty, such as the COVID-19 pandemic, or even to buy out exiting shareholders.

There are two principal types of finance that the business can obtain: equity or loan finance. Quasi-equity exhibits characteristics of both equity and loan finance. Often a combination of financing methods will be used – it is rarely a binary choice.

2.1 Equity finance

A company limited by shares would obtain equity finance by the issue of share capital; LLPs and partnerships would obtain equity by the contribution of capital by the partners.

Equity finance is typically a riskier form of investment from the perspective of the equity holder as there is no mechanism for them to demand repayment or a guaranteed return thereon; and equity will rank behind debt in a creditors' waterfall.[2] Conversely, the equity holder may have influence through voting power, receive dividends and benefit from the growth in value of the business as the business succeeds.

---

2 'Creditors' waterfall' is the order in which a company's assets would be applied in discharging its creditors, which may include lenders, suppliers, employees and shareholders.

A family business may seek equity investment from family members only to maintain full control of the business by the family. There may be a limit as to how much finance family members are willing to provide, in which case it may be necessary to consider external finance.

Should equity finance be obtained from non-family members (eg, professional investors such as business angels, private equity or venture capitalists), the family will need to consider the terms of the investment, including the rights and returns and any impact on the family's ability to control and run the business as they are accustomed.

2.2 Loan finance

Loan finance may be obtained from family members, banks and other financial institutions or other third parties, such as business angels or venture capitalists. It is less risky to the investor as the loan agreement will, generally, include provision for future repayment of the capital and interest thereon. The loan finance will also often be secured against assets of the business. Conversely, the lender will not, typically, influence the business through the power to vote or benefit from any upside where the business is successful, although there may be covenants imposed or conditions around board representation that require the business to be operated in a particular fashion.

Lenders will typically receive interest as their return, which means that cash has to be expended from the business to service the debt, albeit some forms of loan may allow for interest to be rolled up against the loan principal.

The advantage of loan financing is that it does not dilute the family ownership of the business. However, external loan financing can be expensive and difficult to access for new businesses which do not have an established track record or asset base against which to secure lending. Lenders will charge an interest rate which is commensurate to the level of commercial risk they are bearing.

2.3 Other forms of finance

The business may be able to seek other forms of finance, such as grants, if it undertakes research and development, activities for community benefit, etc. Alternatively, if the business is profitable, the funds for future growth may be accumulated by reinvesting the profits into the business.

As mentioned above, there are also forms of finance which have hallmarks of both equity and loan financing. For example, redeemable preference shares are legally a form of equity, but will often carry a coupon or preferential right to dividends which is akin to interest; and can be redeemed or effectively repaid like a loan. On the other hand, loans can be structured as convertible loans, which allow for them to be converted into equity in certain circumstances.

The tax, legal and commercial implications of financing structures should be carefully considered when concluding on the preferred financing structure.

3. People – family/non-family

A family business, at least in its earlier days, is likely to be driven – from a managerial and strategic perspective – by its owners.

Strictly, however, the management of the business is the responsibility of the board of directors, who will be appointed by the shareholders. Directors assume personal liability in certain circumstances and are required to perform their duties in the best interests of the company. At least initially, the board is likely to be comprised of the owners.

External appointments to the board may come in time, when the direction and operation of the family business has become established and the culture is well understood. At this time, the introduction of non-family members may be more viable since individuals with the right expertise, trust and cultural fit may then be identified.

As the business grows, business reasons to appoint non-family members in senior and directorship positions are also likely to increase. These will include the need for specific skills and expertise; which could include:

- an independent and commercial perspective from their own experience;
- an objective opinion where emotional baggage could otherwise cloud judgement;
- improvements to governance;
- development of the team;
- the ability to challenge/question approach and strategy; and
- the mentoring of new family members and support around their integration; and the ability to hold boundaries.

With the passage of time, a more established family business evolves as well as increasing numbers of family members with different skills to contribute to the family business, varying levels of interest in being involved in the family business and divergent expectations around the contribution to, and reward from, the family business.

Establishing the route into the family business, and its accessibility, for family members is likely to help in creating a well-respected structure and avoid perceived favouritism. In particular, this may include a policy around the requirement for external experience, the interview and onboarding process and the remuneration as well as clear parameters around the existing hierarchy or structure and how new family members can expect to fit into that.

Some form of equity participation is often helpful to align the interests of working and non-working family members, as well as non-family members. Equity participation could take several different forms. There may be opportunities to structure equity participation tax efficiently, depending on the jurisdiction of residency of the individuals seeking a return and specific circumstances of the business.

In addition to share schemes, other interesting employee ownership models may be available in different jurisdictions. An option which is being used increasingly in the United Kingdom is to establish an Employee Ownership Trust. This is a statutory trust recognised in the United Kingdom which provides a mechanism to pass ownership, indirectly, to employees with UK tax advantages and a motivated workforce as resultant benefits. There are specific requirements associated with such a trust: on a high level, it provides a mechanism for shareholders to realise their interest (perhaps in part) in exchange for staged payments funded by the company's operations. The realisation is capital gains tax-free for the shareholders and provides them with comfort that the succession of the company is secured since it will be necessary for the trust to own a controlling interest in the company. As the trust is for the benefit of the employees, it allows for non-family members to benefit (indirectly) from equity-like participation. It also allows family members who wish to remain involved in the business to benefit in a similar manner, thus aligning the interests of those individuals who are committed to the ongoing success of the business.

In conclusion, there are various roles available to both family members and non-family members in a family business. The breadth of roles allows for a range of individuals, as well as operational directors, employees and shareholders. Experienced individuals, who are withdrawing from day-to-day involvement, or have no desire for close involvement, could take on the role of a non-executive director. Establishing the eligibility requirements of these roles and a competency framework within which the individuals operate will support the smooth running of the family business and continual motivation of family and non-family participators.

4. Constitution

A family business has to manage the same operational challenges as any other business, with added complications. Inter-familial relationships and family relationships with the business need to be carefully managed.

It is the culture of the business that is commonly the principal driver for families to want to go into business together and the key factor which enables families to continue to work together in times of change and adversity. It should, therefore, be considered how the culture of the family in the context of their family business is established and sustained across generations. In this context, the formal constitutional documents governing the family business can play an important role.

The articles of association are a requirement for establishing a company in the United Kingdom and set out the company purpose, its administrative structure, powers and duties of company directors, and the declaration of dividends. They are in place to regulate how a company is managed and are legally binding. The articles can be changed by shareholder agreement, normally by way of special resolution, requiring agreement of at least 75% of shareholders. It is common, however, for a shareholder group to adopt model articles which provide a very basic framework and enter into other separate agreements, legally binding or not, to set the governance framework of the company.

A shareholder agreement is such a document; it is also legally binding and provides a blank canvas for shareholders to define their relationship. It will often incorporate provisions requiring approval around director remuneration, entering substantial business contracts and commercial legal proceedings, for example. It is a private document, in contrast to the articles, which are publicly available, certainly in the United Kingdom.

The shareholder agreement will typically address operational matters and provide a framework which the shareholders and directors operate within, particularly where contentious scenarios present. It could equally go into detail around how to deal with specific foreseen circumstances, limit the shareholder group (eg, to include bloodline only, or to prevent a family branch acquiring control), address director recruitment and removal, set a company valuation methodology, or provide controls over the transfer of shares, dividend policies and policy on an internal market for shares. The scope may, therefore, be wider and it is for the family to agree how prescriptive such a document is.

A further document to consider – and continually revisit throughout the operation of the family business – is a 'family charter' or 'family constitution'. This is where the core mission statement of the family can be found; and may set out a framework for decision making within the family environment.

The document is entirely private – and not usually legally binding – but forever evolving with the family. Ideally, it serves to support the family in a much wider context than just the family business across a family office, trust structures, investment attitudes and the family's conception of its overriding purpose, values and ethos.

A family charter may be written in a relatable way, encompassing core values and the mission of the family operating in parallel with the legal agreements referenced above. The family charter is most effective where there is deep and quality engagement from the family, across generations and branches, encompassing the current and the future custodians of the business. This facilitates the buy-in and understanding to put the family in good stead to deal with the business challenges which present themselves.

5. Practical

5.1 Adviser team

Although many of the skills and resources required by the business may be provided by family members or employees, professional advisers will be essential to the smooth establishment and operation of the family business. Professional advisers are likely to include lawyers and accountants at the very least. How best to identify suitable advisers and invite tenders for these services should be considered as well as the defining of the professional relationship.

5.2 Compliance

The business may need to register with the local corporate registry. Processes will need to be put in place for accounting and record keeping, and appropriate software used to support this. Tax registrations will also need to be made, including for corporate, employment and sales taxes. Ongoing compliance is essential to the good standing of a business.

5.3 Banking

The time required for opening a business bank account should not be underestimated, particularly if there is an overseas element, as the bank will require detailed information and supporting documentation about the owners of the family business and the source of funds being used to establish the business. Existing banking relationships may be helpful as a starting point.

5.4 IT/AI processes

IT systems appropriate to the size and complexity of the business's operations should be established. Initially, this is likely to include accounting software, website (including the capability to take orders, where necessary), email and office applications.

Engagements will need to be established, in particular, for IT maintenance, disaster recovery and security. IT support may be in-house or outsourced, and with cyber security being the biggest threat to many family businesses, it is crucial to effectively manage data protection, fraud and phishing attempts. Oversights here could lead to reputational risk for the family.

Depending on the nature of the family business, consideration may also need to be given to potential applications of artificial intelligence (AI), which may help to streamline business processes. Some AI functionality may be built into commercial software products which the business uses, but more bespoke applications may require input from a specialist consultant.

5.5 Premises

While it may initially be possible to operate the business from the home of a family member, where this is not possible, or in due course, it will be necessary to locate premises for the family business. These will often be leasehold and, among other things, consideration will need to be given to the location, the length of the lease, whether the premises provide sufficient capacity for growth during the lease term and, of course, cost.

5.6 Disaster recovery

A plan should be put in place to ensure the ongoing operation of the business in case of adversity or unforeseen events. Such events might include natural disasters, or the COVID-19 pandemic, for example.

5.7 Insurance

With many vulnerabilities for a family business, insurance should be considered with professional advice. This is likely to include employers' liability insurance, buildings insurance, business interruption insurance, and any specific insurances required according to the nature of the business. Directors would also be well advised to take out directors' and officers' liability insurance.

6. International

Globalisation means that businesses are increasingly international in their operations, whether this involves digital businesses selling to an international customer base, establishing operations overseas, or employees working remotely.

This process has been further catalysed by the advent of working from home and advances in technology. However, tax legislation often does not keep pace with rapid technological advancement, particularly when it comes to international matters.

While the Organisation of Economic Co-operation and Development's (OECD) Base Erosion and Profit Shifting (BEPS) project and the recent minimum global tax rate are coordinated global measures, they are at this stage primarily aimed at the largest businesses. In the meantime, some countries have acted unilaterally, such as the United Kingdom's introduction of the Digital Services Tax.[3] Businesses need to be aware of tax laws applicable to the countries in which they operate, and regularly horizon-scan given the ever-evolving legislative landscape.

Below are further examples of international matters which can be relevant to family businesses. In addition, there may, of course, be many other non-tax-related considerations in operating overseas, such as local regulatory issues, exchange controls and protected markets.

6.1 Transfer pricing

Transfer pricing is, broadly, a concept which requires that transactions between related parties are priced on arm's-length terms, so that pricing is not used as a means of artificially diverting profits to a related business in a low-tax jurisdiction.

Many jurisdictions will have a size-based exemption from transfer pricing. For example, in the United Kingdom, many small and medium-sized enterprises

---

3 See www.gov.uk/government/publications/introduction-of-the-digital-services-tax/digital-services-tax.

are not required to operate transfer pricing. It is, of course, necessary to understand the rules and exemptions which may be applicable in the different jurisdictions in which a business operates. Notwithstanding this, the United Kingdom's exemption for small and medium-sized enterprises does not extend to entities which, broadly, are tax resident in a jurisdiction with which the United Kingdom does not have a comprehensive double tax treaty.

Arm's-length pricing is therefore relevant for international family businesses that may have structures located in jurisdictions that do not have the relevant treaties in place, such as the British Virgin Islands, Channel Islands, or other international financial centres.

6.2 Tax residence

Companies are generally regarded as tax resident in their jurisdiction of incorporation as a default. However, central management and control or effective management of an entity can also result in a company being regarded as tax resident elsewhere.

In such cases, where there is more than one relevant jurisdiction, companies may either be dual tax resident, or if there is a tax treaty between the two jurisdictions, this may provide for a 'tie-breaker'[4] to determine tax residence. Usually, the taxing rights of the jurisdiction of central management and control, or effective management, will override the taxing rights of the jurisdiction of incorporation. Therefore, the location from which directors and senior management run the company will be important for tax residence.

It may be that certain directors are resident overseas or that whole family branches that are closely involved in the control and management of a company may choose to relocate. It is possible that such relocations cause the company's tax residence to change.

In the United Kingdom, individuals (or families) can become non-UK tax resident with no exit taxes, but the same is not true of companies. If a company ceases to be UK tax resident, then it is deemed to have disposed of and reacquired its assets for market value at the point of exit – which can result in a 'dry' tax charge.[5]

While these are the United Kingdom's rules, other jurisdictions may have their own version of such rules.

Therefore, international families who are appointing overseas directors or relocating should be alive to the potential consequences for their business interests; and professional advice should be sought, as it will often be possible to arrange affairs in such a way that a company's tax residence can be managed.

---

4 'Tie breaker' clauses within a tax treaty provide a series of tests to be applied or a procedure to be followed, in order for the tax residence of a taxpayer to be determined for the purposes of that tax treaty.

5 A 'dry' tax charge is where tax arises on income or gains which have not actually been received; and so there is no liquidity with which to fund the payment of the tax charge.

6.3 Permanent establishment

If a company establishes an overseas subsidiary, then clearly that overseas subsidiary will have a local tax presence. However, 'permanent establishments' can result in a company having a taxable presence overseas without a separate structure or, indeed, intention.

Broadly, permanent establishments arise when a company is doing business in another jurisdiction, rather than doing business with another jurisdiction. Often, double tax treaties will include provisions in connection with permanent establishments and will include carve outs for activities which are preparatory or auxiliary in nature. Permanent establishments, as the name suggests, require some element of permanence and may take the form of an office overseas or a retail store.

It can also include a place of management. It has been found that an individual working from home could give rise to a permanent establishment, so in the context of a family business, if a senior family member were to relocate overseas and continue to operate from there, or perhaps more commonly were to spend substantial amounts of time working from a second holiday home, then this could give rise to a permanent establishment.

Less common for a family business, but a recent trend nonetheless, is the hiring of senior members of staff internationally, as technological advances and ease of travel make this viable. This results in the same permanent establishment risks outlined above.

7. Conclusion

The establishment of a family business requires many decisions for the founding family members from an operational, strategic and structural perspective. Well-thought-through early decisions will provide a solid foundation from which the business may develop and grow. Continual reflection and preparedness to adjust where aspects are no longer fit for purpose will put the business in the best possible position to survive and thrive into the future.

The views expressed in this chapter are the personal views of the authors expressed in that capacity and are not made on behalf of Rawlinson & Hunter LLP.

The value of family governance

Ken McCracken
MFBC Limited

1. Family enterprises

Behind every family business and family office is an enterprising family whose lives are connected through the ownership and enjoyment of various assets and activities. Hence the terms 'family enterprise' and 'enterprising family' are used in this chapter to refer to both a family business and a family office.

2. Family governance

Family enterprise governance is everything that maintains a functional balance of interests among three groups of stakeholders: (i) the people who work in the enterprise; (ii) the current owners (including any beneficial owners); and (iii) relatives of the owners who we will call 'family'. Effective governance helps these stakeholders to perform their respective roles satisfactorily and to participate in a network of relationships in the family and the enterprise.

Family governance is always part of this overall governance for several reasons, such as:

- the enterprise could be the source of the family's financial security, so family members who are neither owners nor employees have a vested interest in its performance;
- some family members might view the enterprise as a future career opportunity;
- the conduct of the enterprise could affect the family's social status and sense of self-worth, and, equally, the behaviour of family members could affect the enterprise's reputation; and
- how the enterprise deals with its stakeholders and accounts for its impact on the environment and society could all be based on the beliefs and aspirations of the founding family as well as commercial considerations.

2.1 Discovering family governance

Some family enterprises are attracted to formal family governance, such as having a written family constitution and policies that govern potentially sensitive areas like employing family members. Some of them create formal structures with rules of engagement and participation, like a family assembly or family council. However, it is important to grasp that all family enterprises have family governance and not just those with an appetite for formality.

The family governance that always exists is in the form of customs and conventions, assumptions, expectations and understandings, which we will call 'natural family governance'. This governance initially emerges spontaneously from innumerable interactions among stakeholders, and from decisions that are made to cope with whatever life throws at the family and their enterprise. It is sustained by a successful family enterprise having the good sense to continue governance practices that have worked well for them in the past, while also seeking to avoid repeating their previous mistakes – that is, learning from experience.

An absence of formal family governance should never be mistaken for an absence of governance. The mere fact that natural family governance has not been written down does not mean it does not exist – it just means it has not been written down. When advisers become involved, the first task is to discover and describe the natural family governance that already exists, then perhaps to modify some aspects of it or fill any gaps that become apparent.

There is a very practical reason for adopting this discovery approach. Successful family enterprises naturally resist making radical changes to existing governance practices that have helped them become successful. Change can easily be perceived as a threat to the existing order, and so will be accepted only when the need for it is clear. This attitude to change is sometimes described as a preference for evolution over revolution, and it means that family enterprises tend to move forward by adapting their existing governance so that it can remain functional.

This makes it essential for advisers to understand existing governance before making suggestions that might result in change. Suggesting changes while choosing to remain deliberately ignorant of existing governance risks arousing the innate resistance to change in a family enterprise, which once mobilised can easily overwhelm the desire or even the need for change.

The task of discovering and describing natural family governance can involve:

- articulating existing norms in relation to family governance;
- identifying the overall purpose of the family enterprise and the governance practices that serve this purpose; and
- identifying who is eligible for important governance roles.

3. Every enterprising family is normal

Every family enterprise has unwritten rules that determine what is acceptable, or normal, behaviour. These norms will be based on the history and culture of the family, and sometimes a world view that is shaped by their religious faith, political ideology or other belief system. Norms will also have absorbed influences from education, travel, other social groups and the media.

Norms are different from values. Norms identify behaviours that are currently accepted as normal, whereas values are principles that express what a family enterprise aspires to become. Accordingly, the process of discovering family governance involves discovering existing norms of behaviour rather than creating a statement of values.

Norms can be discovered wherever the curious observer cares to explore. The simplest enquiry would be "What normally happens in relation to ...?", followed by the subject of enquiry. This could be applied to the following areas of governance that are often important.

Table 1: Enquiries about norms

Norm	"What normally happens in relation to ..."
Communication	... sharing information about the enterprise with the wider family?
Conflict	... dealing with disagreements or conflicts among family members, including any that involve the enterprise?
Conflict of interest	... family members working for, investing in, or buying products or services from the family enterprise's competitors?
Cultural attitudes	... attitudes about work, wealth, financial and other types of risk, philanthropy, gender roles and the status of different generations?
Cultural beliefs	... any belief system that shapes relationships in the family and/or the enterprise's strategy, such as a religious faith or political ideology?
Decision making	... making decisions in the family? Is any family member who is not an owner, director or employee normally involved in or able to influence decisions about the enterprise?
Education	... educating the family about the enterprise, including its history, ownership and current operations?
Family glue	... family events or rituals that help to maintain family cohesion, for example, a regular family gathering or event?

Enquiring into the unique version of normality in a family enterprise will reveal a lot of information about family governance. This can then be enhanced by the other approaches described below.

4. Purpose

The owners of a family enterprise will be striving to achieve a version of success that matters to them, which becomes the purpose of their enterprise. Governance, including family governance, will be what it must be to achieve this purpose because that is what all governance does – it serves a purpose. Good governance supports the purpose and bad governance gets in the way.

The accepted view is that to discover the purpose of a family enterprise, it is necessary to identify the financial objectives and any non-financial returns on investment to which the owners attribute value. The value generated by non-financial returns is referred to as socio-emotional wealth, which describes a range of positive emotional responses to a family enterprise that create a powerful sense of psychological ownership among various stakeholders.

These could include feelings of joy or pride that are connected to the family enterprise and its operations, or to its success and its brand. It could be a sense of identity, status or self-worth that derives from being part of a family enterprise. The feelings might also relate to the impact the enterprise has on a geographical community, an economic sector or the physical environment.

There are some family enterprises for whom the idea of a non-financial objective would be a good definition of 'non-sense'. However, the pursuit of socio-emotional wealth is common enough among family enterprises to make it worthy of enquiry.

4.1 Financial purpose

There is no universal financial purpose that applies to every family enterprise. It could, for example, be to:

- build the enterprise and pass it to the next generation;
- focus on providing a desired level of financial security and standard of living for the current generation; or
- build and sell all or part of the enterprise in the foreseeable future.

Each of these is a worthwhile financial objective that requires different governance, including in the domain of family governance. For example, how will family members receiving benefits, or perks, through the enterprise be governed?

These could include travelling at the expense of the enterprise, or using its property and vehicles, or attending sporting or cultural events that prioritise the family's preferred leisure activities. It could extend to receiving discounts on goods or services supplied by the enterprise or some of its commercial partners.

Discovering how perks are governed could be the subject of a direct enquiry, but it can also be inferred from the purpose of the enterprise based on the assumption that a purpose will lead to governance practices that are consistent with the purpose. As mentioned, good governance supports the purpose of a family enterprise, while bad governance gets in the way.

Family perks would be more likely to be acceptable when the financial objective is to provide financial security and a desirable standard of living for the current generation. In contrast, if the financial purpose was to build the enterprise and pass it on to the next generation, family perks could be considered unnecessary costs that would be better reinvested in the growth of the enterprise. If the purpose was to build and sell the enterprise in the foreseeable future, the existence of family perks might be viewed as risky if a prospective purchaser could use these as a reason to reduce the price.

When the financial purpose is known, it becomes possible to infer governance practices, including family governance, that would be consistent with the purpose. This approach to discovery can be expressed in the maxim: "If this is your financial purpose, this is how you would expect to be governed to achieve it." Applying this maxim requires a little imagination – and experience – and can be used to explore areas of family governance that might otherwise remain undiscovered.

4.2 Non-financial purpose

Examples of non-financial objectives drawn from research and practical experience that could represent a source of socio-emotional wealth for stakeholders in a family enterprise include:

- maintaining family harmony or cohesion;
- keeping a growing family connected through an interest in the enterprise;
- maintaining a positive image and respect for a family; and
- providing careers for family members.

If these objectives matter, there will be governance in place to ensure that they matter in making decisions, creating strategies and implementing plans. In building the picture of natural family governance, it is reasonable to enquire how a family enterprise achieves these objectives by exploring questions such as:

- What is done to maintain family harmony and cohesion?
- How is a growing family kept connected through the enterprise? Does this involve sharing information with the family or holding regular family get-togethers involving discussions about the enterprise?
- Does maintaining the family's image mean there are things the enterprise cannot do that might be acceptable to competitors? Does it

involve family members as brand ambassadors attending commercial events, or meeting customers, or making presentations to long-serving employees? Does it include family being involved in civic roles that support the enterprise, such as working for a charity or being involved in politics?

If providing careers for family members is important for the family enterprise, how is this governed? Questions could include:

- What degree of nepotism is used in hiring employees?
- What support is given to help family employees advance their career that might not be available to other employees?
- Are family members expected to work harder for the same reward as other employees, or do they receive special benefits in terms of flexible working, study leave, holidays and remuneration?

These enquiries based on the non-financial objectives in a family enterprise will help produce a nuanced and realistic picture of family governance. The next enquiry will add even more detail to the picture.

5. Who is family?

So far, the term 'family' has been used without definition. This needs to be considered because it is likely that a family will use the term differently when identifying who is eligible for different roles in governance. The adviser might ask: "Who is family for the purpose of …" becoming an owner, joining a board of directors, getting a job in the family enterprise, or attending a family event that involves the enterprise?

The answer in relation to ownership could be that family is restricted to bloodline descendants of the founder. However, the definition for the purpose of joining a board could be expanded to include spouses or partners of current owners.

All the above are welcome to apply for a job in the family enterprise but on this occasion the definition of 'family' is redefined and extended to include stepchildren and adopted children who would not be within the more restricted definition of bloodline when it comes to ownership. Meanwhile, the founder's siblings and their direct descendants will all be invited to a family gathering that is related to the enterprise.

This illustrates how important aspects of governance, covering ownership, leadership and family governance and the way in which employing family members is governed, can emanate from how a family – note, a family – define relationships for the purpose of each of these roles.

6. Enforcing family governance

Natural family governance does not have formal enforcement mechanisms and instead relies on a system of subtle and not-so-subtle incentives and sanctions. A shorthand way of describing this might be that this governance works because it has moral force.

Family members could be encouraged to conform with existing governance practices by emulating ancestors who are revered as exemplars of the right behaviours, and avoiding the misdemeanours committed by other relatives. Those who do this will be praised, which is a form of reward, and will expect to be preferred when it comes to deciding who is eligible for ownership, or a job in the enterprise, or attending a family gathering.

In contrast, recalcitrants risk being criticised for their unacceptable behaviour. This could involve being accused of rebelling and causing upset and might even be punished by a breakdown in family relationships. These sanctions, or even the threat of them, are administered in the hope of causing shame, guilt and remorse that will lead to changes in behaviour that re-establish the primacy of existing family governance.

In this environment, individuals can choose to fit in by behaving in the way they believe others expect them to behave, and they expect others to do likewise. These shared expectations based on family governance enable stakeholders to anticipate how others will act and thereby to coordinate their overall behaviours. And all this is achieved without any formal governance.

7. Change

The process of discovering family governance could lead to some practices being endorsed, but it could also be a catalyst for change. For example, a family might not like some of the prevailing norms or existing practices that have been revealed, such as how conflicts are dealt with, the consumption of family perks, or employment of family members. At this point, change becomes permissible and desirable in relation to these areas of governance.

The process could also have identified gaps in governance that a family decides need to be filled with a view to the future. For example, while there has never been any conflict between the career or investment decisions made by individual family members and the activities of the enterprise, it might be accepted that this should be addressed in case it happens going forward.

In these circumstances, advisers can make suggestions based on their broader knowledge of this field of practice and experience of what other family enterprises have done. However, their understanding of natural family governance will help to ensure that these suggestions are sensitively attuned to this existing reality and thereby more likely to gain acceptance.

8. Formal family governance

Having gone to the effort of discovering family governance and agreeing any changes that may be necessary, a family enterprise and its adviser might decide that this deserves to be recorded in writing for future reference.

The strongest case for formalising family governance is that it makes things clearer. On the other hand, formality can lead to rigidity because formal governance cannot adapt and evolve as easily as natural governance. There is an element of personal taste in this choice, with some enterprising families being attracted by formality, while others are repelled. However, this should never descend into a debate over which approach is better or best; every enterprising family must approach family governance in the way that makes sense to them, and they should expect advisers to respect this choice.

If a family wants to document its family governance, it is likely to be called a family constitution or charter. The contents will include some or all the information that has been covered in this chapter, in particular:

- a description of the overall purpose that is used by the family enterprise to measure success;
- family governance practices that are aligned to and support this purpose, including, for example, family perks and employing family members;
- which family members are eligible for the key governance roles; and
- norms of behaviour that matter in the relationship among family members and between them and the enterprise.

A family might also want its family governance to be supported by formal institutions like a family assembly. Like any forum, club or association, the role of a family assembly in governance needs to be clarified, and when this is done the detail can be included in the family constitution or charter. Questions to identify the role of the family assembly might include the following:

- What is it that the assembly wants to achieve? Is it mainly a social purpose or does it include educating family about the enterprise or creating policies in areas like family perks or employing family?
- Who can attend?
- Who organises it (the secretarial and chair functions in a group)?
- How often will it meet?
- How does it make decisions?
- How is it funded?
- How is it held accountable for its contribution to governance?
- How does it communicate with its members and other institutions of family enterprise governance, like a board of directors?

Where a family assembly becomes large, it can be helpful to appoint or elect a separate group – the family council – with responsibility for running the assembly. The questions listed above can be applied to defining the role of the council.

9. Value of family governance

Family governance is a unique feature of family enterprises. It will not be found in a company whose shares are listed on a public stock exchange or in a business that is backed by private equity. It will also be irrelevant to an employee-owned company, a cooperative or a charity.

The value of family governance is in maintaining a functional balance of interests among members of an enterprising family and between them and the enterprise. This enables these stakeholders to coexist and collaborate effectively, which makes a vital contribution to overall governance of a family enterprise.

As mentioned earlier, the mere absence of formal family governance should never be mistaken for an absence of governance. In a successful family enterprise, there will always be customs and conventions, assumptions, expectations and understandings that need to be discovered and described before any attempt is made to introduce changes. This is worth the effort because it clarifies the governance that already exists, which may sometimes be unclear, and it ensures that any changes are compatible with this existing governance.

Enterprising families who want to formalise their family governance would be well advised to engage advisers who can help them with the interesting task of writing down what exists, before modifying it if necessary, so that this governance remains functional in pursuit of whatever purpose motivates the family enterprise.

Stages of the family business

Yannick Archambault
KPMG Canada
Kaajal Prasad
KPMG Australia

1. Understanding family business life cycles: when a family office may be the next step

Throughout the life cycle of a family enterprise, both the family and the business evolve through several distinct business and generational changes. Each stage has certain milestones that mark a significant shift in the business, and new challenges and opportunities that have an impact on the family and its dynamics.

Continuity is key to ensuring the long-term sustainability and success of the business while also preserving the family's values, legacy and relationships. As an operating business grows into a multi-generational family enterprise, it requires careful planning and the implementation of formal governance, education, communication, strategic planning, financial management and succession.

This chapter provides an overview of the various stages in the family business life cycle and the complexities of intergenerational transitions that begin to emerge as the family's wealth grows alongside that of the business.

2. Ensuring continuity

There is a pivotal transition point in the life cycle of a family business when managing the full scope of the family's business operations, investments, real estate holdings, philanthropic endeavours and human capital all require a high degree of sophistication, coordination and professionalism. It is also where the family's financial, business and personal affairs have reached such a level of complexity that dedicated, full-time management is required to ensure that the efficient, effective and secure handling of every aspect of the family's financial and human capital continues to contribute to the family's personal goals as well as its wealth. This is when the capabilities of a family office often become a key consideration for the continuity of the family enterprise.

2.1 Considerations for advisers

Advisers can play a crucial role in helping their family enterprise clients determine the right time to consider the potential benefits of transitioning to a family office. Often, they provide guidance through a structured and broad-ranging approach to assessing the family's needs, educating family members on a variety of wealth management and preservation options, and developing a strategic plan for the next stage in the life cycle of the business and the family.

Each stage requires careful planning and strategic decision making. Advisers who understand the unique characteristics of each stage can help to support the continuity of the business and the family through ongoing assessments of their needs, helping in the development of a strategic plan that aligns with their long-term goals at different stages and educating them about the benefits of different family enterprise structures. It all begins with the entrepreneurial ambition and inspiration of the business founder.

2.2 Family business life cycles: from an entrepreneurial vision to a family enterprise

Figure 1: A family business life cycle

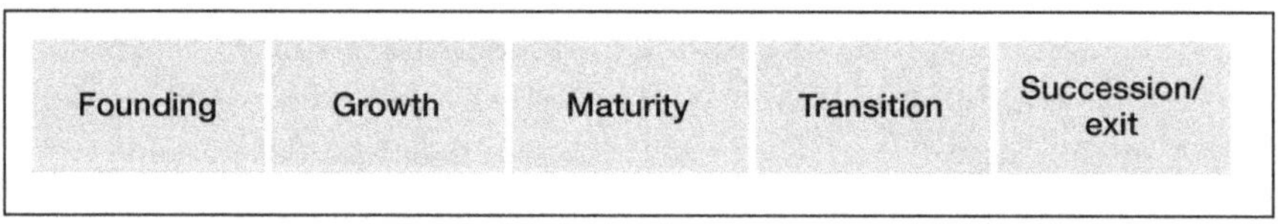

Source: KPMG International.

(a) *Stage 1: Founding a family business*

The business begins with the entrepreneurial vision of a founder or a group of founders. As a first-generation family business, this crucial first stage lays the foundation for the business's future growth and success. The founders' vision and entrepreneurial drive play a pivotal role, beginning with the identification of a potential market opportunity, realistic financial targets and a clear direction for the business with legal and operating structures in place.

(b) *Stage 2: Growth*

The business expands, increasing revenues and market share. At this stage, the business has become a robust and scalable entity, positioned for long-term success and stability as a second-generation family business with more family members involved. As it continues to expand beyond the start-up phase, new opportunities may arise for increasing market share through geographic expansion, targeting new customer segments, diversifying the product offering and introducing operating efficiencies.

(c) *Stage 3: Maturity and continuity*

The business stabilises with established products and processes. In progressing to the maturity stage, up to three generations of the family will often be involved in the business. The goal is to sustain the business, manage its resources effectively, and plan for the future to ensure that it remains viable and prosperous for subsequent generations.

At this stage, the business has typically established a strong market position, a steady revenue stream, a loyal customer base and productive, cost-effective operations. Ensuring continuity is vital to maintain the business's reputation, customer loyalty and market position.

(d) ***Stage 4: Transitions***

Leadership and ownership are passed to the next generation. Eventually, every business family faces the prospect of transferring the leadership or ownership of their business, and it is a normal part of this evolution. The goal of any business transition is to optimise results, including the successful transition of control among family generations. Harnessing the talent of next-generation family members and reimagining how the business can sustain its growth in a new digital world is a powerful way to progress the journey of the family's business.

But, as the family enterprise grows, the family's wealth grows in many different directions as well – from the financial performance of the operating businesses and real estate assets to heirlooms, annuities, private family foundations, impact investing and the non-financial human capital of the family itself. This is not necessarily a linear progression, and different generations of the family influence the focus and direction of the business as it potentially evolves into a more complex enterprising family.

Transitioning from a family business to a family enterprise involves strategic planning, diversification and robust governance structures. While a family business centres around a single entity managed by family members, enterprising families represent a broader, more diversified approach to business and investment, with formal governance and professional management aimed at long-term sustainability and growth.

The family enterprise model in Figure 2 overleaf, developed by Judi Cunningham and Family Enterprise Canada, illustrates this complexity, where the family business has often grown from one operating business to many different businesses.

(e) ***Stage 5: Succession/exits:***

Within a family enterprise, it is not uncommon at this stage that the next generation takes over; or the business is sold or closed; or the family office is professionally run by non-family executives. Succession of leadership (as opposed to ownership/control) becomes a critical factor in the continuity plan within the enterprise.

Giving up control is never easy, but every business owner must eventually face

Figure 2: The Family Enterprise model

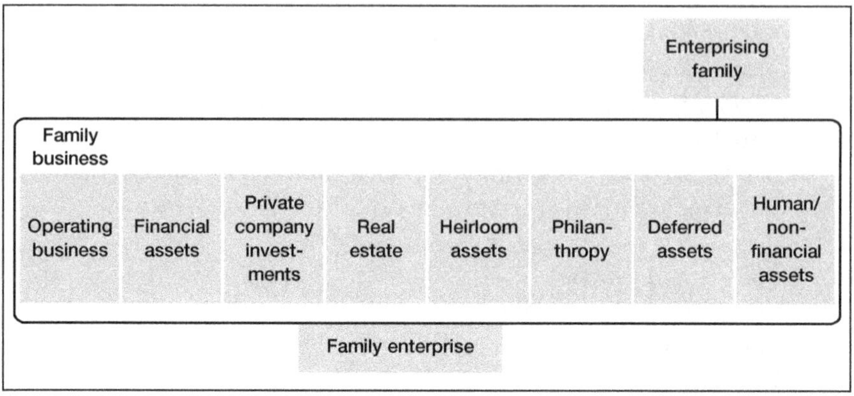

Source: Adapted from Family Enterprise Canada © Judi Cunningham 2010–2024.

reality when it is time to move on, and it is important for family enterprise leaders to reflect on the uniqueness that comes from their family history, values, dynamics and governance to ensure lasting success for the enterprise and the family.

It is unlikely that the founding generation will be the one that experiences a significant transfer of leadership or ownership or exit process. But, starting the process sooner rather than later not only allows the next generation to succeed, it also ensures that the family's legacy continues to grow for generations to come.

2.3 Understanding the complexity of family transitions

Next-generation family members often play a critical role in reshaping the strategies and priorities of their family enterprises. With a focus on the wealth of the family's human capital, they tend to be purpose-driven leaders who help to align the vision and mission of the family enterprise with contemporary values, leading social and environmental sustainability efforts and accelerating the adoption of new technologies and innovations.

Younger generations are also increasingly becoming 'wealth conscious'. They understand the need to cultivate a positive, empowered and responsible approach to the family's wealth and well-being, built on a mindset that recognises abundance, practises gratitude and takes responsible actions to preserve the long-term success and stability of the family.

2.4 Considerations for advisers

The family enterprise model is a holistic approach to a family's wealth, with both tangible and intangible assets that are not managed in isolation. Instead, they are seen as interconnected and mutually reinforcing sources of wealth that are crucial for preserving the long-term continuity of enterprising families.

Advisers play an essential role in helping family enterprises work through a structured, inclusive process to ensure that the family's assets – including the family's socio-emotional wealth – are preserved and continue to flourish.

3. The role of a family office: when and why?

There are many ways to extract wealth from an active family business: through employment income, for example, or dividends, special dividends, loan repayments or sales of specific parts of the business. Partial or full liquidation events can transfer the family's wealth from the business to a portfolio of investments. Family executives who would otherwise require specialised digital transformation, globalisation or sustainability skills to fare well in the next phase of their business's life cycle, find themselves able to make personal transitions into different types of roles.

Recognising when it is the right time to begin preparing for the next chapter of the family enterprise and its wealth is the first step in the process. It requires careful consideration and planning to determine why, when and how to begin the transition from an operating business to a family office structure.

3.1 Rising interest in family office structures

Family offices have been common since the start of this century in the United States and Europe – even earlier in some cases. Over the course of the past 10–20 years, family offices have been finding their place in Asia, Australia, Canada and New Zealand as well. Most family offices globally are the domain of families with wealth exceeding US$1 billion. An increasing number of wealthy families are now exceeding the US$500 million threshold and need to further reflect on their family office requirements, and those with US$100–$500 million are beginning to get organised as well, looking to further formalise their family office setup. Those with wealth ranging between US$30–100 million will inevitably need to reflect on the additional core expertise they may require from external providers, without having access to a fully-fledged family office.

The growth in family offices was first accelerated by the financial crisis between 2008 and 2009, which caused many wealthy families to reconsider their funding priorities as the private market realised its place in funding economic activity. Importantly, family-owned wealth, as a subset of the private market, was able to provide patient, long-term capital that not only added a financial stimulus, but also immense value in the form of business experience, insights and swift decision making without the red tape.[1]

The second major catalyst was the onset of COVID-19, which had another huge impact on economies globally. The agility and ability of family enterprises to sustain their positive long-term performance was put to the test during and

1 KPMG Australia, "Wealth in Transition — Family Offices in Plain View", 2021.

subsequent to the pandemic. Compared to other business types, they demonstrated their resilience and fared very well. The global financial turmoil that followed contributed further to the growth of family offices with wealth realisation events triggering the creation of family-owned investment portfolios.

The creation of family offices was already on the rise, but the pandemic itself caused (and sometimes forced) family enterprises to adapt their strategies quickly and pivot their enterprises into other avenues of growth. For many, this meant bringing forward the process of transition – from operating a business to managing an investment portfolio, ceding control and decision making to the next generation, or exiting their business and realising their wealth.

3.2 The impact of a great global wealth transition

The world is now on the cusp of one of the largest transfers of wealth in history. As the wealth in families grows, so does the complexity of managing their collective assets. It has never been more important for families to find ways to build and maintain their wealth. And the services of a family office are designed to support that objective.

Not only are traditional services such as investment management, philanthropy, and legal, tax and estate planning required, but also business advisory services, governance, financial education and lifestyle management opportunities for current and next-generation family members.

In this environment, advisers require the right skills and competencies as well as a full range of experience and knowledge in many different areas of family wealth, for example, investments, tax, estate planning, governance, leadership, family development, health and wellness, and philanthropy.

Family offices are made up of integrated, multidisciplinary teams that support wealthy multi-generational families by organising, managing and overseeing their complex financial and non-financial assets, wealth, goals and aspirations.

Why establish a family office?

There are often many, complementary reasons for enterprising families to establish more formal family office structures. These include the desire to:

- manage complex financial affairs;
- coordinate family activities;
- preserve family wealth and legacy;
- professionalise the business;
- increase the focus on impact investing;
- achieve a positive social and environmental impact;
- emphasise the engagement and education of next-gen family members to ensure continuity and the preservation of the family's wealth, values and legacy;

- support the business and family transition/continuity planning of senior generations; and
- access advanced technology and data analytics – which are increasingly being leveraged in family offices to enhance their investment decision-making and reporting capabilities.

3.3 Family office types

Over the years, a small number of family offices have served the needs of very wealthy families in many global markets. While they come in different shapes and sizes depending on the family's unique needs and the complexity of their affairs, they are generally constructed from one of two main types: (i) single-family offices (SFOs) that support a single individual and their family; and (ii) multi-family offices (MFOs) that support a number of different families and benefit from economies of scale.

Families with assets of US$1 billion or more will normally have the critical mass of resources to justify a dedicated single-family office and employ many in-house staff. Depending on the services required, families worth tens of millions may enlist a third-party MFO, where they share resources with other, unconnected families. Through the MFO, they are able to leverage the economies of scale and access high-calibre advice from a team of specialists.

When they start to move into the territory of several hundred million or more in investable assets, wealthy entrepreneurs and families may opt for some form of an internal SFO, with some specialist services outsourced to external providers.

4. Navigating the dynamics of multi-generational ownership and wealth

Family offices have continued to evolve in becoming wealth management and planning resources that encompass all aspects of the families' wealth. A family business that experiences a liquidity event while the family is still young, for example, may be the starting point of a first-generation family office by setting up an investment structure that provides for the future wealth of the children as they mature.

The capabilities and experience of family office professionals help families plan for the multi-generational transfers of their wealth, including educating and preparing future generations to manage their wealth and achieve their philanthropic and social impact by also addressing the dynamics of the family itself and governance practices to help families establish and maintain effective communication, decision making and continuity planning.

Transitioning away from the standard family business life cycle is a multi-faceted process – not an event. Families understand business and recognise that there are rules, models and frameworks to help guide them through the business transition process. But generally, there isn't enough emphasis on planning the family's transition as well.

Planning the business and family transition in parallel is paramount so that both are prepared to navigate the complexity of a successful business exit, family office setup and next-generation integration. In many established family offices, the traditional family business continues to be included, and is often led by an independent executive team. The shares of the business are one of the assets that the family owns and, in these cases, a considerable amount of education and coaching is undertaken across the generations to ensure that the family business is managed as an active operation, and not a passive investment.

4.1 Professionalising the family's assets

The professionalisation of the family's assets is key. A family that has been in agribusiness for four generations, for example, is skilled in all aspects of farming, but they don't necessarily know how to manage a diverse investment portfolio or grow and manage their wealth when they have left farming behind. Family offices can play a crucial role in helping to preserve that wealth for future generations. They also play an important role in facilitating the family's decision making and training and educating each generation regarding the management of a portfolio of assets.

As Joe Calabrese, a member of the Ultra High Net Worth Advisory Board, has pointed out,[2] families with successful wealth strategies share a common view that integration adds value in effective wealth management. All the elements need to work together towards a common purpose with clear accountability and coordination across all the functions by recognising the importance of two key factors:

- *Understanding and managing interdependencies:* As Joe Calabrese suggests: "Every UHNW family that has run a successful business understands the importance of coordinating the work of various teams – human resource management, finance, sales and marketing – when making critical decisions and plans. Ultra-wealthy families benefit from applying many of the same governance and management practices to the management of their wealth."
- *Seamless execution:* A well-designed wealth strategy requires thorough, comprehensive planning. "However, no strategy can be counted on to achieve important goals without timely and effective execution," Calabrese says, "which requires ongoing oversight, adaptation as circumstances change, and full integration of the work of professional team members and constituents."

---

2 Joe Calabrese, "Achieving Best-in-Class Integration in Wealth Management", Ultra High Net Worth Institute, 2021.

4.2 Next-gen impact: the rise of 'wealth consciousness'

Next-generation family members who are ready and eager to assume leadership roles in their families' businesses have often developed specialised knowledge and skills related to digital transformation, market globalisation, environmental, social and governance (ESG) regulations and requirements in the current environment.

However, some younger family members who have different attitudes towards entrepreneurship and the family enterprise are placing more importance on mission and purpose, with less concern for the family's quantum of wealth. Many have a preference to pursue alternative careers in areas where they can have a positive social, environmental and societal impact.

Over the next two decades, an enormous transfer of wealth is expected to take place from members of the baby boom generation to their heirs. With a focus on governance, a renewal of their mission and purpose, and the value of merging tradition with innovation, these next-generation beneficiaries increasingly want a reason for the family office to exist beyond accumulating money for its own sake.[3]

Figure 3: Where will you focus your energy?[4]

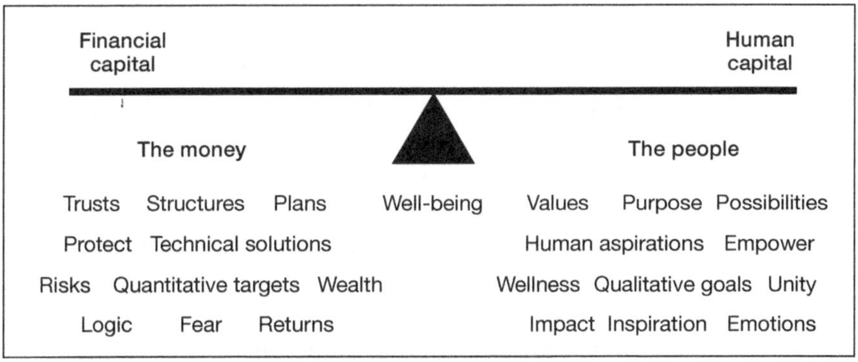

The term 'wealth consciousness' is being applied to next-gen family members who are focusing their energy on how the family applies its human capital as well as its financial capital for the benefit of the family, its communities, the environment and society. They recognise that wealth comes with responsibility and scrutiny, and wealth owners have recognised the need to rethink their approaches. Reputation matters, and having a clear purpose is helping them to demonstrate good citizenship and their families' continued well-being.

3 KPMG Australia, "Wealth in Transition – Family Offices in Plain View", 2021.
4 Adapted from "The strategic inflection point for family wealth", Family Office Exchange, May 2023.

4.3 Facing up to complexity: the value and benefits of a family office

Many factors determine whether a family office should be considered by enterprising families. Perhaps the largest factor is the complexity that individuals and families are currently encountering when they manage their affairs on their own.

Imagine a juggler trying to keep several 'balls' in the air, be they household administration, legal and tax matters, personal investments, family dynamics or charitable ventures. At some point, these tasks become a full-time job, and the juggler could use more 'hands' and expertise to ensure no balls are dropped.

Complexity also relates to asset management itself, since current low-interest rate environments, volatile financial markets and increasingly unstable geo-political conditions, prompt wealthy families to seek better returns, which often leads them to consider more complex investment vehicles, from private equity to real estate to hedge funds, often in foreign markets. This level of complexity demands more sophisticated money management and coordination of holdings, which can strain a family member or even a single trusted adviser.

With the emphasis on thoughtful planning and strategic decision making, transitioning from a family business to a family office structure may be integral to the success of many multi-generational family enterprises.

This professional and structured approach enables families to navigate the complexities of multi-generational ownership, ensuring the long-term prosperity and harmony of the family enterprise through the following:

- *Professional management:* By handling complex financial and administrative tasks, the family office allows family members to focus on strategic and governance roles.
- *Alignment of interests:* The family office ensures that all family members' interests are aligned through structured governance and clear communication channels.
- *Enhanced cohesiveness:* Regular family meetings and coordinated activities organised by the family office foster unity and a shared vision among generations.
- *Continuity and stability:* The family office ensures continuity of management practices and strategic direction, providing stability during generational transitions.

4.4 Scope of family office services

Most family offices were created initially to manage the family's financial wealth; however, the scope of services is now virtually unlimited in enabling families to navigate the complex dynamics of multi-generational goals, values and purpose, and ensuring the long-term prosperity of the family enterprise through:

- integrated wealth management and preservation;
- investment management;

- financial planning;
- estate and tax planning;
- continuity planning;
- family governance and education;
- technology transformation and cybersecurity;
- M&A activity;
- philanthropy, social impact and ESG planning;
- strategic business planning;
- trusts and wills;
- liquidity events;
- managing global taxation; and
- achieving family harmony.

5. Opening a new chapter with a future-forward mindset

The confluence of multi-generational events is leading some family enterprise leaders to revisit their options for the next chapter of the family enterprise – as well as the family itself. Is it time to sell the business or make a partial exit through a liquidity event? Should there be more encouragement and preparation for next-generation successors to step in and help sustain the long-term growth of the family business? What other options does the family enterprise have?

Preparing the senior generation for pivotal transition decisions requires a significant mindset shift. As the key decision makers, they have likely been controlling the business for decades. Now they are faced with changing norms and career aspirations while also marrying digital literacy and tech proficiency with a very traditional business operating model.

Not only is it necessary for business owners to adapt, now they must also consider how to most effectively pass control to another generation or owner while also keeping the family's values and wealth intact. Navigating and managing the combined complexities of wealth, career and family is a constant juggling act. Often, it can become a business unto itself.

For advisers, there is an increasing need to provide guidance and support to wealthy business families through many different business transitions and succession events. The transition planning process itself is pivotal to ensure that the transfer of the business – as well as the family's values, wealth and harmony – all come together. It is where family offices often play a crucial role as the 'ecosystem' that people build around themselves to manage their wealth, business, financial and personal matters.

5.1 Joining the evolution

The transition to a family office structure is a critical life cycle stage. It is important for advisers to recognise when it is the right time for their clients to begin considering their transition process, and bring it to their attention. This requires the integration and coordination of all areas of professional expertise, and there is exceptional value in having specialist advisers working together collaboratively with a singular view of the family, its assets, strategies and wealth.

It involves careful thought and planning to determine when, why and how to begin the transitional journey from operating a legacy family enterprise to engaging the professional services of a family office to manage their wealth, philanthropic activities and personal affairs.

5.2 Key considerations for advisers

Over the past 15 years, the trigger points have generally remained unchanged in determining whether a family office has become the right structure for enterprising families. The one change, however, is in the areas of focus. Socio-emotional wealth and human capital have stepped into the spotlight and are playing a major role in determining what is important to next-gens as their families' wealth begins to transition to them.

Generational change and the transfer of wealth both have a long-term impact, and it will be important for advisers to help clients understand where they need to focus their energy and what the right balance may be.

Most will understand the 'corporate' elements – the structured rules and regulations governing ownership and business operations – but the family's wealth is more subjective. There are more grey areas, and advisers play an important role in bringing clarity to the options and decisions they may consider.

An adviser has access to multiple clients and multiple industries that have gone through various stages of growth, and has insights into a variety of ways of structuring various options. Advisers are also at the forefront of thought leadership of recent changes and developments in regulations, best practices and firsthand experiences.

Specifically, advisers can begin by helping their clients to:

- clarify their personal and collective goals, values and mission;
- develop a plan for transitioning the business and the family towards a new family enterprise model;
- determine the scope of services and functions of a family office that would be most relevant;
- clarify the roles and responsibilities of the family office and the roles and responsibilities of the family;
- obtain relevant coaching and consultation for family members, particularly those in the incumbent generation who are moving from an operating business mindset to an investment portfolio/asset allocation model and those in the next generation who may stepping into active roles within the family enterprise for the first time; and

- understand that when thinking about the future of their family business, any transition, whether it be in ownership or leadership, will be a process, not an event.

5.3 Family offices: a disciplined approach to wealth management

By transitioning to a family office structure, families can adopt a disciplined and holistic approach to managing their assets, fostering unity and securing the family's financial future across generations. The insights and strategic advice that advisers provide will be instrumental in aligning family goals, mitigating conflicts and enhancing the overall governance and operational efficiency of families' wealth.

These are crucial roles to play in guiding clients towards a better understanding of the significant benefits that a family office can offer and the path for getting there. Through expertise and experience in navigating the many life cycles of family businesses, advisers can help families manage the complexities of wealth management, succession planning and legacy preservation.

Within the next 10 years, three catalysts have the potential to drive even more growth in the family office space: (i) a massive generational transfer of wealth; (ii) increased digital disruption; and (iii) greater transparency in communications between current and next-generation family members.

Advisers can help empower families throughout this dynamic environment in making informed decisions about the potential value of various types of family office structures to achieve sustainable growth, maintain family harmony and solidify the family's legacy for generations to come.

Advances in human longevity and the impact upon family business transition plans

Hayden Bailey
Boodle Hatfield LLP

1. Introduction

A child born today has more than a 50% chance of living to over 105.[1] The World Health Organization predicts there will be 426 million people over the age of 80 by 2050.[2] For generations born before 1945, a relatively standard three-stage life of education, work and retirement (with a modest life expectancy of around 75) meant that someone retiring at 65 would have a 10-year retirement before death and sufficient pension income for that period.[3] Longer active lives now mean greater potential to keep working for longer, with it being highly likely that the number of 90-plus-year-old owner managers will only rise over time. The [Ayurvedic] mantra 'healthy at 100'[4] may start to become a reality, with dementia and Alzheimer's being considered treatable conditions.

For family businesses, this means the founder (or senior managers and shareholders) may feel able to remain in seat for much longer periods. While they may be able to fulfil their roles for longer, and provide decades of practical experience and wisdom, increased longevity will inevitably disrupt the established sequence of succession.

For an effective transition, family business owners and their advisers must now consider potentially three or even four generations being able simultaneously to contribute actively to the business. This challenges the traditional linear generation-to-generation concept of business succession. We now face the scenario where the incoming generation of family shareholders are reaching the traditional retirement age before the outgoing generation is able (or willing) to complete the transition of control and ownership.

This chapter considers the impact of a longer lifespan upon family business

1 World Economic Forum, "Here's What Young People Think Is Key to a Long and Fulfilled Life", 12 August 2021, www.weforum.org/stories/2021/08/heres-what-young-people-think-is-key-to-a-long-and-fulfilled-life/#:~:text=A%20child%20born%20today%20in,rise%20from%20451%2C000%20in%202015.

2 World Health Organization, "Ageing and Health", 1 October 2024, www.who.int/news-room/fact-sheets/detail/ageing-and-health.

3 Lynda Gratton and Andrew J Scott, *The 100-Year Life, Living and Working in an Age of Longevity* (Bloomsbury Publishing, 2020).

4 From the Vedas/Ayurvedic motto. See also John Robbins, *Healthy at 100* (Random House Canada Ltd, 2006).

transition (section 2) and looks at what can be done in practice to both maximise the opportunities and mitigate the risks (section 3).

2. What do advances in human longevity mean for family businesses?

2.1 Why are business owners not retiring?

(a) Purpose

People can fear that they will suddenly die for lack of purpose when they retire. For business owners, if it is a business they have lived and breathed which has become completely intertwined with their personal and social lives over many decades, there is often no sense of separation between work and home, making it less easy or attractive to take a step back. There is a fear of being 'put out to pasture' if they are not involved in the stimulation of daily work and decision making.

If the business carries the surname of the owner, separation is virtually impossible and business contacts will inevitably continue to seek out their established contact within the family, always assuming that they are talking to someone with influence and control, as their name is still over the door.

Living *healthier* means that business owners are active and physically and mentally capable of carrying out demanding management and strategic roles into their eighties and nineties. Many business owners are now comfortable with hybrid or remote working, making it even easier to continue a senior strategic role from the 'home office', meaning that physical ageing does not necessarily inhibit working.[5] As a consequence, older business owners will continue to work for longer, particularly if this strongly ties into their core sense of purpose.

Commentators on longevity have proposed that longer lifespans will ultimately lead to multiple careers over a lifetime, coupled with a mindset that views work as a necessary element to be intertwined with social life over a much longer time period overall.[6]

(b) Income

Living longer creates an economic incentive not to retire unless financial plans have been put in place well in advance. Entrepreneurs commonly delay taking a salary for several years in the early stages of their company's life. Once the business is established, there may be some income and capital extraction from salary, bonus or dividend. However, standards of living can change and expenditure can quietly rise in line with increased income, often without the

---

5 There are other consequences of senior management being less physically present in the office that can impact how succession is communicated but those considerations are outside of the scope of this chapter.

6 Lynda Gratton and Andrew J Scott, *The 100-Year Life, Living and Working in an Age of Longevity* (Bloomsbury Publishing, 2020).

business owner making strategic decisions over this income requirement and how it will be sustained long term.

Business owners can, therefore, often find themselves in a situation where they cannot afford to continue their lifestyle without reliance upon the business, making succession planning more difficult, particularly in jurisdictions where the tax rules prohibit gifts of businesses where the donor retains the income.

(c) *Family expansion*

Families can grow at an extraordinary rate. Take an example of two sisters founding a business in 2024, each with three young children. The business needs to support two individuals, but indirectly there are already 10 people essentially relying upon the business for income (including the sisters' spouses). In 40 years, when the sisters might be in their seventies and still leading operations, it is reasonable to imagine there being 12 or more adult grandchildren and the total family size including spouses to have reached something of the magnitude of 70–90 individuals (including spouses) who may all, to a greater or lesser extent, be looking to the business for some benefit, be that income through employment or dividends, or less tangible benefits such as status or family brand and social connections. This places further pressure and expectations on business owners to stay in the business and not to extract significant sums of capital. It is not uncommon for an analysis of the expenditure of a business owner to evidence that they are in fact financially supporting multiple family members across a number of generations.

(d) *Power*

It is difficult to give up power; there is a fear of change on relinquishing control, and this can be particularly true where multiple family members across different branches are connected to the business.

Family expansion over a long time period without proper governance will impact the decision making and management of the business. If, at each generation, family members take up positions of authority unchecked and without a governance plan in place, the potential for inertia and lack of agility in decision making can create additional pressures and lead to a loss of focus. This can be another reason why older shareholders might consider it safer, given the financial pressures from the wider family, to remain in seat for longer, keeping the management and ownership streamlined under their control.

However, the next generation do not always want to rely upon a timeline imposed on them by the older generation, where the goalposts can move for

7 Stanford Graduate School of Business, "Search Funds", www.gsb.stanford.edu/experience/about/centers-institutes/ces/research/search-funds.

reasons outside of their control. The rise of search funds[7] in the United States is evidence that power is being retained to such an extent that no natural heir has been sufficiently clearly identified, leading to established businesses being purchased by new entrepreneurial management teams. Additionally, members of the next generation do not want to risk spending a large proportion of their lives waiting in the wings before they inherit, and may prefer to pursue the certainty of careers of their own, away from the family business.

(e) *Differing mindsets*

There is a difference in the psychology between entrepreneurs and custodians, the former showing a focus on investing in the business, and the latter predominately wanting to ensure that the family sees a return on the ongoing investment to be stable financially while wanting to grow the business at a rate that can cope with increased requirement for dividends from a larger pool of stakeholders. This can put a strain on the 'business first' mentality that the founder generation may propound. A company's dividend strategy might be focused on reinvestment for the first generation, who very much 'live' the business. In contrast, future generations may need to establish their non-business lives with carefully managed dividend or capital event planning.

There can be a scepticism around different management approaches, with the older generation, who have worked 'on the factory floor', sometimes intimating that the younger generation do not have the skills acquired during the earlier years of business growth. Successor generations may have been purposely educated and trained as managers from the outset. Without an appropriate facilitation, these differing mindsets on business management can lead to disagreement on style and approach between the generations.

(f) *Age discrimination*

It is important to bear in mind that many jurisdictions have introduced rules against discrimination on various grounds. There can be civil penalties applied against businesses who discriminate on an age basis. For example, including in the constitutional documents that family owners must step down at 60 is potentially unenforceable and against public policy (depending on the jurisdiction in question). The removal of formal retirement ages in company constitutions because of anti-discrimination laws can lead to the topic of 'stepping back' being left unaddressed unless the governing documents for the family business introduce a replacement mechanism that ensures the topic is discussed.

For example, alternative mechanisms that dictate how long a family member should be in seat, without reference to age, may be acceptable options, prompting review and discussion.

(g) *Taxation*

Some jurisdictions provide for tax relief for shares in qualifying businesses. A discussion of taxation is outside the scope of this chapter, but it should be acknowledged that the tax policy can often drive behaviour. For example, a tax policy that does not tax family businesses on death can act as a disincentive to lifetime transfer.

2.2 Benefits and impact of longevity of a founder's lifespan upon family business

Having a founder or incumbent owner in-role over decades has a material impact on brand and internal stability, which needs to be borne in mind before control is handed over to the next generation.

(a) *The brand*

For many family businesses, the identity of the founder or incumbent owner is a mirror to the external perception of the business brand. It is easy to think of a number of longstanding international brands that are family-managed and the brand itself is seen as a reflection of the founder's values. The security of that brand and the value attached to the 'face' that sits behind the brand can be powerful marketing.

A change from one generation to the next will naturally have an impact on this brand. Therefore, ensuring that the outward-facing brand of the business retains the values of the founder is important and requires careful public relations management. If the values of the differing generations are not agreed upon and set down in writing, then it can lead to a muddled public image, which can lead to confusion of the brand direction for the family and staff. Brands that have embraced this change have endured, while others now feel outdated with anachronistic brand identities, out of kilter with the political norms of the time.

The challenge is to identify and have processes in place to continually assess the longevity and relevance of the brand; and to constantly review and cross-check whether the brand is dependable and reliable and in keeping with generational values. Involving the next generation in such a review shows confidence in their ideas and will lead them to familiarise themselves with the current brand before making changes.

(b) *Internal stability*

Family businesses attract long-serving employees partly due to the stability and familial relationship between the staff. The consistency of a single individual at the top who understands and lives and breathes the business can be inspirational and rewarding for employees. However, that stability can equally, in theory, lead to complacency in the workforce.

Worse, a situation can arise where the CFO, COO and CEO are all potentially of a similar age to the founder/owning generation and, fearing that they themselves may have become inflexible, they may not welcome a challenge to the autonomy of their position. A lack of a succession plan that is publicly shared with key employees can exacerbate this situation. Key staff may make their own private contingency plans for retirement or a move to another business if they become overly concerned. Those plans may not be shared honestly in appraisal or with the current owners, for fear that it makes them look loyal to the current administration rather than the business itself. A planned and transparent succession strategy that is created with a core team before being shared can reduce risk.

An associated concern is that existing management teams can sometimes fear making challenges to the family leadership and become deferential in their approach. Consideration must be given to whether that deference will continue for the next generation of owners, and if not, how challenges to new ideas will be managed to avoid disagreement and inaction.

3. What can be done to manage the risks of human longevity?

There is a tendency for founders to view the business as entirely theirs and for them to have total unfettered control over its future. Entrepreneurs often take the view that their children should make their own way, instead of automatically benefitting from the previous generations' endeavours.

Succession planning can therefore become an almost taboo subject, as founders are wanting to ensure their children engage with the same self-starter mindset with which they built the business in the first place.

The power dynamic of family businesses means that for many years the older generation holds most of the power and decision-making authority. As a result, younger family members may have limited autonomy and may be treated as subordinate to their older counterparts, feeling unable to fully express their views and ideas. A great deal of trust must go into consciously reversing this dynamic and entrusting the younger generation with significant responsibilities.

The counter to this is when a family business has too many stakeholders as the next generation, in multiples, are given too much say. This is not a recipe for a credible business strategy as the business can easily become, or at least appear to be, fractured and without clear leadership. It is therefore important to find a balance between encouraging family involvement and putting in place effective governance and decision-making processes.

In light of this, there are some key tools to consider as part of the transition plan for the management and ownership of a family business.

3.1 Start the conversation early

Entrepreneurs may not accept that they have 'made it' from a business perspective. However, at a point in time, essentially when they have children, they need to consider whether their venture is a family business or a business to sell.

The answer is often to keep doing it for as long as they enjoy it, but to be aware that they owe an obligation to the next generation not to leave something problematic when they die. Therefore, they need to know if they are going to pass on the business, or sell it, and when.

Generally speaking, and regardless of the jurisdictions involved, succession planning requires:

- the setting of clear objectives;
- agreements within the core family group;
- good communication;
- agreed governance structures; and
- appropriate recognition of risks.

Thankfully, we have (to an extent) been given the gift of time if the predictions around human longevity are correct.

Advisers must stress the need to have these conversations well before they are needed and to put in place a blueprint for succession that is robust but flexible.

3.2 Working out the right time to retire

All businesses will have a general expectation of when the current CEO's service will end. If this is an external CEO, it is likely to be on the standard retirement age for the jurisdiction. If it is a family CEO, the timing is much less certain. Subject to consideration of rules about age discrimination discussed above, if a family business forms a strategy to say that family will step down from board positions at a certain time, this can manage expectations for the next generation as to when they will be able to or expected to 'step up' to that role. However, there will be a number of points to consider when setting this strategy, such as the following:

- Some companies have mandatory retirement ages for their CEOs set at 65, but some reverse these decisions.
- Whether the desired retirement age is different for succession of first-generation CEO-founders than for third-generation inherited family businesses. Should each generation make their own decision on when they step back?
- People are having children later in life and often have second, or even third, families as they lead a longer life. It is foreseeable that many family business leaders will be at a traditional retirement age, yet still have young families, and so may not wish to stop working from a financial perspective.

3.3 Set a timeline

Timing of events, such as death, incapacity, political or economic events are all outside of our control. If a business owner makes clear to the board and the family their own plans, then suddenly it can make the board feel that they have authority to discuss openly these otherwise taboo subjects. This can lead to consideration of what might then happen if those plans are ended early for any reason. Putting a date on, for example, stepping back or retirement can be a powerful message. The challenge can be sticking to it or making it meaningful rather than illusory or by name only. Founders can cast a long shadow and so stepping back early can make it easier for the next generation to step into the light.

Being as clear as possible as early as possible is essential. Managing everyone's expectations at the earliest opportunity helps to minimise the risk of being blindsided by big decisions or new ways of working. Ultimately, the aim is to keep the business on track.

3.4 Have a written plan

Family enterprises are often built on strong values, a sense of identity and a commitment to a shared vision. These enduring principles form the bedrock of a timeless legacy that can transcend generations. In navigating the complexities of succession planning, it is crucial to identify and record these timeless elements that make the family business unique and resilient within a written succession plan.

A written succession plan can state who should take over management in the immediate term. It can also set out the founder's expectations of the strategy of the company, particularly in the event of their death. For example, the founder could state that they expect the company will trend towards a more conservative approach to ensure the longevity of the business so that it will be able to provide for their children and future generations.

3.5 Emergency board plan

An emergency board plan (EBP) can form part of a succession plan, creating a protocol for a business to set out what should happen on the board in the short term following the sustained absence, incapacity or death of the CEO, or otherwise head of the family business. It is, in effect a 'break glass in case of disaster' plan, and can be a good way for business owners to understand and engage in the first step of a wider succession conversation.

An EBP should address what processes will be required in the first week, first month and first quarter in the event of a crisis. The family are left confident that the business has a governance and succession plan in place and that jobs are secure.

An EBP should consider the following:

- *Communications:* A communications plan should detail how and when internal and external communications relating to the continuity of the business will be made and by whom. Create a communications plan to report and reassure stakeholders, employees and clients. Consideration would need to be given to public relations and investor relations, and managing the detail of press releases. Should the board nominate the individual who will manage the communications strategy or appoint an agreed external agency for this aspect to avoid disruption?

- *Operations:* Should an interim COO be appointed to provide stability, and who should they report to? Should a management committee be named, with specific individuals recorded on the EBP and their role?
- *Risk and advisory:* Should legal and accountancy advice be formalised together with a process of other external consultancy? Should a general counsel be appointed medium term? How should risk and leverage in relation to the bank and borrowing be managed?
- *Shareholder representation:* Would there be trusted persons to represent the shareholding of the absent member? Should trustees take board seats and represent that party in voting and operational matters? How will trustees and shareholders receive information?
- *Board decision-making protocol and reserved matters:* Consider the need for 'reserved matters' (matters requiring shareholder approval) to consider how decisions on key areas will be delegated between the board and the shareholder/family body.

The EBP must be kept under regular review to ensure it is appropriate and enables the board to continue functioning.

3.6 Use of powers of attorney

Family relationships can further complicate accountability mechanisms in businesses in respect of loss of capacity. Family members may be hesitant to hold a CEO accountable for their senility for fear of damaging personal relationships or creating family conflicts. This can create a power imbalance whereby it is difficult for other family members or stakeholders to challenge the CEO's peculiar decisions or behaviours.

In addition, it is worth noting that family businesses often rely on informal decision-making processes, which can lead to ambiguity around roles, responsibilities and performance expectations. Such difficulties can be particularly acute where the CEO retains mental capacity, but nonetheless is experiencing deteriorating mental cognition, colloquially referred to as 'the twilight zone'. They may be vulnerable and susceptible to influence from others, which may be malign or self-interested. This can create inter-family fighting and hostility, which is obviously destructive to the family business.

Aside from written succession plans, legal documents will need to be reviewed and prepared to fully deal with death and incapacity.

Wills are essential for any shareholder of a family business, ensuring that the shares pass in accordance with their wishes. Often wills are the starting point for focusing on the succession plan, but it is important to note that they are often not enough on their own to ensure successful succession. Communicating and agreeing succession plans with other family members and the board is an essential part of the succession plan. Drafting of wills must dovetail with the provisions of the articles and any other governing documents.

Incapacity is often overlooked and it is critically important that aside from working out what the emergency board plan is, there are also the necessary legal documents in place to support decisions being made during periods of incapacity. Powers of attorney can be prepared in most jurisdictions to allow business decisions to be made in the event of the mental incapacity of a business owner/manager. Powers of attorney can be important tools to mitigate business risk in the event of mental incapacity because, subject to the relevant local laws, it may allow an attorney to step in and make decisions on behalf of the principal in relation to their business interests.

However, this should be viewed as a short-term emergency measure. For more public-facing companies, it could be poor publicity to see a company having to make decisions through an attorney because the owner/manager has not planned effectively enough to hand over the control of business to others in good time. Hence the importance of having the written emergency board plan in place but, even more fundamentally, having a board in place to enable the ongoing operation of the company.

There are often limits to a power of attorney in most jurisdictions, so even if one is put in place, there may be certain decisions which cannot be delegated under the power.

Partnership agreements and articles of association should be checked, as they may prescribe what happens in the event of incapacity or death and should not be inconsistent with the principal having a power of attorney. In addition, it may be necessary to make an application to the relevant local court for an attorney to seek advance approval to such decisions. This is not only a more cumbersome, time-consuming and inflexible process, but it is also more than an unflattering look publicly to end up running a business in this way.

Accordingly, there can be no substitution for full and timely succession planning to ensure the successful continuation of a family business.

3.7 The need to create a functioning board

A common yet sometimes problematic characteristic of family businesses is for founder-CEOs to deteriorate and/or die while still holding the sole directorship and entire share capital of the business. This can quickly lead to deterioration of morale; key employees begin to question the future of the business and 'jump ship'. External buyers may perceive too much business dependence on the founder-CEO. Crucially, the value and reputation of the business could plummet.

Where there is a developed board structure in place and the ability for others (whether family and/or non-family) to step in and manage, this will clearly allow others to further step in and manage the business during such a difficult period. Allowing others to share control and responsibility is a critical part of the succession plan, better catering for both death and incapacity scenarios.

3.8 Monitoring and planning for board transition

Advisers should emphasise more generally the importance of the board (whether that is a formal board or a kitchen-table board!) having an annual review and policy in place around expected timelines for key personnel (including the key family shareholders), and a list of candidates identified (family or otherwise) that can be reviewed and monitored together with appraisal of their relevant skillsets. PwC surveys suggest that nearly half of all boards think more time should be devoted to succession planning.[8]

PwC surveys also suggest that less than half of all directors are confident in their boards' ability to effectively identify candidates for CEO succession.[9] These are difficult conversations and, therefore, often avoided. However, discussing succession regularly, no matter the performance and age of the business leaders, will help make the conversation feel less personal.

The board should regularly assess not only the current CEO position but also the capacities of other executives to take on that role, and address and develop the leadership skills and qualities that might currently be lacking. High-potential candidates should be identified and monitored, as part of any business succession plan. For a family business, this is far less straightforward as there can often be an assumption that the successor chair/CEO will be from the family cohort. That makes reviewing the pool of talent and the process for installing or training them far harder, especially where there are perceived to be several candidates at the same 'level' of the family (ie, several cousins).

Ultimately the board is accountable to and can be removed by the shareholders, and so ensuring these appointment processes are properly thought through in a family business context are essential. Should different branches of the family have the power to appoint a representative director, should there be an independent director or mechanism to ensure the board represents in the right proportions? Where there are family trusts, how will trustees appoint directors to represent their interests?[10]

---

8 PwC, 2024 Annual Corporate Directors Survey, www.pwc.com/us/en/services/governance-insights-center/library/annual-corporate-directors-survey.html.

9 PwC, 2023 Annual Corporate Directors Survey, www.corporatecomplianceinsights.com/pwc-2023-corporate-directors-survey/.

10 See section 3.12.

3.9 Establish a family council?

Advisers should promote the benefits of establishing a family council. This can take the form of regular meetings, at which the business owners and managers and key family members are present and during which strategic matters relating to the business are discussed, typically including reflections on succession.

Shareholder succession issues can be managed within a family council, such that plans for generational shift and transfer of ownership can be planned and communicated in advance. This can help manage expectations for both the family and the board.

Time can be spent and processes can be implemented in the search for a successor, and emergency board plans can be put in place to deal with unexpected situations arising.

3.10 Role of the next generation – can young and old work together democratically?

The gift of time allows the next generation to engage in external careers that provide invaluable leadership experience. Learning to lead a team, especially where they are not the 'leader by birthright', allows them to cultivate a well-rounded skillset and enhance their ability to navigate varied challenges within the family business. It allows time to develop clarity of purpose where individuals can discover and align their personal passions and values. This clarity contributes to an overall sense of purpose, making their eventual entry into the family business more intentional and driven.

Encouraging external careers also helps dispel perceptions of entitlement and reinforces the principle of merit-based leadership, where individuals earn their positions through competence and experience rather than on familial ties alone.

All these factors build succession planning resilience, creating better-prepared future leaders, and reduce the vulnerability of the business to unexpected disruptions. If a 100-year life becomes more of a realistic prospect for many, then arguably having a varied career with different experiences and different levels of pressure will be a necessity and of much more value to the sustainability of the family business.

3.11 Building up wealth outside the business

It is often difficult for entrepreneurs to adapt to diversifying their focus to include building up wealth outside of their business, often after decades of being laser-focused on growing their business and reinvestment, perhaps at the sacrifice of their personal finances and capital extraction. A report from SCORE found that 18% of entrepreneurs plan on retiring using the funds they receive from selling their respective businesses.[11] The mindset can therefore lean

11 Bridget Weston, "Why Entrepreneurs Should Be Saving for Retirement", SCORE, 11 April 2019, www.score.org/resource/blog-post/why-entrepreneurs-should-be-saving-retirement.

towards feeling that the family wealth and value is in the business, and that the family should remain 'business first' rather than 'family first' and continue to reinvest as much as possible.

However, this mentality fails to consider succession and transition for a multi-generational family enterprise. If the older generation have in mind that part or all of the business might one day be sold to fund their retirement, this needs to form part of the governance documentation for the family within the charter or constitution so that the next generation can agree and consult on those plans and make preparations for the growth of the residual business.

It is vital for the family to consider a strategy that creates a sufficient pension for older generations. Failure to do this can lead to significant problems because (as noted in the income section above at section 2.1) a reliance upon the business for funding for an entire lifetime does not allow for a cut-off point and ability for the older generation to become self-sufficient.

Various strategies can be pursued. Trusts (discussed below) can be used as a strategy to exit the older generation without making them feel 'bought out'. Funds can be built up in trust over time to create a pension-style pot to be drawn down after retirement.

Pension planning within the business can be improved with realistic modelling on income and capital requirements for the family shareholders. Financial advice and financial discipline from all members of the business family should be taught and enforced. Adopting a policy whereby, for example, 10% of dividends paid over a lifetime are paid into a pension or invested outside of the business to provide an income and pension pot is generally sensible.

Care must be taken and a coordinated approach adopted. If the business strategy is to build up money outside of the company for retirement, these best laid plans can be blown apart if the shareholders decide to earmark this pension pot for some other purpose or start to spend it. A common challenge (for traditional inherited wealth just as much as for family businesses) is for shareholders to adopt a succession strategy that leaves their company shares to their business heirs, and leaves their residual assets to other family members, such as spouses or other children. However, by earmarking capital for others, the purpose of the pension pot is partly defeated as the shareholder will feel unable to spend down those funds, and instead seek to preserve them to pass on. This can then undo the plan, and stop the shareholder from feeling able to draw down on those funds themselves for fear of eroding them. If such circumstances exist, shareholders will need to consider this in advance and adopt a strategy of building up wealth outside the business that is sufficient not only for themselves in retirement, but also for any other dependants they may wish to provide for on death.

There can be a staged exit where income reduces with age and/or there is a capital event to give the older generation enough to retire on. This capital event should be agreed for each generation. Another strategy is to turn the older generation's equity into debt and pay them out over time, perhaps through the creation of a separate class of redeemable preference shares.

It must be remembered that there is a great difference between a management role and taking actual ownership. The succession strategy must create a timeline that effectively deals with the transition of both.

3.12 Use of trusts

Trust planning forms an important part of the governance of a multi-generational family business. Trusts are a good tool for handing over ownership of a family business (eg, shares in a company) slowly to the next generation. This type of structure can assist with the common fear of giving unrestricted autonomy to a successor outright. The outgoing generation often prefer to hand over power slowly.

Trusts can facilitate the orderly succession of the company's shares and the long-term preservation of wealth for the benefit of future generations. They avoid fragmentation of ownership when someone passes away and can centralise decision making regarding board appointments for operating companies. However, any such succession plan requires the buy-in of the founder generation and incumbent owners, who will need to understand and appreciate the importance of creating their own independence from the business as an income source upon which they rely.

Utilising trust ownership, coupled with a capital allocation committee at a family holding-company level, can be useful tools to create a framework for succession that can anticipate changes in longevity and put processes in place.

(a) Trust distributions

Benefits for the younger generation can be regulated through controlled trust distributions, with options for more strictly regulated entitlements for specific family members if required. Using trusts ensures that assets are not passed to children or other vulnerable beneficiaries outright and until they are mature enough to hold them.

(b) Shareholdings

The older generation can own voting shares in the company in their own names. The capital shares can be given to a trust for the benefit of the children and future generations, with the parents as trustees. In this way, income/economic rights can be passed down to the children while they are not involved in the management of the business, without giving them voting rights. The shareholdings remain consolidated in the trust, with trustees retaining control. Once held in trust, the ownership of the business remains unchanged by the passing of the settlor or any beneficiary.

This provides a greater degree of asset protection for the next generation while the children are young. By the trust owning shares (eg, via a holding company or the use of different share classes), the trust can benefit from increases in share value, without necessarily receiving dividends which would be taxable on the trustees. The directors will control when the trust receives income, or any capital extractions.

4. Conclusion

The time that each generation of a family business has at the helm can unwittingly set a precedent for the culture and ownership of the business. The length of tenure has a profound effect on the engagement of future generations and how they perceive the timing and importance of their role and position in the business. It impacts the success of the business and its ability to innovate and remain relevant as generational attitudes change.

It is essential that founders or incumbent owners consider the position early and engage in an analysis of their own position *vis-à-vis* the business. If the founder intends to continue the business until they decide they have had enough, then the next generation's expectations need to be managed early on so that they do not make life decisions based upon false assumptions. In a multi-generational business this may not be a decision that the incumbent should take alone, and an acknowledgement that they are a custodian for a period of years will need to be understood and accepted.

Increases in life expectancy should be properly modelled out as timelines, together with proper cashflow forecasting that takes into account potential changes to taxation, economic cycles, geopolitical risk and 'black swan' events. If the current generation can set down a marker by which time they agree not to be involved in business management that is one thing, and most families do manage this in some way or another. However, the extent to which owners should remain economically reliant upon the business is a more difficult discussion and divorcing the two risks a situation where the younger generation are managing the business for the benefit of the elders. Issues can be exacerbated as the family tree expands over time.

With longevity comes benefits. Family business advisers will be able to use the suggestions in this chapter to ensure that the experience, knowledge and stability that having a consistent individual in seat for a long period of time is safeguarded, during an ownership and management transition.

Next-generation planning

Matthew Fleming
Stonehage Fleming
Maria Villax
Bedrock Group

How can next-generation education and development best be handled by advisers to support successful succession?

1. Introduction

Preparing the next generation for the great generational wealth transfer might best be viewed through two different lenses:

- individual and personal: helping them to find personal purpose based on their abilities and ambitions; and
- the family context: equipping them with the right tools and skills for their future roles in the family structure, whatever they might be.

Before breaking down the best approach to develop these separate yet overlapping lenses, some industry context is useful. Family governance advisory is a cottage industry with unstandardised processes. One explanation for this is that the real value that is offered by family governance advisers goes beyond the technical knowledge of family governance academia and best practices. They must also be able to bring out that knowledge in a meaningful way for each family based on their unique circumstances, to affect real change. This support becomes hard to define and even harder to sell!

Although in a much stronger position than 20 years ago, family governance still struggles to get the recognition it deserves. Indeed, when it comes to succession planning, this is often swept under tax and legal advice. However, the first step in succession planning should be considered through the lens of the family, as a stand-alone service. Before any estate planning or tax structures are put in place, there is a wider conversation to be had, focusing on very personal aspects that form the family members' expectations for the future.

The younger generation want family advisers who understand that the technically wrapped gift of family assets is not enough. They want advisers who have the emotional intelligence to provide support beyond technical matters – who help families understand the different intergenerational perspectives and priorities, who ensure that where agreement is elusive, there can be understanding – and who appreciate that often the process of reaching this understanding is as important as the transition itself.

Succession planning is a two-way street, which entails supporting the next generation as they step up while simultaneously enabling the current generation to let go. When it comes to next-generation development, the market offers a prolific mishmash of academic courses and development tools. However, they rarely address the crucial element of the long-term journey necessary when developing the next generation, and they tend to focus on a particular set of immediate skills. What is needed is a more holistic approach to preparing well-rounded, fulfilled individuals who are capable of being future leaders, owners and beneficiaries. On the other hand, the market offering to support the current generation to let go is considerably less prolific compared to the support available to the next generation – why is that?

In this chapter, we will explore different ways of thinking beyond the typical academic approach to developing the next generation. Addressing emotions and feelings is an integral part of the process, but it is usually dismissed as a lesser consideration. It should be possible to advance a different narrative about succession planning, one that empowers advisers to help families to have difficult conversations in an environment of openness and transparency. It often requires as much courage and tenacity from the adviser to guide these discussions, as it does from the family to be open to them.

2. The different backgrounds of the next generation

The central concern for the next generation is about having both the necessary skills and feeling ready for the responsibilities ahead. However, the next generation come from different backgrounds, each with their own nuances that are worth exploring before considering development and succession.

2.1 Generational wealth versus entrepreneurial wealth

With generational wealth, the family often emphasises the preservation of wealth and they have a conservative mindset to investing and spending. The education of the next generation often focuses on wealth management and philanthropy. Succession planning tends to be formalised and structured (as they have been doing it successfully for a few generations already), with clear guidelines on how wealth is transferred and who will manage it, with values around stewardship and legacy. There is a strong sense of heritage and continuity, and family members can be brought up under a significant sense of responsibility to uphold the family values, the existing purpose and sometimes its name.

Entrepreneurial wealth brings a different mindset. These families often value innovation and risk-taking. Education of the next generation tends to focus more on business skills, entrepreneurship and innovation, with a focus on learning how to create and grow wealth rather than just preserving it. Here, values revolve around meritocracy and professional success, where the next generation are often more hands-on in managing the family assets. Succession planning is typically less formalised, especially if the wealth is relatively new, and usually focuses on identifying and nurturing entrepreneurial talent within the family to continue growing the business and wealth.

2.2 Family businesses versus family offices

With family businesses, there is a tangible asset, which usually makes it easier to rally the family around a shared sense of purpose. The benefits of committing to long-term family ownership are easier to identify around an entity that creates value for society, generates employment and pays taxes, as well as providing the family with jobs and a livelihood. The development of the next generation focuses on creating a cohesive group of educated, informed and active shareholders, aligned in their long-term vision for the business. Succession planning is complex and will revolve around identifying the future leaders and governors of the business, which should inform a clear transition plan and a skill development path for the next generation.

In cases where there's been a liquidity event and the family own a pot of investments together, the shared sense of purpose as the basis of the commitment to family ownership becomes less obvious. The family becomes a 'financial family' where it's harder (yet not impossible) to derive emotional value from family ownership. Philanthropy can play an important role in these circumstances, providing the rallying cry around a new shared purpose for the family. Succession planning will focus on ensuring the continuity of wealth management and the family's financial/philanthropic legacy. It involves preparing the next generation to manage a diverse portfolio of assets and possibly taking over the management of the family office.

3. What do they all have in common?

Regardless of their background, all next-generation individuals have a desire to separate their role in the collective purpose from their own personal ambition and to ensure a healthy balance between the family's collective purpose and the individual's personal ambition. Clarity of roles and responsibilities will determine the path to develop the right skills, and ensure the next generation is developed by design and not by accident.

Another consideration that holds true regardless of background or future goals, is the fact that the 'wealth mindset' takes years to develop. Understanding wealth as a means of opportunity and the ability to create value for society (as opposed to entitlement) does not happen overnight, or with a few courses around financial literacy or leadership. It is honed through the years, shaped not just by lived experience but also through conversations with parents and advisers, that range from understanding what is value for money and developing healthy financial habits to what purpose(s) is served through the family wealth.

4. The challenges of succession from the perspective of the next generation

The most enlightened families consider succession through the lens of both generations. Wealth, privilege, responsibility and leadership are often neatly packaged and transferred as if they were a present. While some might enjoy the surprise element of a gift, most would rather have been involved in the discussion about the size, type and timing of that 'gift'.

Emotions of guilt and self-worth can be hugely challenging to developing a successful succession plan if not properly addressed by the advisers. Common questions from the next generation and challenges to work through in this respect include:

- What have I done to deserve this?
- Will I ever be good enough to be a wealth holder?
- Should the purpose of our wealth be reassessed?
- How do we revaluate purpose with different generational views on social and cultural capital?
- Can we be involved in or lead the discussions on purpose and values, to ensure that our period of wealth ownership feels relevant for us?

So much of the challenge for families is finding advisers who have the imagination and courage to support them in dealing with these questions, as they consider at a deeper level the nature of the 'gift' and whether it might be perceived as understood, expected, fair and appropriate by the recipient and the wider family.

Success can look different to the next generation and defining success is a crucial part of handing over the baton. Without all these discussions, neither generation has a framework for decision making.

The recognition and mitigation of the risks to families and their wealth is an important element to succession. When plotting impact and likelihood, most families focus on business/wealth management and structuring. These are significant risks, yet they are most often the least challenging to mitigate. Recognising that family rows, ineffective leadership and next-generation fulfilment are often more likely and impactful risks can require a level of honesty and self-awareness that consigns the mitigation to the 'too hard to do' list.

Good and effective leadership is critical. There is healthy debate around the most appropriate leadership models for families: absolute dictatorship, benign dictatorship, democracy – or somewhere in between. In truth, all families require effective leadership, and that can look different for every family depending on scale and circumstance. One of the reasonably common denominators of successful multi-generational families is the democratisation of the process that leads to the creation and maintenance of their leadership model. Most families want the best and most appropriate leaders shaping the future and making decisions; ensuring that everyone has been involved in, understands and accepts the process that selects or appoints the leader/leaders and the governance structure that they operate in gives a family the best chance of success.

Historically, families have often chosen to impose a purpose on the next generation, which acted as a framework for their decision making. This hierarchical approach sits uneasily beside societal changes. It feels as though the democratisation of the process of agreeing or revisiting a purpose gives a family a far greater chance of intergenerational success.

5. Aligning next-generation development with succession planning

5.1 Best practices: elements that show readiness to address succession

Each generation is looking for the answer to different questions. The current generation is looking for signs of readiness from the next generation: Are they ready? Can I let go? On the other side, the members of the next generation might be trying to understand the part they will play: Where do I fit in and how do I make myself heard?

To start addressing succession, both generations should begin by answering the question they are asking from each other. To do so, on the side of the current generation, the following elements should be in place:

- A clear purpose and vision for the family, where the family members understand the goals they wish to achieve together.
- Clear communication channels and forums (such as family meetings), where the two generations (or more) can speak to each other and discuss their views openly. These forums should be used to clarify the roles and responsibilities the next generation should be getting ready for. Equally, the current generation should also consider the evolution of their own roles, to make way for the next generation.
- A consciousness of the current generation's own mortality – the awareness that whether the next generation is ready or not, the day will come when it is their turn to lead and own the family assets.

On the side of the next generation, the elements in place should be:

- Knowledge of the family assets – what there is, where it is, who is involved, why it is there and the story behind it. Unfortunately, sometimes this information is sprung on the next generation under complex circumstances unconducive to a healthy understanding of such important information. Transparency and knowledge transmission from early on are key.

- Needs, or more specifically, a compelling reason to get out of bed every day. This is a sensitive topic, but even more important for it. It is not uncommon to see 20/30-year-olds who have everything catered for. But if there are no needs – financial, lifestyle-related or drivers of professional/personal fulfilment – are parents not taking away the deep sense of satisfaction that comes with self-sufficiency? It is worth noting that the existence of needs is different from the pressure to achieve, which is not constructive.
- A deliberate and thoughtful long-term development plan that identifies the roles in the corporate, governance, investment or charitable structures available to the next generation. This way, the next generation can identify the roles they are interested in and define a path to acquire the hard, soft and inner skills to become ready for the role. (See later in the chapter for the elements of good development.)

By creating this set of circumstances, each generation reconciles what they are looking for from each other.

Figure 1: A good starting point to address succession planning

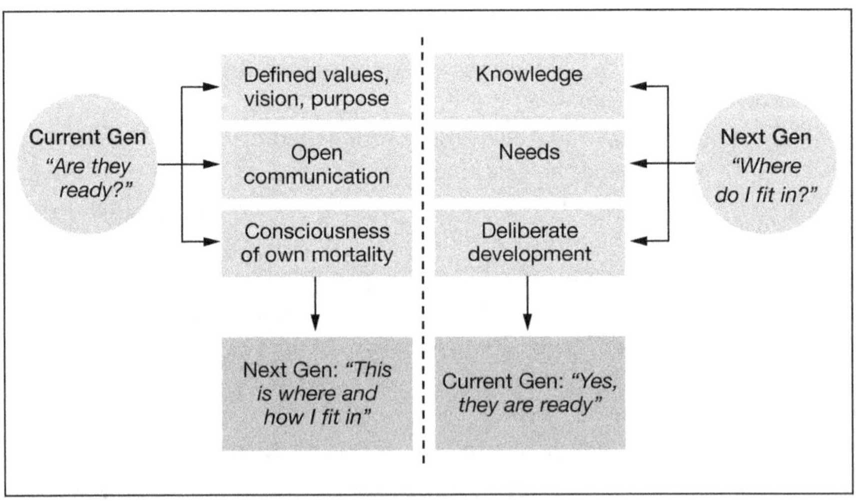

6. The reality: too little, too late

The above best practices demonstrate circumstances where the family has spent a considerable amount of time organising itself. It is not lost on us that this scenario does not represent the reality for most wealthy families. Most do not have the luxury of time, as they have all too often left succession to play out after an event – a death, a relationship breakdown, a major event in the business. Overlaying succession considerations with grief or a difficult situation makes the process even more challenging.

Families tend to consider that the right moment to address succession does not exist. But those who wait will not get it right. This is where the role of family advisers becomes crucial, by starting to introduce these conversations ahead of their need.

7. Developing the next generation by design

The great challenge for the next generation is not only to be ready for their responsibilities, but to also feel ready for them. It is also about being enabled to execute these responsibilities while having earned the right to do so.

On the other hand, the current generation has a specific skillset and characteristics which the next generation will not mirror perfectly – nor should they be expected to. Developing the next generation should take this constant evolution of roles into account and not be directed at recreating the child in the spitting image of the parent.

It is a complex balancing act.

A good development plan will include aspects that support the personal and professional development of the next generation, revolving around who they are and their innate strengths. Concurrently, it will also create a supportive ecosystem which helps them interact with the institutions that they may join in the future. The plan should therefore integrate specific individual development (inward plan) and a defined interaction with the family's and/or business's structures (outward plan).

We already mentioned that it is key to start with defining WHAT the next generation is being developed for. We therefore recommend that the development plan defines the outward elements first, including the following points:

7.1 Definition of roles available to the next generation

Some families are looking for the next generation to take up the management of the family assets. Others may view that the sole duty of family members should be one of responsible ownership. Others may wish to involve the next generation in their governance structure, preparing them to be family council members or board directors, or perhaps even cultural guardians. And then there are cases where roles are available for the next generation at all levels, including in wider structures such as a foundation or a family office. The crucial point is for those roles to be clearly defined and their availability to be communicated to the next generation in no uncertain terms. This practice will clarify expectations on both sides and help the next generation decide the path they wish to take.

7.2 Principles and requirements for involvement

In addition to clarifying what is available for the next generation, it is equally important to define the requirements for them to access these roles. These principles establish the credibility, preparation and experience required to earn the right to step forward. There is no right or wrong standard here and a degree of flexibility may accompany the requirements. The aim should be to equip the next generation with the right level of preparation, but also enable them to be perceived by their peers and colleagues as competent and able. Examples include:

- academic qualifications: postgraduate qualifications, a master's degree or more specialised accreditations;
- time spent in other companies gaining experience or other previous experience;
- a successful track-record in previous work experiences; and
- principles highlighting desirable characteristics, such as mature, competent, hard-working, humble and self-respecting (and who therefore can be respected). This may sound superfluous, but it is always relevant to define expected behaviours, or undesirable ones may appear out of lack of awareness.

7.3 Employment processes and policies

A formal policy creates the process through which the next generation should access a certain role. They should create a robust enough procedure to ensure that the next generation are accessing the role in a fair way, but also acknowledge that they are a different type of employee. They will have pressures that other employees do not, including being recognised for their merits rather than their name. This is a balancing act between ensuring the right people to the right role and acknowledging the vital importance of encouraging and welcoming the next generation into the fold.

Employment policies include some or all the following elements:

- Entry points in the corporate structure – internships, work experience, full-time employment.
- The various steps of the recruitment process, and the people involved in the decision(s). The assessment of the candidate's suitability should ideally be done collaboratively by the family and the business, to bridge the different agendas. Some families consider the involvement of the next generation so important that they will create a role for them that otherwise would not exist within the corporate structure. While we understand this reasoning, it is more advisable to employ them in roles that would have to be filled anyway, to enable them to be viewed by other stakeholders as deserving of the opportunity.
- How performance is assessed and by whom. Reporting lines are

important to clarify, as well as career progression. This journey must be fulfilling for the next generation, with goals and milestones clearly defined. Too often, we see members of the next generation 'lost' within a structure, with no idea of how to progress.

- Remuneration principles – ideally, the remuneration will be dictated by the market, benchmarked to similar roles in different companies. If the next generation is earning above their peers, this will reinforce the idea that they only got the job because of who they are. Also, remuneration for work delivered should be separate from revenues gained through shareholding.

An employment policy is particularly relevant in family businesses, but a less formalised process also has value for roles in a different type of entity. Whether it is the involvement in a family council, committee, foundation, etc, defined steps for entry ensure fair process. This is a key governance principle that will guarantee that all members of the next generation in a certain family will be awarded the same opportunities. The outcome can be different as person X can progress more quickly through the ranks than person Y, but the steps followed for access should be the same for everyone. This way, no one can say they have been treated differently.

We now move on to exploring the inward aspect of next-generation development, focused on professional and personal skills. It is important to mention that any plan should be developed with the input of the next generation.

7.4 Hard skills

This includes formal education and training that gives the next generation an understanding of, for example, business, finance, law, economics and management. These skills are necessary to be able to assess the health and the performance of the family assets, whether the next generation are managing them themselves, or whether they are overseeing professionals in a capacity of shareholders. These skills can be complemented by more specialised courses on family ownership (eg, board membership and responsible ownership).

7.5 Soft and inner skills

These skills help the next generation discover who they are and how they can impact those around them. Hard skills have for a long time taken precedence in the education of the next generation, but emotional intelligence should be viewed as equally or more important. Alongside their technical roles, the next generation need to cultivate influence, learn how to bridge different viewpoints and in certain families, interact with a large group of shareholders. A high degree of self-awareness and the ability to develop healthy interpersonal relationships equips the next generation in a way that hard skills can only do up to a certain point. Communication skills (including active listening and presentation), leadership development, conflict resolution, time management and strategic thinking are a few examples of soft and inner skills. It is worth mentioning that personality profiling is an excellent starting point to develop these attributes.

7.6 Coaching and mentorship

Having access to coaches and mentors creates a support ecosystem which guides the next generation through family pressures, relationships, roles and feelings. A professional coach can support the creation of a personal development plan and help the next generation maintain the course to reach their goals. A trusted mentor (ideally, not a parent) can help the next generation navigate the complexities of family and business dynamics. This person can be an important point of contact between the next generation and the family's affairs, acting as a safe port of call when there are questions that the next generation may not feel entirely comfortable discussing with family members.

7.7 Cohort learning

We have discussed individual development at length above. However, in families with a larger group of siblings and/or cousins, the importance of learning to make decisions as a group cannot be understated. For a successful generational transition into a larger group of shareholders, they must be aligned in their vision for the family assets and know how to take hard decisions together. This only happens if the group in question has undertaken a journey where they got to know each other, understand and respect their differences in personality and have practised discussing different views. Just like in professional high-functioning teams, healthy group dynamics take work and effort to develop; it does not happen overnight.

The approach above showcases a 360° process for a holistic development of the next generation. Not all elements will be relevant to all families, but the key takeaway is that development should enable the next generation to hone their natural skills, build their confidence and empower them to choose the parts they wish to play in relation to the family and their assets. None of it should be an imposition.

An aspect that should be present in the education of the next generation, regardless of their background, is enabling them to fail and believing that this contributes to their personal journey in a positive way. Parents tend to steer their children away from making mistakes to protect them from pain, but this is how the most valuable lessons are learned. That is not to say that the risk of failure should not be mitigated; failure should be allowed but overseen by checks and balances to avoid points of no return.

Finally, alongside a development plan, the next generation should be involved in the succession plan, which we consider in the following section – asking their views, involving them in the decisions and allowing them to shape their own path forward, aligning their development with succession goals.

7.8 Responsible ownership

It may be that the next generation decide to take professional paths that take them away from the family assets. This should not be regarded as a failure, but rather the mark of a family accepting of choice and able to respect that an individual's personal purpose may not align with the family's affairs.

There are also cases where the family has become too large or the business too professionalised for all the members of the next generation to find employment within the family structures.

This is where the concept of responsible ownership becomes a key development point. Developing the next generation is not just about preparing the next leader. Creating a group of engaged, knowledgeable and active shareholders is as important, as they will still have the responsibility to develop an ownership strategy underpinned by their shared vision for the future. They need to hire the right people to deliver it and to assess the health of the family's assets. The element of cohort learning becomes particularly relevant in these circumstances.

8. Operating succession

Having defined the right context in which to start addressing succession planning and clear steps to align the development of the next generation, we move on to detailing concrete strategies to operate a generational transition.

8.1 Create the right forum, with the right people

A generational transition is a puzzle of people, skills, roles and relevant moments in time. A governance forum such as family meetings, a family council or a family board should be in place where these decisions are formally discussed and agreed by all those involved. Too often, succession is dictated by one person and imposed on others. In these cases, succession is operated under a one-way street and can become quite burdensome to those who must follow rules they did not agree to. In fact, a key governance principle translates into a person being a part of creating the rules they must abide by.

8.2 Map it out: who, what, how, when

The complexity of a generational transition can vary according to the number of people involved and the roles in question. In more complex transitions (eg, in a business where succession relates to management, board seats and ownership), it is helpful to create a clear map defining the following:

- Who are the people concerned?
- What are the roles in question, including the responsibilities? Skills matrices can help highlight the readiness of the person next in line, or the need to further develop a certain aspect.
- How is the transition going to be operated regarding each role (including what happens to those leaving said roles)? Considering role evolution is an important component to being able to let go.
- A timeline defining when each phase is deemed to start and conclude. Succession planning is not an overnight event, it spans over many months and sometimes years as it should consider the effective readiness of each person to each role. A deliberate, thoughtful approach has a better chance of getting it right.

8.3 Write it down

A succession plan formalised in a document becomes the guiding reference for the relevant stakeholders. It creates process and accountability. If it is not written down, it is merely an idea, subject to change and misinterpretation.

8.4 Develop a communication strategy to the relevant stakeholders

While the key decisions on succession are made by a small group of people, they typically impact a much wider group of stakeholders. It is important to define a plan where those decisions are well communicated to those impacted, so they know what to expect. Different communication methods will prove relevant at different levels, ranging from private conversations in an informal environment, to company-wide press releases.

In addition to the process-led steps above, it is also important to consider that there is a deeply emotional element to generational transitions. It means the end of an era for some, and the beginning of a new one for others. Feelings of anxiety, sadness or fear are not uncommon, and the right space should be created for an open discussion to acknowledge them – a practice which a 60-year-old may look at in horror. Yet, feelings drive good or bad behaviours, which will impact the success of the transition.

Therefore, creating the openness to address feelings and behaviours can be very helpful. A family member having acted as CEO for 10 or 20 years may have trouble in stopping behaving as such from one day to the other. In fact, leadership is a lonely place to be in, where it is not always possible to seek the support of close ones. Conversely, a newly minted director may experience moments of lack of confidence (*"Can I do this?", "Do I deserve it?"*). Advisers need to be particularly attuned to this emotional dimension, and provide support, reassurance and help beyond the technical aspect.

9. The adviser's role

9.1 The problem with 'shirtsleeves to shirtsleeves in three generations'

A favourite statistic of advisers in this field is that only 13% of family businesses survive through the third generation. Few know where this number comes from and whether it is representative of the world of family wealth. The industry ascertains that the first generation builds, the second enjoys, the third destroys without considering that all businesses have life cycles and that selling may be the result of a healthy choice by the family rather than conflict-based.

The perpetuation of these sayings has exacerbated the insecurities of first-generation wealth creators and led to a belief that loss is inevitable. For some, succession thus became a means to exert control over the family and the assets long after they have gone. But if the next generation is viewed as pre-destined to fail, and succession is aimed at protecting them for themselves, the result can only be a self-fulfilling prophecy. We encourage advisers to step away from this narrative and stimulate the understanding that succession should be communication-led, open, transparent and inclusive, as opposed to control-led, opaque and decided by the select few.[1]

9.2 Stepping out of the comfort zone

Families increasingly have the need for advisers in this field to become aware of dynamics beyond technical aspects. This is a key message: there is a growing need for advisers with the moral courage to help families address the multi-dimensional complexity of the issues highlighted above. Succession planning starts first and foremost with some very personal and emotional realisations that play directly into ego: mortality, ceasing to be the person in charge, making space for other views and priorities, lack of confidence, self-doubt ... Advisers are encouraged to initially spend time to understand the emotional concerns and pain points of not only the client, but of the spouse/partner, children and other relevant people involved so as to address the ecosystem as a whole.

9.3 Some helpful questions

Here are some exploratory questions that as advisers, we've found useful as conversation starters:

- What keeps you awake at night?
- What should your business look like in 10 years?
- What should your family look like in 10 years?
- What are your expectations for your children?
- What are your children's expectations of the future?

---

1 James Grubman, Dennis T Jaffe and Kristin Keffeler, *The Future of Family Wealth Advising – Wealth 3.0* (Family Wealth Consulting, 2023).

- What will make your children happy and fulfilled?
- What do your children need to know that they currently do not?
- What does success look like for you all individually and collectively?
- Do you all know the why and the how, as well as the what?

10. Conclusion

Hopefully, this chapter illustrates that the development of the next generation in the context of succession should be built around them, instead of centring around the family assets. Well-rounded, happy and fulfilled individuals make for good leaders. Being a next-gen brings privilege and opportunity, but it also brings an unavoidable responsibility. It is healthy to offer a *quid pro quo* through which the next generation is encouraged to find personal purpose, enhance what they are naturally good at and choose freely the part they wish to play. The current generation should be supported in figuring out their "What's next?", in a way that makes way for the next generation yet enabling them to continue to share their extremely valuable experience, as guides and mentors.

Communication, defined processes and clear expectations are the bedrock for healthy interactions between two generations. Advisers can best support families through facilitating these difficult conversations. Their presence in the room ensures a structured conversation with less opportunity for emotionally charged exchanges between family members, and means that every voice, even the quietest, is heard.

Preparing for transfer of ownership

Dan Frosh
Family Firm Institute Inc.
Andrew P Hier
Cambridge Family Enterprise Group

1. Introduction

The transfer of ownership in a family enterprise represents a pivotal transition from one generation to the next that can shape the future trajectory of the business, the wealth and the family itself. Ownership, as the power centre of any family enterprise, carries with it the authority to make critical decisions that affect all dimensions of the enterprise. These decisions include determining the types of businesses to own, guiding investment strategies, allocating wealth for investment and distributions, structuring ownership, providing resources for development of the family members (including successor owners) and designing governance frameworks that determine who makes what decisions and how. The impact of these choices extends beyond the operating companies to include family offices, family foundations and who will sit on governing boards and who will be successor owners.

Effectively preparing for this transition is essential to ensure that the enterprise not only survives but thrives across generations. The concept of a 'family enterprise' encompasses more than just one or more operating businesses; it includes all activities that family members pursue collaboratively that contribute to the family's well-being, alignment, success and enjoyment. These activities might include investments, real estate holdings, family offices, philanthropic endeavours, family councils, meetings, family constitutions and even community activities and holidays. This broad definition highlights the complexity of the enterprise and underscores the importance of a well-prepared transition process.

To successfully navigate this process, families must adopt a holistic approach that takes into account the entire scope of the family enterprise. Key elements to consider include developing a shared vision for the future of the enterprise; preparing future owners for their critical roles; refining current ownership structures and governance practices; and developing a comprehensive wealth strategy that addresses the needs of the family as it evolves. Cross-generational collaboration in succession planning is also a vital component, ensuring that leadership and ownership are passed on in a manner that supports continuity and preserves the enduring aspects of the family's legacy.

Each of these elements, which will be addressed further in this chapter, play a crucial role in achieving a seamless and effective ownership transfer. By carefully planning and strategically executing the transition, families can nurture their legacy and ensure that their business interests are sustained well into the future. This process not only safeguards the family's wealth but also reinforces the values, vision and commitments that have guided the enterprise through generations. In this way, the transition of ownership becomes not just a change in leadership, but a reconsideration and affirmation of the family's long-term goals, and its dedication to the success and sustainability of the enterprise for generations to come.

2. Developing a shared vision for the future of the enterprise

As family enterprises navigate the complexities of transitioning ownership to the next generation, one of the most critical elements in ensuring long-term success is the development of a shared vision by the owners for the future of the enterprise. This vision serves as a unifying force, aligning the diverse aspirations and expectations of both current and future family members. Through articulating this common vision, families are better prepared to approach business continuity decisions, portfolio strategy and growth opportunities with a cohesive and unified mindset.

This vision should help the family to answer the fundamental question of "What are we trying to achieve together?". To do so, a well-crafted vision provides an aspirational, yet realistic snapshot of the future, outlining how the family defines success within a specific time frame. In today's fast-paced and turbulent environment, it is often prudent for this vision to focus on a shorter-term horizon of five to 10 years. This time frame allows the vision to remain relevant as the family's circumstances and the external landscape quickly evolve over time.

Once drafted, the shared owners' vision should not sit idly on the shelf. It should be regularly referenced and serve as a guiding star for strategic decisions. Adhering to the vision ensures that the choices made by the family are aligned with the family's long-term goals, thereby helping to preserve the integrity and continuity of the enterprise, especially during a generational transition. The vision should challenge the family to innovate and grow, while also being measurable to track progress. This balance between aspiration and practicality is essential for maintaining momentum and ensuring that the family remains on course to achieve its objectives.

For the next generation, the process of contributing to, understanding and embracing this vision is particularly crucial. A shared vision provides them with a clear sense of purpose and direction, enabling them to make informed decisions that are consistent with the family's values and long-term objectives. This sense of alignment is vital as they step into leadership roles and begin to shape the future of the enterprise.

In the process of developing the owners' vision, involvement of the next generation is not just beneficial; it is essential. Their perspectives are invaluable in crafting a vision that resonates across generations. After all, they are the ones who will be living out this vision in the years to come. Early engagement in this process helps cultivate their connection to the business, fostering a sense of stewardship rather than mere ownership. It also instils a deep sense of commitment and responsibility towards the family enterprise, preparing them for the challenges and opportunities that lie ahead.

Creating a shared vision for the future of the family enterprise is imperative for any family preparing to transition ownership to the next generation. By aligning the aspirations of current and future family members, this vision not only ensures the continuity of the enterprise but also empowers the next generation to lead with purpose and conviction. For family business advisers, guiding families through the process of developing and implementing a shared vision is a critical step in securing the long-term success of the family enterprise.

3. Future owner education and development

One of the best investments a family can make for the long-term strength and success of its enterprise is to spend adequate time, energy and other resources developing members of the next generation for their future role as owners. Failure to prioritise this development can result in disinterest, dysfunctional owner behaviour and misconceptions about the future vision for the business among the next-generation owners. In today's turbulent world, developing united, capable and contributing owners has become an increasingly important aspect of preparing for a generational transfer, and the work to do so can take years.

Given the unique nature of family enterprises, owners have powerful rights, and along with these rights, come significant responsibilities. From a legal perspective, preparing for the transition of ownership from one generation to the next is often approached like a *birthright*, with well-defined guidelines and entitlements outlined in wills, trust documents and other ownership agreements. However, given the critical role of owners, families would be well served to view ownership more like a job, with its own list of qualifications, skills and behaviours. Similar to any other job, these skills and behaviors take time and experience to develop.

This process should be approached strategically within the unique context of each family enterprise and should be tailored to the needs of the rising generation, both as individuals and as a group. Preparing the next generation for effective ownership involves developing a comprehensive set of skills and knowledge.

3.1 The history of the family business

A narrative history of the family business can provide important context to further engender a sense of pride and responsibility in the future owners. Sharing stories about the origins of the business, the founder's vision, and how challenges and key successes along the way helped to shape the business's journey can teach important lessons about perseverance, innovation and operational excellence. This historical perspective not only honours past achievements but also provides valuable lessons and insights for future challenges. The idea is to preserve insights from mistakes and responses to adversity, not just highlights of success.

3.2 Overview of current business and investment activities

All owners must have a basic understanding of how the family makes its money and the activities that comprise the family's wealth. On the business side, owners should be familiar with the company's core products and services, key members of management, primary markets and customers served, and the key drivers of profitability. Additionally, owners should also generally understand the industry in which the business operates, including market competition and industry-specific risks or regulation.

On the investment side, owners need to understand the construction of the family's total wealth portfolio. This includes discussing the types of investments held, the rationale behind these choices, and the expected returns. Emphasising the importance of diversification and risk management can help owners make prudent investment decisions. These discussions and related education help to ensure that the collective investment portfolio continues to meet the family's wealth objectives as the family's needs evolve over time.

Risk is a core concept to understand: What is risk? How is a prudent business risk determined? What are desirable risk management policies? How should effective implementation of these policies be monitored?

3.3 Financial literacy

Family business owners must also possess at least a basic level of financial literacy to make informed decisions to help the business grow and remain competitive. Understanding financial statements such as balance sheets, income statements and cash flow projections is essential for owners to assess the financial health, profitability, liquidity and solvency of their business. It also allows owners to engage in more productive discussions with their board of directors and to evaluate the board's effectiveness. Capable owners will look at performance over a period of time, tracking key ratios in the form of a 'dashboard', and seeking alert notices from the executive team when certain thresholds are reached.

3.4 Capital allocation strategy

In addition to understanding how to read and interpret basic financial statements, active owners (those who are pivotally engaged within the enterprise and help lead the ownership group in making key decisions) must also understand the impact that capital allocation decisions can have in order to effectively prioritise and invest resources in projects that generate the highest returns and help to achieve their long-term objectives. This knowledge helps them identify the optimal balance between reinvesting in the business, issuing dividends and investing in other strategic initiatives. Effective capital allocation can help minimise financial risks and aligns spending with long-term goals, maintaining financial health and stability.

3.5 Interpersonal skills

Equally important are the skills that enable effective leadership and interpersonal relationships among a group of family owners. Communication skills are vital for building consensus in decision making, collaboration, resolving potential conflicts and strengthening unity within the family. Leadership abilities help in inspiring and guiding teams, fostering a positive organisational culture.

3.6 An ownership culture

In addition to developing these skills and competencies, preparing next-generation family members to become effective owners also requires instilling them with an *owner's mindset*. Nurturing this mindset will enable members of the next generation to become stewards of their family's wealth, cultivating a strong connection with value creation within the family enterprise. This emphasis on value creation can empower owners to make the often-difficult decision to get out of a legacy operating business or investment when it becomes necessary to do so, recognising that while the family's business activities may need to change, the engagement of an enterprising family will continue. An *owner's mindset* should also include the perspective that all owners have the responsibility to contribute back to the family enterprise in various ways in appreciation for the rewards that ownership offers.

4. How to develop ownership talent in next-generation family members

Engaging future owners early in business activities is critical for their development. Involvement in family meetings, strategic planning sessions and governance roles provides practical experience and insights into the enterprise's operations. This early engagement helps build their connection to the business, developing a sense of responsibility and ownership.

Below are several examples of practical activities that can be implemented to help facilitate the education and development of future owners:

- *Exploration of key business activities:* Assign teams of next-generation family members to engage in collaborative learning about the main family business activities and then report their findings to the larger group. Family members should leave this exercise with a better understanding of the business operations as well as how to effectively collaborate with fellow owners on a meaningful project.
- *Case study analysis:* Use case studies with family enterprise themes to give next-generation owners the opportunity to work through real-world scenarios together, enhancing their problem-solving skills.
- *Task force innovation projects:* Create task force projects for next-generation members to investigate and learn about possible new innovative business dimensions, services and new ventures, to provide hands-on learning opportunities and reinforcing the need for an entrepreneurial mindset.
- *Governance observer roles:* Create non-voting observer roles on governance bodies to allow future owners to gain insights into decision-making processes and governance practices.

Developing future owners in a family enterprise is a multifaceted process that requires strategic planning and commitment. By educating the next generation about their roles and responsibilities, building robust business, financial and soft skills, and engaging them early in business activities, family enterprises can ensure a seamless transition of ownership. This approach not only preserves the family legacy but also drives the business towards continued success and sustainability. For family business advisers, facilitating this development process is key to fostering resilient and forward-thinking family enterprises.

5. Integration of the new ownership structure: to whom is ownership given and how is ownership to be held?

As families begin to prepare to transfer ownership to the next generation, the process provides a great opportunity to evaluate the current ownership structure and make any necessary refinements to help ensure that it is well designed to meet the foreseeable needs of the next generation.

5.1 Defining ownership eligibility

Among the first areas where guiding principles need to be resolved is whether restrictions should be imposed on who may actually become owners. As the family generally grows from generation to generation, the senior generation may confront increased complexity in addressing this sensitive topic. A majority of family enterprises tend to favour restricting ownership to bloodline descendants to ensure that control remains within the direct family lineage.

However, even within this scenario, there are complexities that need to be adequately planned for, including whether to allow adopted children (often who are legally adopted before the age of 18) and stepchildren to become owners. Additionally, as spouses marry into the family in the second generation and beyond, they often bring a new pool of valuable talent into the family. Their influence on the family enterprise is undeniably significant given their roles of helping to raise the next generation of family owners and as a (hopefully) supportive spouse. Prior to transferring ownership to the next generation, the current family owners must determine their philosophy regarding what ownership roles are allowed to pass to future-generation spouses.

Some families decide that spouses may never hold shares and may require future lineal descendants to execute prenuptial agreements that preclude their spouses from acquiring ownership through divorce. Including these restrictions in shareholder agreements and trust documents are other effective vehicles to protect ownership from transferring to spouses in most jurisdictions. Other families may decide that the shares in the family business must only pass to lineal descendants but permit qualified spouses to serve in ownership decision-making roles as a trustee on behalf of their minor children, or on an owners council (discussed further below). There are also some families who decide to allow spouses to jointly own shares in the business, perhaps with some protections included to keep the shares in the family in the case of a divorce. Potential advantages, disadvantages and implications exist for each of these options. Advisers should help the family to thoroughly examine and evaluate these options within the family's unique context and with help from the family's estate planning and tax professionals.

Other families might consider an alternative approach, deciding to extend ownership to include non-family members, such as board members, key executives, or other stakeholders who have demonstrated a strong commitment to the enterprise. While this approach can bring in diverse perspectives and expertise into ownership decision making, it also represents the inclusion of other values and guiding philosophies on growth and risk taking, which can create potential owner misalignment.

Often, the decision to give ownership to key non-family stakeholders is motivated by the desire to ensure strong loyalty and incentivise their operational performance within the company or through governance roles. Viable alternatives exist, such as phantom stock plans, that can encourage these motivations without passing actual ownership outside of the family. Families who are interested in transferring ownership outside the family should carefully evaluate the potential current and future consequences of doing so, including the creation of non-family minority shareholder rights. Once ownership is given, it can be much more difficult and sensitive to get it back.

5.2 Refining the current ownership structure for the future

Prior to transferring ownership to the next generation, the current owners should devote quality time and resources to examining the current ownership structure and evaluating whether it is well designed for the dynamics and needs of a larger and more complex next generation. This ownership structure must also integrate into an evolving enterprise's broader governance framework, including decision-making centres and operational management.

As family enterprises pass from generation to generation, it can be common for fewer family members to work in the business and the connection between the family and the business can weaken as a result. However, it remains just as critical that the owners who have the responsibility to make important decisions for the enterprise understand the business and its industry and are well-informed about the risks, challenges and opportunities facing the business.

Some families excel at educating the owners who are not active in the business and governance to prepare them to participate in ownership decision making. Others are not as adept at this important task. For those families, there may be some options in the way they structure their ownership to help alleviate the impact of this dynamic. For example, creating voting trusts or dual-class share structure, with voting and non-voting shares, can help families to distribute the economic benefits of ownership equitably while concentrating the voting responsibilities with those family members who are most informed and qualified to make these important decisions.

Additionally, as the enterprise itself may become more complex with the introduction of new business and investment ventures over time, families could benefit from evaluating whether one or more holding companies above their operating businesses may help by providing shared resources, asset protection, and enable more effective portfolio governance and capital allocation decision making.

6. Estate planning and succession

Any discussion of preparing for the transition of ownership must include the topic of estate planning. When approached effectively, it provides the framework for transferring ownership in a way that is consistent with the family's dynamics, long-term goals and governance structure. Family enterprise and estate planning advisers must ensure that estate plans are aligned across the family, with a clear understanding of what assets will be passed to the next generation, how they will be transferred and how decision-making authority about these assets will operate in the future.

The available estate planning options, vehicles and tax implications are jurisdictionally dependent and accordingly, this chapter will not address specific estate planning options. Advisers must ensure that their family clients receive qualified legal and tax advice for each jurisdiction in which they own assets. However, estate planning should be approached holistically – looking at the family's needs and dynamics. In jurisdictions with a significant estate and gift tax in place, there can be a tendency for tax planning decisions to dictate the estate planning process. While estate tax implications are often among the primary concerns for enterprising families, they are never the only concerns present. It is important to explore other possible factors, including the liquidity needs of members in the next generation, personal protections against creditors, ex-spouses, unequal branch sizes and how the branches will approach decision making.

For instance, one branch of the family may choose to consolidate decision making within a smaller group, while another branch may prefer to leave decision making up to individual branch members. These differences must be reconciled to prevent conflicts and ensure that the enterprise remains unified in its strategic direction.

Another critical decision is whether ownership should be distributed equally among next-generation members or allocated based on other criteria, such as involvement in the business or specific contributions to the enterprise's success. Equal distribution can promote fairness and cohesion, but it may also dilute control and complicate decision making. Conversely, unequal distribution, while potentially more strategic, requires clear communication and consensus to avoid conflict.

Evaluating the current ownership structure and the necessary refinements to ensure it is right for the next generation is a valuable process in preparing for the transfer of ownership to the next generation. The process may at times be complicated and will require careful consideration of critical topics, with significant implications. By aligning the new ownership structure with the enterprise's governance framework and using estate planning tools to ensure a smooth transition, families can position their enterprises for long-term success.

7. Design or refine the ownership governance

As a family prepares for a generational transfer of ownership, it creates a natural opportunity to evaluate its current ownership governance practices and contemplate how these practices may need to be refined to meet the evolving needs of the future ownership group. Among the most important aspects of ownership governance that may need to be examined are the established decision-making processes.

Owners are empowered to make the critical decisions to guide the future of their enterprise with the goal of growing its value for current and future generations. Some of these fundamental decisions include:

- setting the strategic vision for the enterprise;
- making prudent bets on capital investments;
- making good choices of key people and talent;

- setting, protecting and adjusting the culture; and
- designing the right family enterprise governance structures, practices and policies.

Given the importance of these decisions on the sustainability of the enterprise, ownership groups must become skilled at exploring available options, evaluating their implications and ultimately making sound judgements in an efficient manner. To do so, they must design and follow high-quality decision-making processes. As the current owners prepare for a transition of ownership authority, they must also ensure these processes are designed to facilitate the involvement and meet the needs of the next owners as well.

Not every generational transfer is the same, and the dynamics of transferring ownership from a controlling owner in the first generation to a sibling partnership in the second generation are inherently different than in later generations. This is especially true when it comes to decision-making processes among the owners.

7.1 Controlling owner to sibling partnership

This evolution involves a shift from centralised, founder-led control to a more distributed form of ownership and governance among siblings. The term 'sibling partnership' is not meant to require a legal form of 'partnership', but indicates siblings working together in control of the enterprise. Shared control requires designing processes that facilitate the participation by a group of owners with diverse interests and a range of knowledge about the business. Effective information-sharing becomes even more critical to keep owners who are not active in the business adequately informed about the business's performance.

7.2 Sibling partnership to cousin consortium

By the third generation, ownership can become even more diffused among a broad group of cousins with diverse interests and backgrounds who are more geographically dispersed than their parents' generation. As a result, these family owners can feel increasingly unaware of and disconnected from the family's business and investment activities. For these reasons, it can be valuable to introduce representative governance systems to foster efficient and well-informed decision-making processes.

8. The benefits of an owners council during a generational transition

An owners council is a representative working group tasked with actively leading the ownership group and is empowered either to make decisions delegated to it on behalf of the owners or to investigate and make recommendations for formal approval by the full group of owners. An owners council becomes more appropriate as the number of owners grows, particularly where it becomes difficult to have detailed working discussions with a large number of individuals, and the range and depth of understanding of key ownership issues is not uniform across all family owners. Another advantage of an owners council is that it allows the selection of the most informed and capable among all family owners to do the analytical work and to arrive at the best recommendations.

Owners councils serve a variety of purposes, especially within a complex family enterprise, including to:

- align the family's ownership goals and strategies;
- serve as the voice of the owners to the board of directors;
- provide a forum to discuss, debate and resolve important ownership topics (as appropriate);
- keep the family owners appropriately informed; and
- support the development of the future owners.

As the family ownership group grows through generational transfers, an owners council can be especially beneficial, serving as a forum to encourage cross-generational discussion and collaboration on important ownership topics as well as the development of future owners. Additionally, a high-functioning owners council can contribute value to an evolving family enterprise in the following ways:

- *Aligning current and future family owners' perspectives:* Owners councils can serve as a forum for current and future owners to engage in meaningful cross-generational dialogue to better understand each other's perspectives in the pursuit of aligning behind a collective vision for the future of their enterprise. This alignment is critical in maintaining the cohesion and unity of the family enterprise.
- *Educating and developing future owners:* The council can take the lead in coordinating the family's initiative to design and implement training programmes, educational workshops and mentorship initiatives to prepare the next generation for their future roles as owners. This educational focus can help ensure that future owners are well-informed, capable and ready to take on leadership roles within the family enterprise when the time comes.
- *Creating opportunities for next-generation involvement:* The council can design and implement initiatives to involve next-generation family members in governance processes. This might include observer roles or opportunities to serve on committees or task forces.
- *Enhancing transparency and communication:* Effective communication is crucial during ownership transitions. The owners council can establish

clear channels for information sharing, ensuring that all family members are kept informed about the business's performance, strategic decisions and governance issues. This transparency helps build trust among family members and fosters a collaborative environment.

- *Facilitating conflict resolution:* Ownership transitions can be fraught with potential conflicts as different family members may have varying perspectives and interests. An owners council serves as a neutral platform where disputes can be addressed and resolved in a structured manner. The council can mediate disagreements, helping to prevent conflicts from escalating and ensuring that ownership transitions proceed smoothly.

9. The critical role of shareholder agreements during ownership transitions

In addition to reviewing their ownership governance practices and processes, families preparing to transfer ownership should take the opportunity to review and update their ownership agreements and policies as necessary.

Shareholder agreements, in particular, are powerful documents for privately held family enterprises. They are legally binding arrangements among a company's owners that describe the key ownership rights and responsibilities and high-level parameters about how the company should be operated.

These agreements offer a number of benefits for family enterprises as they plan for an orderly transition of ownership, including the following:

- *Governing the ownership succession process:* Effective shareholder agreements can include detailed succession plans, identifying potential successors and any eligibility criteria they must meet. In doing so, the agreement reduces possible ambiguity and ensures it is transparent and understood by all parties.
- *Determining a clear plan and process for unanticipated circumstances such as the premature death or incapacity of an owner:* Of course, not all ownership transitions go according to plan. Sometimes, unforeseen events can cause ownership to pass to the next generation sooner than anticipated, and the buy-sell provisions within a shareholder agreement can outline the process to be followed, valuation principles and funding mechanisms to help maintain an orderly transition of ownership to the next generation.
- *Defining decision-making criteria and approval thresholds:* The shareholder agreement should outline a process that promotes dynamic decision making among an expanded ownership group in the next generation, including provisions that outline the appropriate approval thresholds for various ownership-level decisions (eg, changes in capital structure, mergers or acquisitions). By setting appropriately high approval

thresholds for these critical decisions, the agreement can encourage collaborative decision making that protects the interests of all shareholders.

- *Imposing confidentiality requirements:* Unless an owner is also a member of the board of directors, or an employee, there is typically no inherent duty to keep business information confidential. Owners do, however, have inherent rights to receive potentially sensitive information about their businesses (including the right to inspect corporate books and records). As enterprising families prepare to transfer ownership to members of the next generation, they would be wise to consider including a provision that requires owners to maintain confidentiality and help to avoid the risk of an inexperienced owner sharing sensitive information publicly.
- *Imposing non-competition requirements:* Similarly, unless an owner is also a member of the board of directors, or an employee, there is typically no legal duty against competing with the family enterprise. Some families address this concern in a family charter. Others choose to avoid this conflict by including prohibitions in a shareholder agreement. The scope and definition of the non-competition clause requires careful attention. Some legal jurisdictions are moving away from upholding non-competition restrictions.

In these ways, and others, a shareholder agreement is a vital tool for family enterprises, providing a comprehensive framework for the orderly transition of ownership to the next generation. By governing the transfer process and instituting reasonable restrictions, it can help promote stability and foster a fair and transparent transition.

10. Making the ownership succession process more successful: cross-generational collaboration

The successful transfer of ownership in a family enterprise is not just defined by the ultimate outcome. The process of preparing for the eventual transition is just as important as the result. An effective process will provide the family with invaluable experience in having difficult discussions on sensitive topics, articulating their hopes and concerns about the future and refining their decision-making skills. To design an effective planning process, robust cross-generational collaboration will be imperative. This collaboration ensures that the transition is not only smooth but also aligns with the long-term goals and values of the family.

11. The importance of collaboration

Collaboration between generations is essential in bridging the gap between the founding principles of the family enterprise and the evolving aspirations of future generations. Engaging both current and next-generation family members in meaningful dialogue fosters a shared understanding of the enterprise's mission, vision and strategic direction. This shared understanding helps align the goals of different generations, ensuring that the transition of ownership supports the continuity of the family's legacy.

Cross-generational collaboration also empowers the next generation by providing them with the opportunity to contribute to the decision-making process. When younger family members are involved early on, they gain a sense of ownership and responsibility, which is crucial for their future leadership roles. This engagement not only prepares them for the challenges ahead but also strengthens their commitment to the family enterprise.

12. Attention to all stakeholders

In any ownership transition, it is vital to consider the interests and expectations of all stakeholders, including non-family members who may hold key roles in the enterprise. Cross-generational collaboration must extend beyond the family circle to include these stakeholders, ensuring that their perspectives are considered in the planning process. This inclusive approach helps build trust and maintain the stability of the enterprise during the transition.

13. Planning and timing

Effective planning and timing are critical to the success of the ownership transition. Cross-generational collaboration should be an ongoing process, rather than a last-minute effort. Starting the collaboration early allows for the gradual transfer of knowledge, responsibilities and decision-making authority, which helps ensure a seamless transition.

A well-timed and carefully planned transition also allows for the identification and mitigation of potential risks. By involving multiple generations in the planning process, families can develop a more comprehensive and forward-looking succession plan that addresses the unique needs and aspirations of each generation.

14. Conclusion

Preparation for ownership transition in a family enterprise is a critical stage in multi-generational succession. It is best accomplished over years, with some period of shared ownership and shared leadership, to ensure effective continuity and the benefits of innovation. Coordination with other dimensions of the family enterprise, beyond ownership, is desirable to achieve alignment and engagement across the family and the family enterprise. Surprise tends to be counterproductive.

Important steps in preparing for ownership transition include: developing a shared vision with appropriate evolution of goals while preserving still-relevant aspects of legacy; preparing successors to gain adequate skills and knowledge; nurturing an active and responsible ownership culture; and adapting the distribution of ownership, how it is legally held with good ownership agreements, and the structure of ownership governance to meet the new array of leaders and decision makers. If done well, the result is an adaptive, engaged and talented family enterprise able to continue good stewardship into the next generation.

Trusts and family businesses: the ideal succession solution?

Nic Arnold
Victoria Blackburn
JTC Private Office
Bryony Cove
Jennifer Ridgway
Farrer & Co LLP

1. Setting the scene – why trusts?

Trusts have long played a role in managing and preserving family wealth. While historically they originate from a need for medieval landowners to protect their estates in times of war and unexpected deaths, trusts have evolved to be vehicles for succession planning, protection of family and business assets as well as means of potentially saving tax.

COVID-19 exposed vulnerabilities for family businesses which highlighted the need for more robust, proactive business planning and risk management. As well as challenging the operational agility and financial robustness of family businesses, the pandemic underscored the importance of better succession planning in the wake of the sometimes unexpected death or illness of key family members. With families reevaluating their priorities, trusts can be considered as tools to generate continuity and manage the transfer of business ownership in a controlled way which avoids fragmentation and reduces the likelihood of family friction.

Further, geopolitical influences, such as the war in the Ukraine, US/China trade tensions, global inflation and even the departure of the United Kingdom from the European Union, will impact the decisions made by family business owners in an increasingly interconnected and unpredictable world.

This chapter looks at how families can use trusts to protect their family business from such external threats and even, it might be said, from the biggest potential threat: the family itself. As family dynamics and needs change, the impact of just one family member's actions can have extremely negative impacts on the long-term family wealth preservation and success of the business.

It should be noted that this chapter does not seek to replace detailed legal and tax analysis, nor the exact advice which may be given on a jurisdiction-by-jurisdiction, and family-by-family, basis. This chapter does, however, provide useful guiding principles and examples which should assist the practitioner.

We shed light on the advantages, and disadvantages, of passing ownership of the family business to trustees (individuals or professional trustees) to oversee the family's future interaction with the family business, and consumption of the family wealth.

We look at some of the challenges which may occur where families do not appreciate the role that a trust plays in their lives, where trust deeds may have been drafted too rigidly to meet evolving family needs, or where beneficiaries' expectations are not aligned with those of the trustees and/or other family members. Such challenges can give rise to disagreements, and case law provides important guidelines for dispute resolution. Trusts have also faced challenges as tax legislation continues to evolve across the globe, but despite this, it is rare to see the mass collapsing of trust structures due to tax law changes.

2. Trust principles – the basics

Trusts are known within common law jurisdictions for their ability to provide control and flexibility over family wealth beyond the founding generation. Families have found a powerful mechanism by which to manage the family business ownership. In simple terms, the trustee is able to act as a single and often sole shareholder and decision maker who is able to hold a macro view of the family business. This is a position that can be held in perpetuity while the beneficial class(es) who may have either an active or a passive engagement in the family business, evolve over time and through the generations. While other types of structures in civil law jurisdictions may seek to achieve a similar result, trusts have a particular ability to provide meaningful long-term safeguarding of wealth in a way that embodies the values and desires of the wealth creators. This is perhaps especially true when used to protect family businesses, as trustees can play a central role in the long-term relationship between family members and the family business.

In technical terms, most trust law is spread across three sources: common law principles, statute and case law. Each jurisdiction's trust law has evolved differently, and we will seek to illustrate examples through this chapter from key jurisdictions, including England and Wales, which is arguably the original trust law jurisdiction.

The role of trustees and their interaction with beneficiaries will be governed by all three sources and requires careful navigation. Indeed, in order to fulfil their fiduciary duties, professional trustees will usually require regular and ongoing input from professional advisers in their capacity as trustees separate from, and in addition to, professional advice taken by the trust beneficiaries.

In each jurisdiction, trustees will be informed by local statute setting out the nature and extent of their powers and duties (eg, the Trustee Act 2000 under English law in relation to investment powers). Typically, however, case law will also need to be considered across different trust jurisdictions when exercising those powers, and each trustee should bring their own experience to bear.

While the courts may be consulted in relation to larger decisions, often referred to as 'momentous decisions' (per *Public Trustee v Cooper*[1]) – such as the appointment of a large shareholding on a new trust, or to a particular beneficiary, or the decision to sell the long-held family business – the general principle is that trustees must make decisions based on their knowledge of the trust assets, the beneficiaries and the surrounding context.

Trustees will need to review the appropriateness of the decisions they take by appraising all relevant considerations (which includes the settlor's wishes) but disregarding irrelevant considerations (per *Hastings Bass (deceased)*[2]). We look further at this later in the chapter.

A statement or letter of wishes, while not legally binding, is an important reference point for trustees to follow when executing their fiduciary duties. Where most effective, this document should provide guidance to trustees about the settlor's personal preferences for the management and distribution of a trust's assets.

In many cases, additional checks and balances are achieved through the appointment of a protector. While the trustees will typically focus on the day-to-day management and administration of the trust, the protector provides an oversight role, ensuring the trustees are acting appropriately and reasonably, and typically their role is to see that the trust continues to align with the settlor's intentions and the needs of the beneficiary class, albeit within the present context. The protector may have powers of veto (their consent is required for certain trustee decisions) or may have the power to appoint or remove trustees, with powers to add to or exclude individuals from the beneficiary class.

Settlors may also reserve certain powers to themselves. This often includes investment powers, the power to remove and appoint trustees or, sometimes, dispositive powers or vetoes. Such powers may support a bond of trust between the settlor and the trustees, or alternatively may drive a wedge between them. Care is needed. Utilising the skills of the settlor in the first few years can be of benefit, but a plan for succession to the powers held by the settlor should be included to ensure longevity and give the trustees the space to appropriately perform their duties.

Trustees need to be conscious of any limitations on the exercise of their powers, but in the context of a family business, where powers held outside the trustee body (by non-trustee power holders, like a protector) are managed well alongside the trustee role, this will provide an opportunity for good governance and family communication. This is explored further later in the chapter.

There will always be advantages and disadvantages of owning a family business within a trust structure. Key to this will be the care with which the

---

1 [2001] WTLR 901.
2 [1975] Ch 25 (CA).

trust is set up, the experience and quality of the trustees overseeing the family wealth, and the degree to which it is recognised that a trust structure used to protect a family business should be treated as an integrated part of the working mechanics of the family with strong beneficiary communication and education.

3. Control – when it works and when it doesn't

The most common concern that families have when contemplating settling their family business into trust, is about passing shareholder ownership of the business to the custody of decision makers who are not family members and giving up the control they have been used to over many years.

In the context of a family business, concerns can legitimately arise that the trust will distance the family from their business, particularly where professional trustees exert a high degree of governance through the processes and procedures they employ to protect the family wealth.

These concerns can be managed via what is now a classic ownership model whereby the trustees are the shareholders owning a holding company, which in turn owns the trading business(es). This effectively separates ownership, oversight and management of the business. Family members routinely sit on holdings boards with senior executives and have a say in their composition, whether by formal veto, via a family protector or a formal consultation requirement (with these powers or processes typically set out in the relevant corporate governance documentation). The business itself is then run by an executive board for the trading entities which sit below the holding company.

In addition, for larger trusts with complex assets including family businesses, the protector may be a committee rather than an individual, and this can help with issues of protector succession, particularly where the idea of acting on the committee for a set term is introduced.

This idea is exemplified in the case of a second generation £1 billion family business which was held through a Jersey trust. The trust, settled by the deceased patriarch, was discretionary in nature, with wide trustee powers. The business was very successful and was driven by full-time involvement from all members of the second generation. However, it was becoming clear that the nature and level of family input would need to adapt to accommodate the increased number of third-generation family members who represented a wide range of ages and degree of business involvement. The protector provisions were used to implement a family-led protector committee operating on set terms and replacing the role of one person with family members from all branches of the family. Consent is now required from the committee for major trustee decisions, including significant disposals, sale of shares in the business, and the power to remove and appoint trustees. This innovation will play a key role within the family business governance as the number of trust beneficiaries gets larger and the overall family involvement in the business is reduced.

In the case of an elderly shipping magnate who had spent his life making the major decisions to create and run his business empire, the challenge was that, despite the different talents and responsibilities of his descendants, there was no individual who could replace him in the role he had created. There was a real concern that everything he worked so hard to create and the stability this provided for his family would collapse after his death. The decision was taken to put the family business into trust, and with the support of the trustees, the settlor built an advisory committee comprised of key family and business members whose roles and responsibilities were enshrined in a family charter linking in with the operating side of the business. As a result of this careful planning, the talents of the next generation were utilised in a meaningful way alongside the introduction of the trust structure to protect the family business for the long term.

In situations where family members are able to exert power over the day-to-day running of the business outside the role of an employee or consultant, the addition of trustees as stewards and legal owners can formalise roles and responsibilities, and enhance the skills and reflect the goals of the family individually and collectively.

In the case of a settlor who had passed away many years before, the burden of wealth was a real concern for the patriarch's six children. The new patriarch, the eldest son, was intimidated by the responsibility imposed on him, demotivated by having so much wealth and the business quickly declined, as did his focus in life. Using the trust structure as a tool, and with the input from the trustees and other key advisers, a strategy was developed that allowed him to generate a new focus and to appoint people better able to manage the family business. He stepped down as CEO and built an impressive philanthropic side to the trust, which helped him find a renewed purpose and sense of fulfilment.

4. The 21st-century 'great wealth transfer'

It has been well documented for some time that the first half of this century would see the greatest generational transfer on record for the wealth created following World War II up to the 1990s. With this as a backdrop, where trusts are combined with strong family governance, the two can go hand in hand to help the next generation prepare for the transfer of wealth and support the older generations to adjust and let go. Well-thought-through trusts can provide a mechanism for effective intergenerational collaboration and family communication with the trustees as willing participants in the process.

However, it is not always the case that a trust can be used as part of a good model of governance. In the example of a settlor who placed a significant percentage of his well-known business into a UK trust, he was overly focused on tax advantages of settlement, and did not think through or engage with the concept of giving up control and embracing succession to the next generation.

The settlor continued to be very involved in the business as he moved into his late eighties, and actively refused to allow the next generation in their forties to become involved in day-to-day management. Despite being a major shareholder, governance structures and communication were also not put in place to enable the trustees to facilitate succession, and the settlor and his co-directors continued to control the business. As a result, there was no planned succession, and despite the business continuing to be a financial success, when the settlor died, the decision was made to sell the business because, having been excluded for so many years, the beneficiaries felt they were unable at that late stage to come together as drivers of the business, even within the protective environment of the trust structure.

This opportunity also was not taken in the case of a 'next-gen' who, at the age of 21, suddenly noticed cash appearing in his bank account. The payments were from a trust set up by his grandfather some years before to provide for the grandchildren, and he had no idea it existed. When asked how he felt about 'his money', he explained that, on the one hand it was obviously great, but on deeper reflection, he was disappointed that the family did not trust him enough to open up about the true family wealth and prepare him for it.

This story will resonate with many practitioners and is particularly important in the context of the changing values of family business. The 'next gen', some of whom are already in their forties and fifties, are increasingly driven by a greater sense of purpose and responsibility than their forebears, which includes increased tolerance to taxation by national governments and a level of embarrassment for some at having a trust at all, reflecting broader societal changes.

Mechanisms within trust structures can be used to give a voice to future generations and facilitate a growing focus on social and environmental issues, prioritisation of investment in sustainable family businesses, and for initiatives that seek to combat climate change, societal inequality and global challenges. When planned carefully, the long-term nature of business assets being owned in trusts will align with what is often a longer-term vision from the next gen, rather than a historic focus on shorter-term financial gains. To support this, there is also increasing worldwide regulation of the trustee industry around investing and regulatory and fiscal compliance, which reflects the changing times.

5. Provision of information to beneficiaries

This drive for greater transparency about family wealth is reflected in the common topic of providing information to beneficiaries about trust assets.

Beneficiaries' rights in relation to knowing about the trust assets, income and capital will depend on the terms of the trust. However, beneficiaries will always have a right to ensure that the trust is administered correctly and have standing to hold the trustees to account. Consequently, in most trust jurisdictions across the globe, there is an expectation that beneficiaries should be given enough information to enable this to happen.

The key case which sets out the UK law on the provision of information to beneficiaries is *Schmidt v Rosewood Trust Limited*.[3] This case confirms that the beneficiaries' right to seek disclosure of trust information is based in the court's jurisdiction to supervise the administration of the trust. In practice, this means that the beneficiaries do not have an automatic right to trust information, but they do have a right to ask for information, and if this is refused, the court is able to intervene and, using its discretion having heard the trustees' view, order disclosure.

Typically, beneficiaries can expect to know of the existence of a trust and the nature of their interest in it. In most cases, the court will support a request for the trust deed (and any further trust deeds or resolutions that amend the terms of the trust) and the trust accounts. These trust documents are the basic documents that would enable a beneficiary to hold the trustees to account and enforce a proper administration of the trust.

While it is generally a good idea to be open with beneficiaries, trustees need to take care to ensure that in sharing information they are not releasing confidential information relating to other beneficiaries. For example, beneficiaries might typically be provided with accounts redacted to remove personal information about other beneficiaries.

Letters of wishes, unlike trust deeds, are private to the trustees and do not need to be shared with beneficiaries. This enables the settlor to be confident that their guidance to the trustees can be implemented in confidence. That said, settlors might consider whether it would be helpful to prepare a 'beneficiary-facing' letter of wishes which could be shared. Clearly, the guidance in that letter should not contradict the guidance to the trustees, but particularly in the context of a family business, a carefully drafted letter of wishes can be invaluable for future generations to understand the purpose of the trust and the values held by the settlor so that the settlor's intentions can continue to influence the interaction of the beneficiaries with the business and the family's wealth.

A long-held principle established in *Londonderry's Settlement*[4] is that trustees do not need to share the reasons for their decisions with discretionary beneficiaries, and trustee minutes setting out decision making are typically not shared.

Trustees should also remember that privilege cannot generally be asserted against beneficiaries if the trust fund has been used to pay for legal advice. Legal advice provided to the trustees and paid for using the trust fund should usually

3 [2003] UKPC 26.
4 [1965] Ch 918.

be shared with beneficiaries if requested. However, if trustees wish to assert privilege, they may need to fund legal advice themselves or show the reasons why privilege should not be broken within the principles of the case of *Londonderry's Settlement.* If a beneficiary wishes to access the legal advice, they must apply to the trustees and not the lawyer since the lawyer is bound by privilege and cannot waive it unless their clients, the trustees, consent to it or a court orders it. This is a complex area which requires professional advice before a beneficiary asserts their right to legal advice given to the trustees.

6. Investment decisions

6.1 Diversification

For English law trusts, the starting point is that trustees are under a duty to invest, which generally means generating income and capital returns. Under the English law Trustee Act 2000, in making investment decisions, trustees have a duty to consider the suitability of the investment and (to the extent appropriate in the circumstances) the need to diversify the portfolio.

The duty to diversify (or at least consider whether diversification would be appropriate) is often not well aligned with a trust which holds a large shareholding in a family business. The trust may well have been specifically created to own the family business through good times and bad. However, the reality of many private businesses is that in some years performance might mean that the shareholding would not have been retained by trustees exerting their fiduciary duty, were it not for the history of the business being owned by, and for, the family.

It is important that trustees actively consider their investment duties in the context of the family and the business. In most other contexts, a single shareholding in a business would not be a prudent, diversified investment, and that divergence away from normal investment principles needs to be managed carefully. Letters of wishes are especially useful for this, as a settlor can explain that they have created the trust in order to hold the family business and therefore they want the trustees to be invested in a less diversified way than would usually be the case. The trustees (ideally involving the current beneficiaries) might also sign a memorandum of understanding explaining that, with a long-term view and based on the wishes of the settlor and current beneficiaries, they have made a reasoned choice to remain invested in the family business.

A particular dynamic arises where professional investment managers are employed to manage a discretionary investment portfolio for the trust separate to the family business holding. The trustees should take care to ensure that the investment manager is familiar with the family business to enable the discretionary portfolio to be suitably diversified, taking into account the nature of the business. For example, if the family business is in the hospitality sector, the investment manager may seek to avoid this industry as part of their investment strategy.

In some cases, the trust settlement deed may also contain exoneration clauses specifically relating to financial loss caused by the investment in the family business.

6.2 Sustainable/ESG/impact investing

Particular issues can arise in relation to trust investments where some (or possibly all) beneficiaries favour a change in approach. In the context of a family business, there may be a desire to invest more sustainably or with a positive environmental or social impact.

As trustees of private trusts have a duty to protect the trust assets, which in practice means investing for financial return, a desire to invest more sustainably may require professional advice to be taken to support a change in direction and confirm that this will not harm (or significantly harm) financial returns. Where a change in investment strategy would materially impact financial returns, the trustees will need to consider this aspect with even more care when exercising their fiduciary duties.

A number of legal cases over the years have reassured trustees that it can be to a beneficiary's benefit to meet a moral obligation rather than focusing purely on generating financial returns. For instance, by making charitable donations on their behalf (*Re Clore's Settlement Trusts*[5]). In the context of sustainable and ESG investing, while such investments may indeed perform well over the long term thus meeting trustees' fiduciary duties, this may not be an obvious financial outcome in the short term. Some settlors may therefore wish to include specific trust provisions to enable sustainable investing where the investments are chosen for wider impact than high financial returns.

6.3 Sale of the family business – momentous decision

The sale of the family business would obviously be a significant decision to be made by the trustees. As with any other investment decisions, trustees should take professional advice and consider the wishes of the beneficiaries. The 'sacred cow' nature of many family business shareholdings means that the momentous decision to sell will often come with disagreement, particularly where some beneficiaries have more involvement in or emotional attachment to the family business than others. It may well be a decision where the trustees should seek the blessing of the court (set out in the case of *Public Trustee v Cooper*[6]), under the category two route described in that judgment.

5 [1966] 1 WLR 955.
6 [2001] WLTR 901.

7. Trustee involvement in the business

On the basis that a trustee's fiduciary duty is to preserve the value of the trust fund, where the trustee is a shareholder of a business, this might mean that they have a duty to ensure that the business is performing well. The aim would be that the value of the trust's shareholding should be maintained, a return paid to the trust and the value of the business should grow. This therefore raises the question, where the business is operated on a day-to-day basis by directors, how involved should the trustee be?

The concept of 'anti-Bartlett clauses' evolved out of the case of *Bartlett v Barclays Bank Trust Co Limited*,[7] where the trustees of a 99% shareholding in a business were found liable for losses caused by the trustees failing to prevent the business from investing in a highly speculative property development project. The bank trustee had reviewed annual accounts and reports, but did not seek any enhanced levels of reporting or monitoring. This case confirmed that the trustee has a fundamental duty to act as a prudent person of business, taking care to review the affairs of the trust-owned company and take appropriate action if the business is not being conducted properly. This leads to the question of whether the trustees appoint their own independent director (which is not uncommon), or insist on a system of shareholder reporting that goes significantly above and beyond the normal reporting requirements to shareholders.

An anti-Bartlett clause is a specific exoneration clause which relieves the trustee from any responsibility to interfere in and monitor the running of a business in which it owns shares. This can address some of the concerns raised by the *Bartlett* case, although there are limitations to this exoneration. No protection is offered to a trustee who does in fact involve themselves in a business, and for corporate trustees, there is no protection if trustees appoint independent officers on the board of directors of the company. There is also no protection if the trustee is put on notice that there is a problem with the company or is aware of facts which call for enquiry and does nothing.

Despite the relatively old age of anti-Bartlett clauses, plus the use of legislative exoneration of trustees based on laws which have been introduced in some jurisdictions, these concepts continue to be regularly tested in disputes, particularly where the trust-owned shareholding has decreased in value. At the time of writing, conflicting decisions, such as *Zhang Hong Li v DBS Bank (Hong Kong) Ltd*[8] (which held that where there is a properly drafted anti-Bartlett clause, the trustees have no high-level supervisory duty in relation to the underlying company) and *Ivanishvili v Credit Suisse Trust Ltd*[9] (which found that an anti-

---

7 [1980] 1 Ch 515.
8 [2019] HKCFA 45.
9 [2023] SGCA(I) 5.

Bartlett clause would not protect the trustee from liability or losses on investment assets in its custody and control) addressing how anti-Bartlett clauses interact with the trustees' irreducible duty to act in good faith for the benefit of the beneficiaries (*Armitage v Nurse*[10]), mean that trustees must continue to take care and consider carefully the level of monitoring that they should engage in relation to a family business.

8. Avoiding trust disputes

For all the reasons explained, the interaction between the trustees and the beneficiaries can and does lead to disputes. Such disputes can be a manifestation of historic family issues seeded in the relationship between the business founder and their children, or between different generations of a family. Trustees can find themselves in the crosshairs of these relationships because they hold the family wealth.

There is no easy answer to avoiding such conflicts, but careful consideration of the duties and responsibilities in relation to beneficiaries, in particular the potential issues outlined above, will help as will good knowledge of the business, the family dynamics and personal circumstances.

Communication and understanding, or the lack of, is typically at the heart of most disputes. Whether a lack of clarity between family members around the expectations for the next generation, or a lack of interaction between trustees and beneficiaries alongside poor appreciation of the trustee role.

The introduction of good governance and communication protocols with a baseline pattern of meetings and reporting can be especially useful in a trust-owned family business context. Indeed, in many ways the trust structure lends itself well to a strong governance-led approach as this is the fundamental role of a trustee. Typical governance and communication tools will include:

- regular trustee and beneficiary meetings, which take place at least annually and include a detailed review of the family business and enable the beneficiaries to discuss their wishes and needs;
- a protocol for the family business reporting to the trustee shareholder that goes beyond basic annual reports and accounts of the company;
- agreeing a communication protocol with the beneficiaries to confirm what trust information they will, and will not, receive;
- an agreed approach in relation to diversification and the long-term plans for the family business shareholding which involves beneficiaries as they reach adulthood; and
- attention given to the expectations for beneficiaries, focusing particularly on their involvement in the family business, the family's values in relation to long-term stewardship of wealth and the agreed

10 [1997] EWCA Civ 1279.

approach to legal mechanisms such as prenuptial agreements and wills for beneficiaries. These are strategic issues that can be embodied in a constitution or other non-legal governance document and will include fundamental family agreements on matters such as who can be involved in the business benefit and how they will or will not be rewarded differently from beneficiaries that are not involved.

9. Vulnerable beneficiaries

Trusts can be useful to allow vulnerable beneficiaries to be provided for in a way which might not be possible through the family business alone.

This was a key family tool in the case of four beneficiaries, one of whom had a disabled child who would always lack capacity to make their own financial or welfare decisions. The settlor wished to make proper provision for this grandchild and the parents as long-term carers. Working in partnership with the trustees, a sub-trust was carved out for this branch of the family. This included both family business interests which catered for the long-term wealth provision connected to the core family wealth, but also shares in the family business were sold back to the family to enable acquisition of more liquid investments able to be sold more easily and provide income rather than just long-term growth.

10. Can a 'business family' afford not to have a trust?

The costs of having a trust can be prohibitive, particularly given the need for trustees to be well advised in an increasingly litigious and regulated world. That said, there are clear advantages for a family in terms of wealth protection from relationship breakdown/divorce, creditors/bankruptcy, death and incapacity. This can, and often does, outweigh the required expenditure.

It is important to weigh up the advantages and disadvantages of these opposing forces carefully. Families should consider whether a trust would be effective for them in protecting the family business, their legacy and inheritance, from the costs of litigation or expensive family disagreements. Indeed, some settlors view their trust structures as a form of insurance against going down the same path as well-publicised family breakdowns in civil law jurisdictions such as for the L'Oreal family in France or the Oetker family in Germany. That said, a trust is not a panacea and there is no replacement for planning ahead and having a heavy dose of realism about the possibility of a dispute among less bonded family members.

In the case of a principal who was given a terminal cancer diagnosis in January and died in July, an emergency will signed on his deathbed leaving his entire estate including his majority business shareholding to his second wife, did not set the scene for family harmony. The deceased requested the business be kept for future generations, and his second wife promised to benefit the wider family in the long term. However, his three children from his first marriage were exposed to being disinherited and this generated understandable concerns. In this scenario, a well-advised trust set to receive the business and assets, such as the much-loved family holiday property, on the principal's death would have created a bedrock for future family understanding of their rights to the family wealth. It would have also given comfort to the children from the first marriage, which was a lingering worry irrespective of the promises made by the second wife. Importantly, it would have relieved his second wife from the responsibility of being the ultimate decision maker around the inherited assets. Despite her desire to represent everyone's interests, her husband arguably put an unreasonable level of responsibility on her at a very difficult time and this is an aspect of the 'burden of wealth' that can sometimes be overlooked.

11. A word on tax and other 'advantages'

While the popular view might be that trusts are mechanisms to avoid tax, it is an ill-advised family that puts its business into trust expecting this to be the case – tax savings are increasingly hard to come by. Indeed, the asset protection and continuity benefits will in most cases come with a tax outcome that merely replaces one tax regime with another. A more realistic strategy would be one which acknowledges that tax exists, and the family should not rely on none being paid at all. That is simply unrealistic.

For families originating from low-tax jurisdictions such as the Middle East, it is of note that the motivation for asset settlement is almost exclusively for wealth preservation, security and succession planning purposes.

While families and trustees will want to take professional advice to ensure they do not inadvertently fall into a tax 'trap' triggering an unnecessary or unexpected tax liability, families should also focus on the non-tax advantages of legacy, governance and succession planning if they are going to embark on trust structuring for their family wealth, especially family businesses which generally rely on stability and predictability around tax and regulation to succeed.

12. Alternatives to trusts

We know that there are many ways to hold assets whether in corporate settings or structures which include trusts or trust-like options such as civil law foundations. Such foundations should not be confused with charitable foundations, which are discussed below. Many are set up on mainland Europe and key differences include having a separate legal identity with no 'owner', unlike trusts, which have trustees. As we write, there are an increasing number of such foundations being set up as an alternative to trusts.

Other options include family corporate holdings, sometimes referred to as family investment companies (FICs). Some are set up afresh, but for family businesses these may be a tailored holding company with separation of control and economic interests and the ability for family members to sit on the board of directors or during the succession process as board observers or occasional proxies. Many business families find corporates a more familiar structure to work with than trusts and these should be openly considered as an alternative.

13. Charitable foundations

Charitable foundations can be used alongside or within wider trust structures owning a family business or diversified wealth. Like trusts, they provide a formal structure for philanthropy, allowing the family to set and manage their long-term strategic goals rather than being drawn into a disjointed range of *ad hoc* giving by different family members. In establishing a foundation, the family can both leverage professional expertise in grant making, project evaluation and impact assessment, and build on the skills and passions of the next generation. The hands-on involvement of family members in the foundation's activities, visiting projects, assessing impact and reporting back to the wider family, can foster a deeper understanding of family values and meaningfully connect the wealth-generating family business with the family's cross-generational philanthropic endeavours.

14. Conclusion

The topic of family businesses and trusts could be a book in its own right. However, we have endeavoured to summarise the key considerations, danger areas and some solutions for families when they are navigating trusts as ownership structures for their cherished businesses.

Planning involving trusts can be incredibly emotional for families, especially where their businesses are concerned. Our final tip would be to always keep an eye on what the family actually wants, how they thrive as a unit, and what may put them in the danger zone in terms of their relationships and how they interact with their advisers and trustees. Communication, which is covered extensively in this book, is the key to success as a business family as well as for how we as advisers know and understand our clients.

Extracting wealth from the family business

Russell Prior
HSBC Global Private Banking

1. Introduction

Extracting wealth from a family business is a complex topic that involves an intricate web of financial, emotional and even cultural drivers. The decision to extract wealth from a business does not exist in isolation. It will be linked to or influenced by the life cycle of the business and by the personal, family and wealth life cycles of the ownership group.

While research undertaken by HSBC Private Banking has shown that the role and meaning of family businesses to their owning families can vary widely across the globe, since the COVID-19 pandemic we have seen an increasing number of business-owning families proactively considering the topic of wealth extraction.

In this chapter, we examine the reasons why a business owner might extract wealth from their business, the main options through which wealth extraction can be organised and, critically, examine some of the wider considerations and issues that a business owner should think through before undertaking wealth extraction.[1]

2. What are the reasons for extracting wealth from a business?

There are several enduring reasons why directors and owners of family-owned businesses extract wealth from their businesses, including:

- employment remuneration for directors and employees;
- distribution of profits to shareholders via dividends;
- retirement;
- other lifestyle-related reasons;
- personal or family investment;
- new ventures;
- philanthropic gifting; and
- ownership succession or exit.

1 This chapter does not provide legal or tax advice in relation to wealth extraction. The validity of the any of the matters contained within this chapter may vary according to the jurisdiction in which the business, business owners, directors or employees and/or other parties to a wealth extraction transaction may be located or operate. This chapter does not consider all options for wealth extraction, particularly those that are driven by a more favourable fiscal environment in specific jurisdictions.

Yet, notwithstanding the points listed above, many business owners have typically preferred to build their wealth inside the businesses they own or within or close to the sphere of their business interests, concentrating on what they believe they understand and in which they have expertise. They often also refer to the higher level of return that they feel can be generated by the business rather than by investments outside the business. A level of return, they say, within a risk tolerance level they understand and with which they are happy.

Notwithstanding this feeling, this approach does present business owners with potential risks, specifically:

- concentration risk, as similar types of investments may be vulnerable to the same adverse factors and circumstances;
- contagion risk, as investments are not ring-fenced and which may see wider assets vulnerable to negative effects in another part of the portfolio; and
- fiscal risk, where trading and investment assets are within the same legal entity.

Since the onset of the COVID-19 pandemic, we have seen the emergence of a major new driver for wealth extraction, namely wealth risk diversification. One of the unfortunate effects of the pandemic was to expose otherwise healthy businesses to a level of turnover and profit reduction that had not been experienced in living memory, and consequently did not really feature in business owner planning or risk mitigation strategies. It has also raised the spectre of the effects of other unexpected and unknown risks.

Unlike the effects of a more general economic downturn, the effects of the pandemic seemed almost random in the types of businesses they affected. In response, we are seeing many business owners asking if and how they might take some "risk off the table" by diversifying into other investments, even if that means slightly lower levels of perceived return.

Separate to this more recent driver, wealth extraction remains, nevertheless, a key part of the business ownership life cycle, so, as with all aspects of business ownership, it deserves strategic consideration and planning, not only in terms of the wealth strategy for the business owner(s) but also for the business.

3. Options for wealth extraction

To simplify what can be an otherwise wide-ranging list of options, the routes for wealth extraction have been grouped under five headings.

3.1 Self-funded

A first grouping of options for wealth extraction are what we might describe as self-funded, where the funding comes from the business itself. A critical consideration here is the extent to which the business has the profits (both historic and future), reserves and liquidity to finance such payments and that, ordinarily, such payments can be made without harming the prospects of the business.

Wealth extraction funded by the profitability of the business should be considered in the context of where the business is in its life cycle.

(a) Remuneration

Remuneration typically covers the total compensation paid to an employee for the work or services they provide to the company. It will therefore include base salary, bonuses, stock options, pension contributions and any other financial compensation.

The list of items that comprise remuneration can provide business owners with a variety of structuring options for wealth extraction. For instance, base salary is a fixed cost payable regardless of the performance of the company, whereas bonuses and stock options can be tied to metrics that align more closely to the performance and growth of the company. Remuneration may also include other non-financial elements but these will be less relevant for wealth extraction purposes.

While an advantage of using remuneration for wealth extraction is that it can be individually tailored or focused on a small group of key employees, it is worth remembering that, as it applies to employees, it will not work for owners not employed in the business.

As remuneration is an operating cost of the company, it will directly affect the profits generated by the company.

(b) Dividends

In simple terms, a dividend is a distribution of the profits or earnings of a company, recommended by the directors of a company, paid out to shareholders, the owners of the company. The laws relating to dividends and the governance processes that need to be followed can be quite complex, so this section only covers some of the general points relating to dividends, which are as follows:

- Dividends can only be paid in the event that there are sufficient reserves of the right classification and that the company can afford to pay them;
- Dividends are payable to all shareholders of the relevant class of shares in proportion to their shareholding;
- The constitutional documentation of the company (eg, the articles of association) will define the rights to receive dividends; and
- Dividends can be paid out on several occasions during a year, known as interim dividends, but such payments are still subject to the requirements set out in the above points.

Standing back from the specifics of a given dividend declaration, payments of dividends ought to be seen in terms of the financial health of the company.[2] It is not unusual, therefore, for a dividend policy to be established for the company. A dividend policy aims to set out the proportion of profits to be distributed to shareholders over the period the policy is in force, balancing the dividends paid with the needs of the company to retain profits to finance its operations or growth.

(c) ***Purchase of own shares by a company***

This option is also referred to as a share buyback, and involves a company purchasing shares from one or more of its shareholders. Reasons for this can include the distribution of surplus cash in the company, consolidation of ownership or enabling a shareholder, for instance a departing employee who holds shares, to sell some or all their shares where other shareholders are not willing to purchase them.

Such a transaction will need to be permissible for the company and it will be important to check that there are no other prohibitions on such transactions in documents such as shareholder agreements or the company's constitutional documents. The company in question will need sufficient distributable reserves to cover the purchase and will need to have cash available to pay for the shares. Such transactions will need the support of the shareholders of the company and approvals in line with the company's constitutional documents. Where the shares purchased are cancelled, the proportion of the company owned by the other shareholders will rise proportionately.

(d) ***Gifting***

It is possible for companies to make gifts for charitable purposes, which may meet the wealth extraction objectives of the owners of the business. These can include, potentially, stock or equipment, land or property, and even the secondment of employees, in addition to the more straightforward financial contributions. Typically, gifts for charitable purposes can be deducted as a business expense.

(e) ***Members' voluntary liquidation***

The final area to cover in this section is that of a members' voluntary liquidation or solvent liquidation. This process is typically seen when a company has reached the end of its life or where the owners want to retire and close the business. It is an option to be considered as an alternative to selling the company.

A members' voluntary liquidation is relevant to solvent companies, those

---

2 It is worth noting that dividends can also be paid out in shares, known as scrip dividends. In such cases, new shares in the company are issued rather than using the company's cash to settle the dividends. It is also possible in certain circumstances for a company's assets to be used in settling a dividend rather than cash – known as a dividend *in specie*.

that have assets greater than their liabilities, can pay creditors in full and on time, and can meet any contractual obligations and clear any legal disputes. Once the winding-up process is complete, the net proceeds of the liquidation are distributed to shareholders, in proportion to their shareholdings and, subject to various potential conditions being met, may be in the form of capital rather than income[3] in terms of their tax profile.

At the end of the process, the company will be de-registered.

In summary, when considering a company-funded wealth extraction, there are some key strategic issues to consider:

- Taking wealth out of the company leaves less wealth in the company for its future operations and growth. Thinking about the company's need for financial resources and capital, the sources of and potential availability of such funding, where the company is in its life cycle, and the future strategy for the company and its owners all need to be considered in advance of the wealth-extraction process.
- The business owner's wealth extraction objectives and the nature of the funding to meet them should be considered – that includes loans to shareholders.
- The actual financing of the wealth extraction is different from having the profits and reserves available to cover it. This may have implications for the sources of financing the company has in place.
- There will be corporate governance and legal conditions to be considered and properly applied in relation to the various options, which may vary across different jurisdictions.
- The tax treatment of the various options will need to be assessed in detail and will vary across different jurisdictions.

3.2 Third-party investors

A second grouping of options to support wealth extraction from a business is where third-party investors introduce external capital. This section explores several different sources for such capital and also reviews the range of options for wealth extraction that such capital can support.

For companies with a strong, well-positioned business and strong future growth potential, these options provide a highly valuable means of wealth extraction.

However, as we will examine in more detail in section 4.4, the introduction of third-party capital has the potential to bring a fundamental, and typically irreversible, change to the ownership structure of the business. In most cases this will be a change that will have major consequences for the business owner.

---

3 This may be relevant in certain circumstances, such as where tax rates on capital gains differ from income tax rates or where capital losses exist and may be offset.

The introduction of third-party investors may also bring changes to the board and management arrangements of the business, including to the business owner's position as CEO or other senior director of the company.

Consequently, a business owner thinking of pursuing one of these routes should ensure that a full and strategic assessment of the opportunity and its implications has been undertaken.

(a) Private equity

This section looks at the effects of private equity funds investing in private companies as a means for business owners to realise and extract wealth from their business.

Typically, private equity investors take stakes in private companies with the aim of generating a higher level of return from their investment when a subsequent sale of the business is undertaken. For the business owner(s), depending on the structure of the deal, there is an opportunity for them to use this process to reduce their stake in the business, while accelerating the value of their remaining ownership stake.

In taking a stake in a company, private equity investors will look to create an appropriate financing structure that might combine existing and/or new ordinary shares, preference shares, convertible shares and debt. From the current owner's perspective, in terms of wealth extraction, they will be looking to see what level of wealth they wish to extract and can be extracted as part of the financing package, and then how their remaining participation in the ownership of the company is structured. Much will depend on the level of ownership being negotiated by the private equity provider and the extent to which the current owner wants early wealth extraction.

Moving beyond the private equity financing moment, depending on their role, the existing owner will still be able to extract wealth through a number of the routes set out in section 3.1 and/or through a subsequent exit process for the business.

(b) Family office

There has been an increasing trend for family offices seeking to invest in private companies. Investment approaches can include both direct investment and co-investment alongside other external capital.

In many ways such investors share a number of similar characteristics with those set out in the section above on private equity, however, important differences and points to consider include the following:

- Family office investors can have longer investment periods than private equity investors as they tend not to be focused on the same investment cycles as private equity firms.
- As the family office is investing the supporting family's capital rather

than third-party capital, they can be more flexible with the financing structure for investments.

- Family offices are open to minority, as well as majority, stakes.
- Family office investors will often look at the fit with its portfolio of companies and potentially bring industry and operational knowledge and expertise.

That said, family office investors need to be thoroughly assessed as potential investors and not just seen as a potential source of more flexible capital. Their level of expertise and experience in taking direct equity stakes will be an important consideration.

(c) *IPO*

An IPO (initial public offering) makes shares in a private company available to the public via listing the shares on an exchange. Consequently, to achieve a wealth extraction, the pre-IPO owners of the shares have the opportunity for some of their shares to be sold as part of the IPO.

The pre-IPO owners may also hold onto their some of their shares, with the listing of the shares on an exchange providing, in due course, a potentially helpful platform for future share sales.

Business owners may, of course, hold more than just ordinary shares, such as share options and other equity-linked compensation awards. The treatment of these and the opportunities that might arise should form part of the IPO planning.

An IPO has several significant consequences that need to be factored into a business owners' wealth extraction plans, namely that:

- the company will be subject to the reporting requirements of the exchange;
- the performance of the pre-IPO owner if CEO or part of the post-IPO business leadership will come under scrutiny;
- the performance of the company is likely to be covered by stock analysts and proxy advisers, and the performance of the shares is likely to be subject to the outputs of this research; and
- holdings of the shares are likely to be subject to regulatory rules and restrictions, which bring stricter governance and reduced flexibility.

Consequently, a business owner might find themselves with a significant portion of their wealth held in a single stock that is subject to the requirements, expectations and limitations of a number of external parties, including lock-up periods and trading windows.

In summary, the injection of third-party capital to support the extraction of wealth is likely to generate consequences which need to be fully considered and evaluated as follows:

- The introduction of third-party owners potentially brings a set of different perspectives, objectives and regulatory requirements.
- Different performance and return expectations are probable. Alignment of these across the ownership group will be important.
- The start of a process of both ownership and management succession for the original business owner is to be expected.

3.3 Management or employees

Another route for capital extraction for a business owner is a transaction where either management or employees acquire shares from the business owner. Such transactions can appear to be advantageous as the company can benefit from the stability of the existing management and employees taking the business forward, and they can give the appearance of being relatively straightforward as the parties are well known to each other.

Looked at from the perspective of the business owner extracting wealth, rather than from the perspective of the management or employees acquiring shares, it is really important that the business owner conducts their own arms-length strategic assessment of the potential deal. The following are some of the considerations that should be borne in mind.

- Both the quantum of finance required and the financing structure of the deal are important. It is highly likely that a component of the financing of the capital extraction will be paid from the future cash flows of the business. Careful consideration is required as to what the business can afford.
- The financing structure might involve some personal financing from the management team, but this is often modest. Debt and private equity might be required, and the business owner might be required to support the deal structure through, eg, deferred payments via loan notes, which brings additional risk to the wealth extraction.
- The structures for employee-led deals may involve the use of a trust, the implications of which need to be assessed.
- The price achieved through such a transaction may not be the highest.
- It should be recognised that the deal involves parties with access to a lot of information and knowledge, and there are some clear areas where conflicts of interest can arise. The quality of management as they step up to become owners, the future participation of the owner undertaking the capital extraction and the robustness of the plans of the business all need to be considered.

In summary, critical to this wealth-extraction solution is the source and tenor of the payment schedule. The strength of the business and the management team will be key underpinnings of these.

3.4 Trade sale

A fourth route for wealth extraction involves the sale of the business, the sale of an operating subsidiary of the business, or the sale of assets of the business to a third-party trade acquirer.

In all three scenarios, the acquirer is likely to settle the deal in the form of cash, debt or shares in the acquiring company or a mix of them. In the event of the sale of the business, the sale proceeds will be received by the outgoing shareholder. In the event of the sale of a part of the business or of assets of the business, the proceeds will be received by the company selling the assets. In the latter scenario, the business owner will need to think about how to extract wealth from their business, following the options discussed earlier.

While the financial terms of the deal might look relatively straightforward, the other terms of the deal also need to be considered fully and negotiated appropriately. Matters such as representations and warranties would be included here.

Business owners selling to trade acquirers are often also concerned about what might happen to the business they have built and the management team and employees in the business, once under the control of another owner. This is particularly relevant where there is a strong overlap between the businesses.

In summary, a trade sale can appear to be a clean route for wealth extraction, however, the full terms of the deal are important.

3.5 Family

The final route to be considered is where wider family behind a family-owned business is involved in supporting wealth extraction.

This often happens at a time of generational ownership transition within a business-owning family and so ideally what happens should have been discussed, organised and structured ahead of the event arising. This also allows the wealth extractions to fit within the family's objectives for their business. This can involve ownership consolidation between siblings, but also transition to the next generation. Transitions in the latter category are not always straightforward, as there is often a greater number of family members in the next generation than the preceding one, and as a family business passes through the generations, each generation is broader in number and connection.

Potential options include a next-generation buyout and a share buyback, but these require availability of funding or liquidity to support a transaction. Where the business owner seeking wealth extraction continues to be involved with the business, then the remuneration and dividend options set out in section 3.1 will continue to be available, but this can sometimes confuse the generational transition picture. Pension entitlements may be drawn.

Where a family member desires to extract wealth via the sale of their shares within the family, whether at a point of generational ownership transition or not, it can be very helpful for the family owners of the business to have a shareholders' agreement in place that governs such situations.[4] Such an agreement can provide for an orderly process that keeps the ownership within the family and prevents sales of shares to third-party, non-family owners.

In these circumstances a shareholder agreement might set out:

- the conditions under which a sale of shares can take place;
- the basis upon which the shares will be valued; and
- how the share transaction will be financed and will operate.

In summary, wealth extraction from a business owned by family can be complicated. Mixing the issues of business continuity, generational leadership change and wealth extraction within a family setting can be a source of strong emotional reaction. Planning and preparing appropriate family governance well in advance can be very helpful.

4. Key issues and considerations

In this final section we look at some of the key issues and considerations upon which business owners might reflect when considering wealth extraction from their business, and that can help frame the decision making about how the business owner might proceed.

4.1 Wealth philosophy

At the highest level, ideally, the business owner should have developed a philosophy for their wealth (which includes their business interests) and within which any wealth extraction plans can fit.

A wealth philosophy talks to the higher point and purpose of the wealth and should act as a golden thread through the different stages of the wealth life cycle – wealth creation, management, extraction and transition. A wealth philosophy should recognise that wealth is not just measured by its monetary value during a business owner's lifetime, it should equally reflect and be measured by the legacy it can leave, the lessons it can teach and the social impact it can create, and will encompass both financial and non-financial wealth – see Table 1.

---

4 Shareholder agreements can equally be put in place to govern the process for share sales between non-family co-owners.

Table 1: Examples of financial and non-financial wealth

Financial wealth	Non-financial wealth
• cash • investments • real estate • family business	• physical and mental well-being • reputation and social capital • values, customs and principles • education • family history and relationships • legacy

Three well-known examples of wealth philosophies are set out below. It is interesting to note how they capture the tension between two issues that are regularly mentioned in relation to the wealth generated by business-owning families – family and society.

- Andrew Carnegie wrote in *The Gospel of Wealth* (1889)[5] that all personal wealth beyond that required to supply the needs of one's family should be regarded as a trust fund to be administered for the benefit of the community.
- Warren and Susie Buffett stated that they wanted to leave their children "enough [money] so they can do anything but not enough that they can do nothing".[6]
- More recently, in 2022, Yvon Chouinard, founder of clothing company Patagonia, and his family transferred their ownership into two new entities designed to either reinvest in Patagonia or distribute dividends to protect the planet. It was described as "going purpose instead of going public".[7]

Carnegie's approach talks to a wealth philosophy built around understanding the core wealth required for the family, with wealth beyond that to be for public benefit. Carnegie is well known for his philanthropic acts, many of which exist today.

Buffett's philosophy talks to his views on the passing of wealth to his children, but he is just as well known for his intention to give away 99% of his wealth in his lifetime or at death.[8]

The Chouinard philosophy shares the philanthropic underpinnings of

5 Andrew Carnegie, *The Gospel of Wealth* (1889), www.carnegie.org/about/our-history/gospelofwealth/.

6 Berkshire Hathaway Inc, News Release, 25 November 2024, www.berkshirehathaway.com/news/nov2524.pdf.

7 Yvon Chouinard, "Earth is now our only shareholder", https://eu.patagonia.com/gb/en/ownership/?srsltid=AfmBOorHL6t0kPuZyg2WarDy3oB-XDltU9GNj4yB8pUbamPHkd9k5-4w.

8 The Giving Pledge, Warren Buffett pledge letter, https://givingpledge.org/pledger?pledgerId=177.

Carnegie and Buffet's approaches, but the focus on the planet is more explicit and directs attention to the sustainability of the business and the sustainable impact of the wealth.

In my experience, for the overwhelming majority of cases, the development of a wealth philosophy can best be described as "work in progress".

Not everyone has the level of wealth that enables the sorts of choices set out in the three examples above so, more prosaically, there are key questions that can help provide guidance around the development of a wealth philosophy. These can, of course, and do change over time.

(a) What is the overall level of wealth?

The overall level of wealth is a prime determinant of the focus for a wealth philosophy. For business owners with core wealth,[9] the focus is likely to be on having sufficient means, both income and assets, for their needs within their own lifetime. Gifts to family and philanthropy, while still possible, will be more modest in scale.

For business owners with surplus wealth,[10] the emphasis shifts and is much more likely to bring in the debate about wealth transfers to the next generation and strategies for philanthropy.

(b) What is your approach to wealth management and wealth diversification?

Family business owners have differing views as to where they want to hold their wealth, with some keen to keep it in the family business, yet others wanting to diversify away from holding a significant proportion of it in the family business. This difference is likely to be affected by where the business is on its growth journey as well as by the life stage of the family business owner.

(c) Do you have children? And what is your attitude to wealth transfer to the next and subsequent generations?

In my experience, attitudes to wealth transfer to the next and subsequent generations vary quite widely. For many there is a desire to support the next generation, although counterbalanced by concerns about the impact the wealth might have on next-generation motivations. But there are greater levels of concern about supporting multiple generations.

Many business owners would like to see their next generation interested in taking on the family business, but express concerns about the interest of the

---

9 'Core wealth' refers to a level of wealth necessary to sustain a given lifestyle for the life of the person or family. Core wealth should be sufficient to cover planned expenditure and outgoings, with an additional margin for unexpected but reasonably possible events, like ill health in later life (Russell Prior, *Family Governance and Surplus Wealth: Sustaining Family Fortunes* (Globe Law and Business, 2021)).

10 'Surplus wealth' refers to wealth over and above core wealth. Given that surplus wealth is unlikely to be consumed according to the planned lifestyle, its likely use will be restricted to gifting to family or gifting in the form of philanthropy *(ibid)*.

next generation in the family business and about the levels of commitment that would be required.

A final, perhaps smaller, group of business owners are keen to see the next generation make their own way.

(d) What is your attitude to philanthropy?

I have seen a strong rise in the levels of interest in philanthropy as a purpose for wealth generated and released by successful business owners, and this often extends out to a desire to involve the wider family.

Key question: Does the business owner have a well-defined wealth philosophy to guide the wealth extraction plans?

4.2 Vision for the business

Notwithstanding that this chapter is looking at the issue of wealth extraction from a business, the next set of considerations should be about the business itself. Wealth extraction from a business can create a number of implications for the business, so it needs to be thought through carefully.

It is worth remembering and factoring in the different 'side effects' or consequences of each of the different extraction routes.

Higher levels of pay and bonuses generate consequences not just in terms of the cost to the business, but also the future expectations it can set for employees and management. Dividends or share-based extraction routes affect the wider shareholder group, not just the business owner seeking wealth extraction.

Wealth extraction financed alongside third-party investors (whether external or internal third parties) can begin to change the ownership complexion and outlook of the business. For companies with a high investor profile, wealth extraction by the key business owners and directors can risk sending unwanted signals to parties interested in the performance and prospects of the business. Consequently, business owners can be effectively locked into an ownership position that is not easily changed.

For family businesses where the expectation is for ownership transition within the family, wealth extraction can provide a range of different possibilities as well as issues. For instance, it can be used to support the ownership transition from one generation of the family to another, gradually allowing the senior generation to withdraw from the business. It can support the development of intergenerational wealth transfer and growth. Or it can be used in such a way as to reward the different stakeholders in a family business for the impact and success in respect of their different roles.

Consequently, there are some key questions to answer:

- Where is the business in its life cycle? Does wealth extraction fit with this?

- Is the wealth extraction a one-off or part of an ongoing process? If ongoing, is it sustainable?
- Is the wealth extraction strategy effectively the start of ownership transition or exit?
- Does the wealth extraction fit with the business owner's personal ownership strategy, and/or that of the overall ownership group?
- Is there a clear ownership succession strategy? How will wealth extraction affect this?
- Is the financial position of the company able to support wealth extraction – profits, reserves and liquidity? How will the business pay for the wealth extraction?
- Does the company have the possibility for the future injection of shareholder capital should it be required?
- What other sources of finance does the company have access to and are they already in place?

Key question: Do the directors and owners have a clear long-term vision, ownership, capital and financing strategy for the business, within which the proposed wealth extraction plans clearly fit?

4.3 Wealth extraction objectives and process

With a clear wealth philosophy and a clear understanding of the strategy for the business, the positioning of a wealth extraction event should be much more straightforward. Unfortunately, experience has shown that these underpinnings are rarely as well developed as one might hope.

This lack of clarity is often due to the fact that it is big questions that need to be answered, questions that can have a significant emotional impact. Our research and experience show that these are questions that business owners have a tendency not to focus on often right up until close to the point where they need to act or take a decision.

In terms of setting wealth extraction objectives, much will depend on the scale of wealth or value of the business. However, just as important is for the proposed wealth extraction to be seen and positioned within the personal wealth objectives and wealth life cycle of the business owner undertaking the wealth extraction.

Critical questions to consider will include:

At which stage in the wealth life cycle is the business owner?

- wealth building;
- wealth management;
- retirement planning;
- wealth transfer; or
- legacy.

What are the objectives for and scale of the proposed wealth extraction?

- consumption;
- diversification;
- investment;
- divorce;
- gifting to family;
- gifting to charity;
- retirement funding; and/or
- intergenerational wealth planning or transfer.

Which wealth extraction process best supports the owner's needs and objectives?

- remuneration;
- part exit/sale of the business;
- dividends;
- share buyback;
- gifting; or
- members' voluntary liquidation.

It would be advisable to obtain the necessary tax and legal advice to ensure that the approach being taken has been fully assessed and any implications appropriately understood.

Key question: Has the purpose of the wealth extraction been properly assessed and determined, and has an appropriate extraction approach been selected?

4.4 Governance and control implications

Wealth extraction, particularly when at a significant level, has the potential to affect or change the wealth arrangements and structures of a business owner's wealth, which will, in turn, have implications for the governance and control of their wealth. We have set out below a number of areas for consideration.

(a) Arrangements with co-owners

For businesses that are co-owned, whether by family or non-family members, it will be important for the co-owners to be on the same page regarding the proposed wealth extraction.

Co-owners tend to be more aligned through the development and growth phases of the business life cycle whereas, in general terms, wealth extraction from a business is more likely to come at a time when the business is reasonably well established and has enjoyed success. The further into the personal life cycles of the co-owners and of the business itself, the greater the likelihood that the co-owners may have different objectives, views and strategies for the wealth that they have tied up in their business. It is worth co-owners recognising, discussing and preparing for this well in advance.

(b) Investment planning

For many business owners, a wealth-extraction event will be the first step in building a portfolio of investments outside of the business, and might include real estate and financial investments. Everything from investment strategy, objectives, holding structures and portfolio arrangements will need to be considered, and appropriate advice and support obtained.

(c) Succession planning

Where wealth extraction takes place and this affects the ownership arrangements or the business owner's ongoing management role and participation in the business, then appropriate succession plans will need to have been developed and put in place, ideally well in advance of the wealth extraction.

Succession plans are often thought of in terms of the people who might succeed the departed person. It is also worth considering other protection options for the business such as key-person insurance.

(d) Estate planning

The impact of the passing of a business owner, or them becoming incapacitated or seriously ill, is likely to be significant, particularly if it happens unexpectedly.

Ensuring that the effects of wealth extraction on estate planning arrangements are fully understood and that appropriate adjustments or updates are made to those estate plans should help ensure that the wealth extraction does not have harmful consequences.

Shareholder protection insurance, including cross-option agreements, might be considered.

(e) Governance and management arrangements of family's advisers

As business owners start to build their wealth outside the business, their affairs are likely to become more complicated, with an increased range of professional advisers helping and supporting them. It is important that the governance and management arrangements for these advisers are well coordinated, but also understood by the successors to the business owner.

Key question: Have the practical, governance and control implications of the wealth extraction been properly assessed and has an implementation plan been put in place?

5. Conclusion

Extracting wealth from a family business can appear to be a relatively straightforward undertaking. In reality, and in practice, it is far from straightforward.

There are a number of options for wealth extraction but they come with different implications, and these will vary according to the legal jurisdictions of the parties to the wealth extraction. Well-advised implementation plans are key.

Meaningful wealth extraction is likely to give rise to the establishment of a pool of wealth held by the business owner separate from the activities of their family business. While that can be a positive step in terms of, for example, wealth diversification, it can also give rise to unintended and unplanned consequences.

Consequently, clear objectives, planning and preparation ahead of a wealth-extraction event are highly important, but there is an equal requirement for them in respect of what comes after the wealth extraction event.

Selling the family business

Introduction

Clare Stirzaker
Boodle Hatfield LLP

While the focus for many family businesses is very much on passing the business down to the next generation, as advisers we also need to be prepared for families seeking help with selling either a stake or the entirety of the family business. As we are aware, this can be for a wide variety of reasons such as a desire to 'prune the tree' and reduce the number of family members involved with the business, a need to raise additional liquidity, or simply an inability or desire to continue with the family business.

To help us consider this area in greater detail, Dominic Epton and Katharine Taylor of Rothschild & Co have shared their wealth management experience and provided a very helpful breakdown on the different steps families can take to generate liquidity. Their section helps guide advisers on the different available options and points to key practical elements to be mindful of when supporting clients on such projects.

It is also important though to not lose sight of how emotional and difficult a process the sale of a family business (either in whole or part) may prove to be for many families. Nick Mayhew of Alembic Strategy follows on from the Rothschild section and deploys his coaching experience to provide insightful commentary on recognising the emotions in the room during a sale process, with helpful tips for advisers on how best to trouble spot and enable a deal to continue to move forward by "Burying the Dead Cats".

We will often need to play a key role in helping assess and guide our clients on whether selling a stake or all of the family business is definitely the right choice for them. Given the magnitude of taking such a step, I felt it was important to obtain two different perspectives to help support you with such work, which I hope you enjoy reading.

The financial impact of selling the family business

Dominic Epton
Katharine Taylor
Rothschild & Co Wealth Management

Selling a business is a goal that many owners and operators spend years – often decades – working towards. For many, it is the culmination of all the hard work and countless hours they have invested in their vision.

But while a successful business sale is a time for celebration, owners should not pop the champagne corks too early. There are many important decisions to make before – and after – a deal is done. Taking the right steps early is essential to achieving the future goals your clients have set for themselves, their family and the company.

We have worked with many successful entrepreneurs at Rothschild & Co Wealth Management before, during and after the sales process. In this chapter, we share our knowledge and experience, including timing, managing the sale process and post-sale planning.

1. Why sell?

There are many reasons to pursue the sale of a family business, and these could affect the way your client approaches the process. Some common reasons include the following:

- *Receiving an attractive offer*. If they receive an offer that matches or exceeds their own valuation of the company, they may decide to seize the opportunity and sell.
- *Wanting to de-risk*. If most or all their wealth is held in a company, then they may want to de-risk and withdraw some or all of that equity from the company.
- *Financial issues:* They could be concerned about future funding or commitments so wish to consider bringing in external parties. They may also be concerned about wider economic uncertainty.
- *A lack of successors*. Even if a family business has previously been passed down through generations, that may not be an option for the future. If they have no successors, or if other family members do not want to take control of the business, then a sale might be the most appropriate option.
- *Family disputes*. While many family businesses operate successfully, there are instances where a disagreement regarding the future operation or direction of the company means that a sale becomes necessary.
- *Competitors being bought*. There may only be a finite pool of parties they could sell their business to, so they may want to sell now before competitors do.

- *Natural end.* They may choose to pursue a sale as they feel they are unable to take the company to the next level, or because of changing customer demands.

2. Choosing the right type of sale

The sale of a family business is a momentous occasion and can mark the start of an exciting new phase. This could allow the pursuit of new ventures or enjoying hard-earned retirement.

Your client should start by establishing the relationship they wish to have with the company in the future. If they are looking to make a clean break, then a sale to private equity or a strategic buyer may be suitable. If they wish to de-risk and extract value from the business, while still retaining a stake, private equity can again be a good fit.

They may also consider an initial public offering (IPO). Owners typically pursue an IPO when a business has reached a key point of transition, or a significant capital injection is needed in the business. We explain more about these sale options below.

Investor appetite and market conditions can also be a major influence on choosing to sell. Many clients receive an unsolicited approach from somebody who has wowed them with a big offer or a compelling story about the future of the business. This can be persuasive, even if the offer is unexpected.

On other occasions, activity in the markets – particularly the IPO market – can often motivate private owners to sell a business. But while comparing your client's situation to someone else's can be a strong motivator, every business is unique, and they cannot simply apply one valuation to another company.

2.1 Preparing a business

The process of selling can start as much as two years ahead of the sale. Think about the housekeeping your clients will need to do before the sale can take place. This includes making equity transfers, resolving property ownership and restructuring. They should also consider management incentives, such as share schemes.

The financial performance of the business is critical to both the success of an exit and the value achieved. It is important to time the exit to coincide with a moment of great momentum in profitability and overall performance.

The immediate- and medium-term future of the business are what acquirers, investors and the market at large are most preoccupied with. So, being able to demonstrate year-on-year sustainability in revenues and profitability sits at the heart of a successful transaction.

Family alignment is a precursor to stakeholder alignment and both are critical. It is important to ensure existing owners are at one in terms of the goals to be achieved, and the means of getting there. If your client does not plan on staying with the business post-sale, then ensure that they establish leadership teams well in advance of the sale process, as prospective buyers will want to see that the business can succeed after they have gone. It can be hard to integrate new management teams, so start this process in good time.

Owners should also start tax-planning early, to make sure it is robust and to avoid any nasty last-minute surprises. The tax implications of a sale are also worth considering. It is common for a family-owned business to want to give its CEO or another person in the company a stake, but often this is left too late and can result in a less tax-efficient outcome. Owners may wish to transfer shares to minimise certain tax implications, or introduce a share scheme to reward employees prior to selling.

Consider what story owners are presenting to investors. Here are some questions to ask your clients ahead of a sale:

- What do any buyers need to know?
- Who would be a good buyer?
- Who is likely to pay the best price?

2.2 Finding the best way to sell

Trade sales, private equity sales, management buyouts and IPOs are some of the common ways to sell a business.

A trade sale is when the business is purchased by a corporate acquirer. Generally, 100% of the company is sold. Buyers are looking to fulfil a purpose, such as entering a new marketplace or accessing new technologies or products.

In the past, private equity sales would also usually result in a 100% transfer of ownership. Today, the world of private equity is far more complex but can be adapted to your client's needs. There are minority buyouts, majority buyouts, hybrid deals, debt-funded deals, sponsor-less deals and more.

Some owners are happy to give up total control if the valuation is compelling. Others may be less willing to give an investor the power to change the company, particularly if they still have a significant amount of their own wealth tied up in it.

Another option is a management buyout, which is where the company's existing management team purchases the business. This can help ensure a smooth transition to the new owners, given they will already have intimate knowledge of the business.

Finally, IPOs are another potential route for selling a business and they typically involve only a partial sale. IPOs also provide opportunities for a greater proportion of shares to be sold over time, which is less common in private equity deals.

IPOs are often used by families for succession planning, and they are a good way of professionalising the business so it can progress to a new stage of development.

2.3 Timeline of a sale

When the time comes to sell, a structured, competitive auction process between interested buyers is key to achieving maximum returns. The headline price is not everything, though. Your clients should also consider the structure and terms of each offer to determine which buyer is delivering the most value.

All sales are different – some proceed without a hitch but it is common for there to be some bumps in the road. Be prepared. Be ready to conduct multiple rounds of bidding before entering into an exclusivity arrangement with one buyer.

Be upfront with the buyers about the family's level of involvement with the business. Any buyer needs to have a clear picture of what they are buying. This means forewarning them of any potential issues and making sure numbers and performance are backed up.

Consider performing due diligence on the potential buyer. Despite the cost, this will identify any concerns early in the process and means the family can conduct the sale with confidence that their buyers are legitimate.

Even late in the sales process there are potential pitfalls to be aware of. Sales can fall through because the buyer has cold feet, the company has underperformed or because some other aspect of the company has changed. Last-minute legal issues can cause sales to be delayed.

The timeline of a sale is also highly dependent on the objectives of the owners, and the type of sale that is being pursued. Do they want to achieve a clean exit or a certain price? Think about their motivations for the sale.

Generally, your clients should give themselves between six and nine months to prepare for a sale once an adviser is appointed and the process is underway. This time frame enables the adviser to do the necessary housekeeping in advance. But remember, it may take two to three months to find an adviser they are comfortable with.

In terms of timing the sale itself, if they have a business that they expect to show strong performance over the next six to 18 months, that is often the optimal time in which to start planning a transaction.

In the context of an IPO, it takes at least six to nine months – but more typically 12 to 18 months – for private companies to get to a stage where they can be floated.

2.4 Avoiding common mistakes

Business underperformance is the most consistent reason a sale fails. This is why owners must be realistic with advisers about forecasting the company's financial performance from the outset.

Giving an overly optimistic view of the future performance will likely lead to a difficult negotiation on pricing. Owners should therefore be balanced when setting financial forecasts.

If momentum starts flagging during due diligence, then the buyer could step away from the deal or want to revisit terms. Performance, performance, performance is what needs to be delivered during the process.

3. Beyond the business sale

There is much more to a business sale than the transaction itself. On a personal level, your client will also need to prepare for selling a company that they may have been involved with since 'day one'. Mixed feelings are common.

There is often joy and excitement at achieving one's professional dreams, but also concern for the future and sadness over the loss of a business. The psychological impact of selling a business can take a toll, which is why it is important to discuss early in the process how it will affect your client, their family and other stakeholders. Media management assistance can be beneficial if they want help with any press coverage that may arise once the deal is finalised.

It is common for the proceeds of a sale to be based on an 'earn out' or deferral period of anywhere between six and 24 months.

More broadly, selling a business will lead to a change in your clients' financial situation and lifestyle. We like to use an analogy that one of our clients once told us to describe this transition: they will now be drawing money from a 'lake' of wealth, rather than the regular and consistent 'river' of income they had before.

To ensure that lake never dries up, they need a post-sale financial plan to secure their and their family's future. A wealth manager can help with important estate and inheritance planning processes, and also, crucially, with investing the proceeds of the business sale to create a reliable source of cash flow.

4. Beyond 'day one'

Many important questions will be swirling around your client's heads once the business sale completes. Should they save or invest the money? Is there enough to retire early? How much can they share with friends and family?

Before making any big financial choices, however, they should first stop and take a breath. They must consider their options properly, rather than rushing into a decision they may later regret. As the Genevan philosopher Jean-Jacques Rousseau reportedly said: "Patience is bitter, but its fruit is sweet."

Your client's first point to consider is how to keep their cash safe, given holding large cash reserves can be risky and difficult to stay within the compensation limits for cash deposits – in other words, return of cash is far more important than return on cash at this stage.

4.1 Choosing the right option

A range of low-risk, short-term investments and private banking services are available if your client is looking to find a temporary home for their cash while they formulate a long-term plan.

Preserving and growing their wealth over many years is likely to be the ultimate goal. However, most cash savings accounts offer interest rates that run well below inflation, meaning they are only ever a short-term solution.

But while holding cash is short term, it is a decision that deserves some focus. Some of the options available are:

- fixed-term deposit accounts;
- fixed-income investments;
- gilts;
- treasury bills; and
- liquidity funds.

4.2 Taking time out

After receiving a large cash lump sum, it can be hard to look past the here and now, but it is important to ensure that your client's money is managed effectively to secure their family's finances for the years, decades and even generations to come. Seeking good advice is crucial.

With thanks to Simon Cope-Thompson, managing director of Arrowpoint Advisory, who assisted with this chapter. Arrowpoint Advisory is the dedicated mid-market corporate advisory team of Rothschild & Co in the UK.

The process and family dynamic considerations of selling the family business

Nick Mayhew
Alembic Strategy

This chapter brings together case studies and experienced guidance on how to navigate the sale of a family business. It covers timing, options for sale, the sale process, post-sale planning, and the necessary conversations and agreements which underpin the good family dynamic needed to steer a deal to successful conclusion.

Every business sale is unique, and all owners experience an emotional roller-coaster ride during the process. The ups and downs can stretch relationships and affect discussions about critical aspects of a sale. Selling the family business will be a bit of a wringer and families do best when they have an effective approach to navigating their family dynamic so that they can make decisions together quickly during the sale.

1. Why sell the family business?

Owners approach advisers to manage the sale of their business for many reasons. To avoid some truly challenging sale situations, it is a good idea to talk to clients about their options and the essential preparations in advance of bringing a business to market. For most owners, this will only happen once in their lives, will be critical to their financial security and have a major psychological impact, closing off as it often does many years of life, work, hopes and struggles. It is an unfamiliar and worrying process even if owners are well educated about the process and they and the business are ready.

In *The Seven Habits of Highly Effective People*, Stephen Covey says we should begin with the end in mind.[1] Planning to sell any business will prompt owners to implement strategies which make the business more resilient and more consistently profitable to make them worth more. A business which is commercially and financially successful will be equally attractive to successors and buyers.

Rationales for selling might include:

- to culminate plans for the business which the family have all agreed, enabling a secure retirement;
- with changes to inheritance tax (IHT) on business interests, a sale rather than inheritance of shares to the next generation on succession might be more desirable;

---

1 Stephen R Covey, *The Seven Habits of Highly Effective People: Powerful Lessons in Personal Change*, Simon and Shuster (2013).

- to raise significant share capital for innovation and growth;
- to secure the future of the business when it is financially distressed or at risk;
- because succession to the next generation is not an option; and
- to end disputes and the stretched and strained family relationships which can often plague the lives of families in business together.

2. Understanding family dynamics

As an adviser to family businesses, you will be aware that the family dynamic, meaning the usefulness and quality of family relationships, colours everything. Family dynamic results from the emotional attachments of family members to each other being overlayed with the pressures of running the business together. Interpersonal chemistry, emotional intelligence, and the ability to listen to each other when experiencing uncomfortable emotional pressures are key to navigating business decisions, and an understanding of emotional reactions when the stakes are high is vital for advisers. You can probably imagine the emotional reaction family owners might have to each of the reasons listed above for selling, and have empathy about why they may find them difficult to discuss.

Families who can talk through their difficulties well are more likely to navigate the sale process successfully.

Emotions or moods colour our behaviours; they are how we experience life. There is no such thing as an unemotional human – even when we are asleep, the brain wakes us if something needs attention. Emotions are essential systems which the brain uses to keep us healthy and safe.

We call the internal sensations we experience about life *feelings*, m*oods* or *emotions*. Emotions are typically motivating, variable and short-lived. The word 'mood' is often used to describe feelings when arousal is lower. Moods are longer lasting and form the background of our experience – like the base coat on the canvas of an artwork. Being aware of our own moods and emotions is hard, and all of us could do with learning more about them *in order to have control*; to feel safe with strong feelings and experience life fully.

By control, I do not mean suppressing moods and emotions, I mean *knowing how to control them*. Imagine being able to control your feelings like a pilot has control of an aeroplane – we can go faster, fly higher and land safely because of our experience and control. Suppressing feelings would be like an aeroplane which never flew. Let us explore how to recognise emotional tones and energies by using the 'affect model' in Figure 1.

Figure 1: Affect model

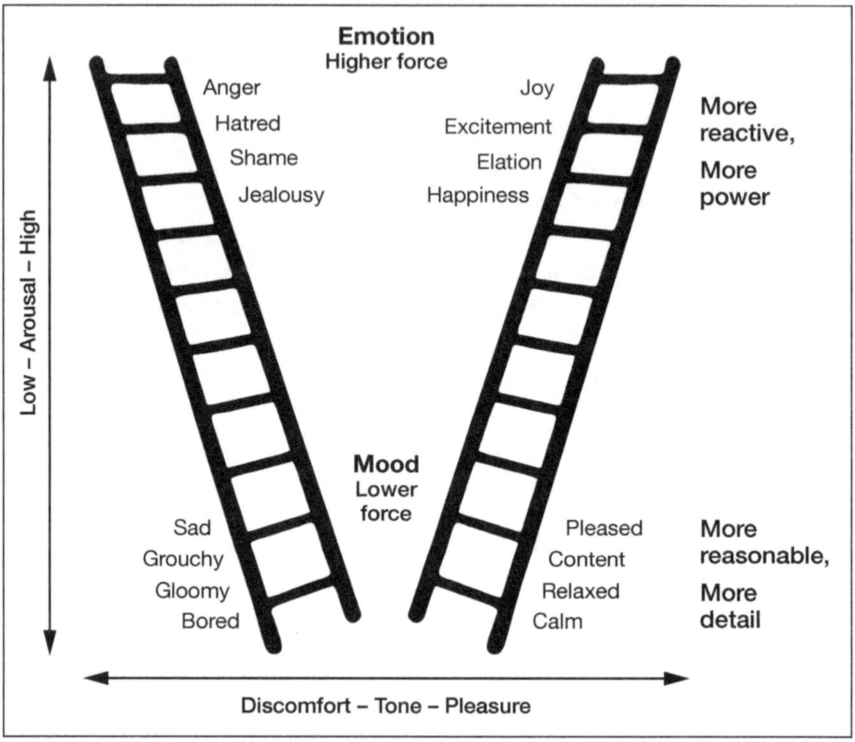

'Affect' is a technical word for moods and emotions. Affective disorders are also called mood disorders, like depression. The 'affect model' helps us visualise these inner experiences. Moods shift to emotions as tone changes to pleasure or discomfort, and as arousal increases.

We have used ladders in the image as a metaphor to help recognise the different feelings involved in dynamics. Imagine being at the top of one of the ladders.

High up a ladder, most people would have strong emotions; fear, or elation, perhaps feeling unsafe and a strong urge to get down and feel safer. At the top of the ladder, we tend to have tunnel vision; with strong feelings comes a sense of urgency. As we climb back down to the bottom of the ladder, we are open-minded and relaxed but may lack that energy or urgency. At the top of the ladder, things are exciting and/or threatening. In the middle of an argument, or while feeling threatened or worried in family relationships, it can feel like being up that ladder. At the top, it is hard to pay attention to other family members' needs, it is hard to listen, and we tend to be more forceful about our own needs and more upset if others appear not to be paying attention – often we cannot even tell that we, or they, are in this heightened state.

The purpose of the emotional state is to be forceful, because it seems to be needed. We behave forcefully because of our feelings; because of how we are interpreting what is happening. These shifts in how we perceive things under pressure can cause confusion and arguments – if we do not *feel* the same way about a situation, we do not *perceive* it the same way and the emotional response is a consequence of failing to understand the different reading of events.

As an adviser, there are two important ways you can help by using the affect model. Firstly, as a neutral party, creating a sense of confidence and ensuring that what each family member says is acknowledged. This is normal professionalism and even more important in family businesses. Tolerating family rows calmly and avoiding judging or taking emotional responses personally is helpful. In doing this, you lower the sense of threat, and ensure dignity and respect is given to everyone. Knowledge and experience reduce uncertainty. Identifying the real threats as they arise also reduces uncertainty – together with perspective and your experience of problem-solving. Secondly, you can think about how to create more motivation when action and decisions are needed to progress things in everyone's best interests.

I will refer to this model throughout, as it can help when family members argue. Consider using it as a map to help you, and them, to navigate their emotional responses, to help explain and understand why each feels as they do.

For now, be conscious that family business clients will experience strong feelings about any decision they have to make together in the business. The tools suggested below apply just as well to any difficult business or life-planning decision.

3. Family dynamics and selling the company

3.1 My name, my history, my life

Selling the family business is a major change in life, and it can be unsettling, with an impact on the family name, reputation and history. Having the same name as the business is common, accentuating the public exposure of private lives, and increasing sensitivity. This sensitivity can lead to 'personalisation'; taking things which are not intended that way personally, and finding it harder to keep things in perspective. Selling the family business feels deeply personal.

3.2 Family business culture

Family businesses are often deeply rooted in their communities and have a strong sense of responsibility for their employees and community. This will continue beyond the sale, which may well feature in community history for generations. The community impact of changes and the direct impact on team members increases sensitivity to buyers' culture, values and approach, and any post-deal integration plans will probably need to take this into account.

Such priorities may narrow the range of buyers and limit value. When some in the family prioritise value and others place cultural fit first, the difference of views will cause tension and may lead to arguments during the deal.

For these reasons, it is vital to obtain and discuss buyers' integration plans, in order to prepare families, and to expect more red lines about this aspect of the deal.

3.3 Family conflict

The crossover of personal and professional identities causes conflict in family businesses. Over the years, conflict can become entrenched. On the one hand, rivalry and arguments could be ended for everyone by a sale. On the other, conflict makes it hard to agree to sell in the first place, or to complete the sale process.

Referring to the affect model, conflict can feel like constantly being up the left ladder. Perceptions become distrustful and magnified – the word paranoid is often used to describe this. Conflict *distorts perceptions* about proposals which have been made in the best interests of everyone, and sometimes owners can make decisions which seem to be made for illogical reasons, like frustration or resentment. When this is happening, advisers should be aware that the emotional foreground is normally a signal that an important need is not being met.

As advisers, we need to acknowledge problems and take the distortion out to get to the root of things, and not seek to avoid, ignore or overrule by force – remember that perspective will often return when feelings are acknowledged, and real needs unearthed and respected. In short, advisers should be patient with emotional expressions and use their skills to explore and understand the hidden needs.

3.4 Intergenerational differences

It is normal for different generations in a family business to also have different life expectations. Being heavily involved in the family business can be fraught with emotional challenges; sometimes the next generation are not given a choice about joining the business, or struggle with imposter syndrome in following in their family's footsteps, which feel like big shoes to fill. Discussions about succession or sale involve facing these expectations and turning in a new direction. It will mean a change of life paths for all involved and many will find adapting difficult.

4. Preparing the business for sale

Ideally, family business owners should "begin with the end in mind"; you can never start too early to prepare the business for sale. As the economic climate ebbs and flows, it is essential to be able to choose the time clients come to market, and to defer plans if markets are not suitable without it being a problem.

Advisers should help clients clarify their goals and timescales, and guide them to build resilience and flexibility into their balance sheets. Resilience and quality are vital components of the business model too, including leadership, assets and knowledge, products and services, customer base, supplier networks and adviser relationships.

It can be valuable to talk through the diligence process a buyer will require, to bring focus to helpful ways of ensuring the business is in good order. Consideration can be given to the structures in which property assets, trading and investment assets are held, and ensuring that contracts and legal rights and obligations are in place and up to date. Even in the absence of a deal, this is an excellent way to review business risks which arise due to informal business arrangements which rely on trust and practice.

While keeping governance appropriate to the scale and environment, the effective work of the board of directors to govern the business should be given attention. The essential role of effective governance in maintaining competitiveness, ensuring consistent performance and improving decision making through experience has a significant impact on confidence, which is an essential part of business valuation.

It will be useful to consider valuation, and realistic expectations and targets for exit value. It is also important to discuss how a well-managed sale process can create a market for a company which, in turn, improves valuation. If possible, shareholdings and incentive schemes need to be organised well in advance of a sale process, to ensure the desired outcomes are achieved, and these also help align family and non-family leaders and their team with the same goal of improving value.

4.1 Finding the best way to sell the business

Trade sales and management buy-outs are the most common ways to sell a family business. In recent decades, private equity firms have become a more significant source of sales, particularly for larger businesses and those with growth potential. Initial public offerings (IPOs) are a possibility for significant (ie, very large) businesses and are rare.

The best approach to sale will be decided by the owners at the start of the process.

In a trade sale, unless the business has been approached by a competitor or fellow supplier with an attractive offer, the key role of the mergers and acquisitions (M&A) adviser will be to organise a marketing process. This will include preparing a thorough information memorandum (IM), setting out important information about business operations, key people, markets, potential, past and future performance expectations, all in sufficient detail for possible buyers to make an initial offer. Based on this document, advisers will normally prepare an anonymised summary, agree a list of potential buyers to approach, and write to them inviting interest. Those willing to sign a confidentiality agreement will receive the full IM. The aim is to try to receive two or more acceptable offers. The information provided and the generation of offers are two key components for generating the best price and terms. Offers can be negotiated and improved before agreeing heads of agreement (a summary of the key commercial agreements) with one buyer, granting them an exclusive period to check information (diligence), prepare legal contracts and try to conclude a deal – a process which will take months.

Trade sale – a real example

A trade sale of a regional professional practice bearing the family name, led by third-generation cousins, solved years of politics. In this case, the family tried to resolve the difficulties with some success, but inflexibility in one cousin, who personalised decisions because of the shared name, drained the energy of the family at partners' meetings. It worked but was not fun.

The deal offered a great solution for clients and staff, and was therefore supported by all the family. A 100% buy-out gave the partners the option to choose to leave with cash or continue in the larger firm, but this was no longer a family-led business after the sale. The solution matched the family's emotional needs, ensured the preservation of the culture and values, improved services, and reduced the family resentment.

In a management buy-out, similar information is exchanged, but as the management team know the business intimately, the process will feel very different and will not be competitive. The information provided is fundamentally so that the management can organise their funding in order to complete a deal with the family. There is likely to be more continuity for trade and culture in a management buy-out, but the value is unlikely to be as high as can be achieved in a competitive trade sale process.

Buy-out – a real example

Geoff raised £50m of debt to buy out his sister and nephew from the family business. Equity was held 50:50 between Geoff and his sister. His logic was to bring the equity back into the control of his side of the family and adult children on his death.

While his sister was a director, she and her son no longer held executive roles due to years of conflict with Geoff. Even though he had been keen for them to continue to have shares in the business, Geoff became resentful of their receipt of dividends from the company's success. Families are complex and people can have contradictory needs.

This buy-out was not necessary. The business was performing well and paid good dividends. Tackling the conflict was more likely to preserve good family relationships in the long term and avoid loading the business with debt. If the transaction did not work out, Geoff's resentments would likely worsen.

Private equity investment – a real example

Two sisters founded their business together. It had grown, creating pressures, and as they did not understand how to talk to each other about their feelings, they became unable to talk openly.

One of the sisters proposed private equity funding to accelerate the growth, which seemed a great plan. Her hidden agenda was to professionalise the board as a solution to their interpersonal difficulties. On the day of the transaction, she checked out of the relationship with her sister, rather than celebrating with her sister and the team, and the situation spiralled out of control; avoidance of each other, cold meetings, and even threats to exit one of them.

A different family member suggested "Burying the Dead Cats" and within two months, the sisters had understood and resolved their communication difficulties. They were able to work in partnership once again in an enjoyable way. The business is still challenging but the experience of it has been transformed for both. Given the conflict, the deal could have caused the business to fail, but resolving the conflict and re-establishing trust means the deal is more likely to work out well.

4.2 Tripwires which derail a deal

Deals typically run into problems in four ways, namely:

- not getting on well and building good chemistry with the buyer's team;
- too many unexpected issues arising during diligence, putting the buyer off;
- business performance dropping during the deal process, which can happen simply because it takes up so much of the owners' time; and
- an inability of the family to agree on contentious detailed points of negotiation on the deal, like warranties, deferred payments or post-deal changes.

All of these can be avoided with planning and preparation so that the family can get to completion successfully.

5. Making it all the way to completion

Once the decision is made to sell the business, whoever is leading the process will need to maintain unity and an effective decision-making process through to completion.

5.1 Consider getting expert help to manage relationships during the deal

Usually, the sale is managed by the corporate financier or banker who is handling the transaction for the shareholder, although sometimes it is led by the solicitor. These professionals are very used to the cut and thrust of the deal process but can be less experienced in handling difficult family dynamics.

It is important to hire someone who is prepared to act as 'lead adviser'. Brokers normally act as introducers and do not expect to mediate the challenges arising during deals. Trying to keep the family aligned as well as keep the buyers on board can be overwhelming. It is better to work with an experienced and trusted family intermediary who understands the sensitivities, to manage the relationships during the sale.

6. Tools for managing family dynamic during a sale

6.1 Burying the Dead Cats™

At Alembic, we have developed a brilliant facilitation for fixing the rifts and rows which develop in family businesses because of the stresses on family dynamics, called Burying the Dead Cats. A dead cat represents an unpleasant, stinky mess, which affects everyone, but which no one really wants to deal with. They must be cleaned up for everyone to move on. Our facilitation focuses on helping participants face the realities, discuss and resolve the difficult issues themselves. With expert coaching and facilitation for emotional situations, people can normally fix the problems themselves and at the same time learn how to fix such issues in the future, preventing things from getting out of control again.

Experienced facilitators help the family talk about their difficulties (Dead Cats) in a safe space, where everyone is heard, resentments and misunderstandings get aired and cleared up, relationships can be improved, and goals are set. To gain the strong shareholder and family support needed for selling the business, the Dead Cat issues must be sufficiently resolved at the outset so that rifts do not derail the sale, and a difficult conversations process can be set up to be used when challenges arise during the deal process.

6.2 A family council

It is essential the family agree a process for having their Dead Cat conversations well. Where there are larger shareholder groups, a good way to do it is to create a family council or an owners' board, with the express intention of solving any problems and to support the deal, enabling clear and consistent instruction to negotiators. The group needs to be empowered to make the bigger calls on behalf the families and to give their steer to advisers. If you do not have experience of family councils or owners' boards, take advice before you start the sale process.

These groups can also help with appointment of advisers and keep a strong channel of communication and agreement with the shareholders and wider family, remaining open to their sensitivities and needs.

6.3 Patience

Patience is essential with family businesses. Emotional responses are going to be more sensitive due to personalisation, imposter syndrome, family culture and history, and the different needs of individual shareholders and different generations. When emotions arise, it is normally due to needs not being met, but the arousal and feeling of threat (see Figure 1 above) distorts perceptions, creating potential for misunderstandings and damaged relationships. While it can feel distracting and stressful to have angry family members on the phone when you are in the middle of a difficult negotiation, you must take time and talk the issues through to a conclusion.

It is not worth sacrificing family relationships, which surround clients for life, for the sake of a deal. Focus on trying to make the transaction work for everyone.

6.4 Develop the family's ability to process emotional issues together

Selling the business is a major decision. Getting to a successful sale is more likely if clients have done their preparation. When family disagreements come up, think of them as an opportunity to improve how the family deals with disputes.

Embrace the emotionally difficult stuff and you will find a much richer set of relationships, and better decisions will follow.

A good way to start is for individuals to learn about their own emotional responses. After a difficult conversation, find a time to explore each party's emotional journey reflectively using the affect model in Figure 1 above. With a little practice, it is possible to work out how to map out what happened, talk about misunderstandings and how they happened, and explore alternative options, all of which improve emotional awareness, and flexibility. To do this, use the arousal and tonal indices to map how interactions changed emotions, moods and behaviour.

Did you begin relaxed, alert, stressed or tense? These place you somewhere on the arousal scale. Were you feeling neutral, discomfort, or threatened and anxious or alternatively very positive? This places you on the tonal scale. What emotion words could you use to describe your state? When the row started, what happened to your feelings? Track how things changed emotionally and what that meant for your behaviour. Mapping your emotional journey can help reveal your patterns of behaviour and in due course give you greater control.

If possible, encourage family business clients to get involved in constructive approaches to difficult conversations with their children. The earlier they start, and the more they do it, the better they will get at it. Even though the frustrations are normal and will never go away, people gradually experience useful emotional conversations rather than confusing, pointless or damaging encounters which lead them to avoid topics which practically need to be addressed.

7. After the sale

7.1 Life is changed for everyone

A successful sale should feel great – there will be more money, or if the sale was due to a crisis, losses will have stopped. However, attachment to family businesses can be very strong and people are complicated, so, alongside relief, there can still be uncomfortable feelings: purposelessness, and even a sense of guilt or loss may still need to be dealt with.

7.2 Multi-generational wealth and imposter syndrome

If the sale goes well, owners will have life-changing amounts of money with implications for future generations.

In wealthy families, while money solves many problems and can lead to much happier lives, it still needs to be managed well. A normal part of growing up is learning to survive 'on your own two feet'.

Surviving is a struggle for many throughout the world. While it may seem ideal to remove the struggle, striving is a critical part of learning how to survive, involving many interpersonal skills.

To get on in life, we need to learn how to make money and how to work with other people.

When the main source of money is through the family, striving focuses on relationships inside the family system, and it can distort relationships and limit independence for generations following a successful exit. One source of imposter syndrome is this lack of independence. Unlike the generation which made the money, the younger generation may feel they would not be able to maintain their lifestyle if left to their own devices. A lack of striving can also lead to a sense of purposelessness together with a feeling of standing in the shadows of their forebears. There is more to do to identify how these complex emotions are helping or hindering wealthy family members in their lives, and to guide healthy development.

Conclusion

Selling a family business can be a time for celebration, but there are many ways it can be more complicated than selling another kind of company. Human emotions, family connections and ownership structures can all play a huge part. Our key message is to seek advice, and to seek it early during the sale process.

Selling your business is also a good opportunity to take a holiday or reconnect with family. After years of building and growing a business, and all the sacrifices that can entail, the sale can be an opportunity to take stock and reset.

Family offices set up after a sale can be used to establish a sense of purpose as well as to manage the wealth you have received from the sale.

Managing family dynamics: how to improve communication and deal with conflict effectively

Tony Cohen
Alexandra Sharpe
Kinestra Partners LLP

1. Introduction

It is not hyperbole to say that successful and sustainable family businesses must be underpinned by healthy family dynamics. Achieving this, however, is not an easy feat. Family dynamics can be tricky in the simplest family setup, let alone one where there are shared decisions to be made about money, leadership and power, all against the backdrop of shared history and, typically, love.

So, what do we mean when we refer to family dynamics? For the purposes of this chapter, when we refer to family dynamics, we are considering the patterns of interactions, relationships and behaviours among and between family members. These dynamics are shaped by various factors, including generational differences, individual personalities, and the history of family relationships as well as the individual perspectives held by the family members driven by their role within their family business ecosystem.

Understanding family dynamics and how they can impact everything within a family business is crucial for the business's long-term success and sustainability. It is critical to take purposeful steps to manage the complex dynamics which inevitably arise to create positive collaboration and teamwork, facilitate good decision making and promote a harmonious working environment. It is also our experience that most families identify maintaining family harmony as an objective in and of itself, independent of the influence of healthy family dynamics on commercial success.

Family dynamics in a business setting are complex due to the overlap of familial and professional roles. Unlike non-family businesses, where relationships are primarily professional, family businesses intertwine personal and business relationships. Family members wear multiple hats at once – they are siblings as well as business partners, parents as well as bosses. This intertwining can lead to unique strengths, such as deep trust and going the extra mile, but also unique challenges, such as emotional conflicts and blurred boundaries.

In this chapter, we seek to discuss what 'good' looks like when it comes to family dynamics. We will identify the key challenges which might prevent a family from nurturing healthy family dynamics, positive communication and the effective resolution of conflict, and we will offer some suggestions on how those challenges might be best met to enhance the opportunities that are unique to a family in business.

2. Understanding family dynamics

2.1 Healthy family dynamics – what does 'good' look like?

Most business-owning families want their relationships to flourish as well as their business, and it is our thesis that healthy family dynamics are a necessary ingredient for the long-term success of a family business. However, it is very difficult to define what 'good' looks like in this regard. Every family is different, with its own special quirks, history, culture and relationships. Some have very close relationships with each other and live their lives 'close', while others are more remote and the 'glue' is their shared business interests. A family is a living, breathing, evolving system and there is no ideal family dynamic.

Having said that, in a family business, we would suggest that any owning family should be aiming to be able to:

- communicate well;
- respectfully disagree;
- recognise each other's talents and strengths;
- trust and collaborate with each other; and
- deal with conflict.

Such capabilities enable good decision making. There are some special features of family businesses, however, which can make achieving these goals particularly difficult, and in the balance of this section, we explore some of these challenges further.

2.2 Generational differences

One of the most significant factors influencing family dynamics is generational differences. Family businesses often involve multiple generations, each with distinct values, work ethics and perspectives. For instance, senior generations might prioritise stability and tradition, while younger generations may advocate for innovation and change.

We frequently see the senior generation wanting to 'stick to their knitting' while the next generation pushes for diversification. Such a disagreement in approach is just an expression of the fact that in a family business you tend to have a much broader age range than in other business settings, meaning the perspectives of those involved is partly shaped by their place in time. Many of our clients have had family members in their nineties still involved with the business in some capacity, which you are unlikely to encounter in any other business form.

2.3 Family hierarchies

In addition, one could say that a multi-generational family structure creates a natural hierarchy – the older family members being more senior. Very often we find that this can create a dynamic whereby the next generation feel reluctant to speak openly and honestly with their seniors, in many cases for fear of being seen to be disrespectful.

This can even impact dynamics and decision making after a key family member is no longer alive – "What would Dad have wanted us to do?" is a question we hear a lot. It can seem on the surface like an easier question for a group of siblings to ask themselves than asking themselves and each other what they really want.

2.4 Personal emotional factors

Personal factors also play a significant role in family dynamics. Family members can have deep-seated feelings and histories that might influence their interactions and decisions. We have encountered families in business together where their dynamic has been shaped by important emotional childhood events such as a bereavement, an estrangement or even witnessing abusive behaviour within the family.

2.5 Spouses

Similarly, as family members marry and in-laws join the family, we see that the family dynamic is often significantly impacted. This is no surprise when you consider that a spouse brings with them their own history and personal values. It does mean, however, that as a family shifts from being a nuclear family, perhaps very focused on their business to one where additional 'outsiders' have their own perspective, that challenging dynamics can arise. Indeed, one family client of ours calls their in-laws "the outlaws".

While spouses may not have shares or be directly involved in the family business, they frequently have an important influencing role and will, of course, always have a fundamental role in terms of rearing the next generation.

3. Different stakeholders, different perspectives

In family businesses, family members have multiple roles as they balance family and professional responsibilities. This duality can create a real sense of loyalty and commitment, as family members are usually deeply invested in the business's success. However, this duality can also create significant complexity when it comes to dynamics.

The 'Three-circle Model', originally developed by Renato Tagiuri and John Davis in 1978 at Harvard Business School, looks at the family business system as three overlapping sub-systems of family, business and ownership. The model allows us to neatly consider the perspective of different interest groups within a family business through a three-way Venn diagram. The overlapping of the three circles identifies seven distinct stakeholder groups, as can be seen in Figure 1.

Figure 1: Three-circle Model

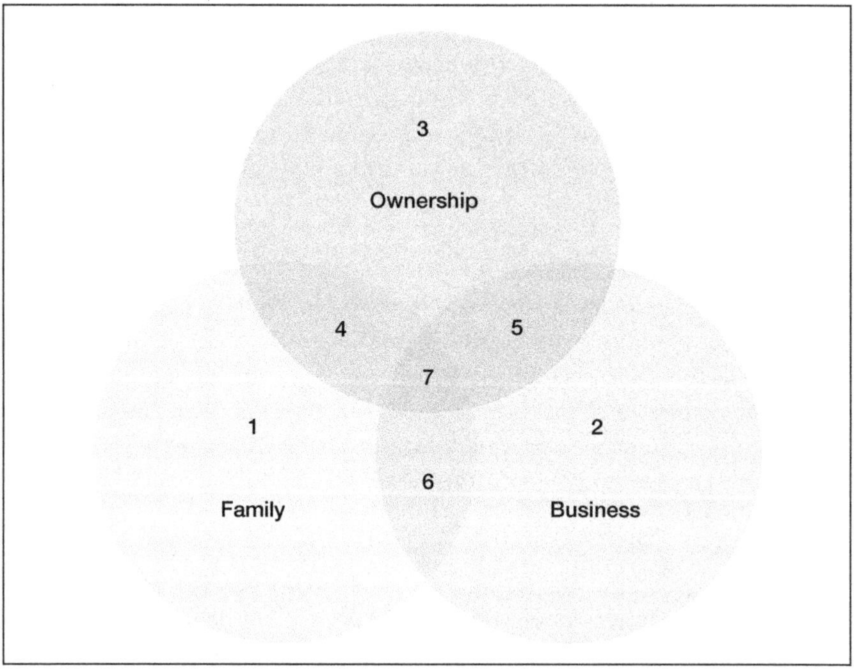

Source: Authors, adapted from Tagiuri and Davis.[1]

1. **Family members**
2. Employees
3. Shareholders
4. **Family shareholders**
5. Employee Shareholders
6. **Family working in the enterprise**
7. **Family shareholders working in the enterprise**

A person's perspective within a family business is very much shaped by where they sit within the system. There are four different roles that a family

1 See https://johndavis.com/three-circle-model-family-business-system/.

member might have (in bold in the list in Figure 1). The dynamics of a family business will be heavily influenced by who and how many family members sit in each role. For example, if there are few family members working within the business, but many shareholders outside, this is likely to create its own particular relational quirks. Likewise, if there is only one shareholder, for example, but several family members working in the business, the balance of power can lead to different challenging dynamics.

It is also important to consider that the different systems may have different goals, for example:

- **Family:** harmonious relationships
- **Business:** commercial growth
- **Ownership:** wealth preservation

Importantly, the respective goals and values of the three systems may not be entirely compatible – is accountability in a business setting consistent with unconditional love, for example? The dynamics that are created by the overlapping systems explain much of the complexity of the dynamics within family businesses.

As a result, we always encourage our family business clients to plot their key stakeholders on the Three-circle Model as we find it helpful for them to better understand some of the dynamics which might be at play. It can also help families in business understand that perspectives will inevitably be different, depersonalising and sometimes even defusing issues. (See also the "Theories and models in family enterprise advising" chapter of this book.)

We think it is also important to note here that within any family system, different family members frequently have roles (unofficially) ascribed to them, for example 'the favourite', 'the maverick' or 'the helper'. These roles all have an impact on the dynamics within a family business and can be hard to shift even if they are unhelpful in terms of contributing towards an inclusive, aligned and collaborative group.

4. Common sources of conflict in family businesses

Even within the most empathetic and sophisticated family businesses, differences will inevitably arise. This is natural and desirable as a diversity of perspective is a core family business strength if harnessed correctly. However, differences can evolve into full-blown conflict. Often the genesis of conflict within a family business can be traced back to the family domain or system, originating perhaps before there was even a shared family business to fight over, childhood patterns playing out in adulthood. Similarly, personal conflicts between family members such as sibling rivalry, marital issues or simply differing personal values can spill over into the business setting and can materially impact business operations and decision making.

However, there are common themes which originate from within the business and ownership domains which can lead to conflict and the unsettling of family dynamics. We find that those most regularly encountered are related to:

- financial disagreements;
- succession planning;
- role and responsibility conflicts; and
- family vs business.

4.1 Financial disagreements

Family disagreements over shareholdings, salaries, dividends, bonuses and the reinvestment of profits are common.

Shareholding disputes often come to the fore after the death of a key family member, particularly when they have kept their business and financial affairs private. When information is not shared and communication is poor, family members may make assumptions which, when proved incorrect, can be bitterly disappointing.

Typically, financial disagreements boil down to perceptions of unfairness. Later in this chapter, we explore the concept of adopting fair process as a methodology, which can help mitigate the risk of such perceptions arising.

4.2 Succession planning

Succession planning is another one of the most significant sources of conflict in a family business. Transitioning the leadership of a business from one generation to the next can be fraught with tension.

It is a particularly frequent source of conflict during the transition from a founder to their children. A patriarch or matriarch choosing a successor from among their children can lead to intense sibling rivalry and competition.

Succession planning when it comes to ownership can also be a source of conflict. Who will inherit what? This is an especially difficult question since it is not a universal truth that equality is always fair – for example, perhaps the daughter who has been working in the business for several years should receive more shares than her sister who has never contributed to it. Or perhaps not? In one particular family business case, we have seen a divergence in thinking on this lead to some considerable conflict.

Later in this chapter, we share some principles to adopt when approaching succession planning to improve the chances of success from a family dynamics perspective.

4.3 Roles and responsibility

Closely connected to succession is conflict arising from ambiguity as regards roles and responsibilities.

We have a client case where a very significant conflict had arisen based on one member of the family asserting that another was not pulling their weight within the business. Here it was expectations around not only their day jobs, but also the 'extra curriculars' associated with being a business-owning family which caused the conflict, for example, socialising with non-family colleagues, giving a speech to thank employees and writing condolence letters. The conflict was managed with the help of a skilled therapist but the scars of that falling out are still felt by the family.

It also demonstrates how important it is to have role clarity and defined responsibilities, even related to activities which sit outside of the day to day. More generally, it probably goes without saying that differing opinions on the level of contribution that any one family member may be making to the business whether spoken or not will always raise the temperature in the board room and around the dining table.

4.4 Family vs business

Conflict can also arise when business decisions are made for family reasons. For example, a family member is employed when they are not actually up to the job or a business line is retained because it is a passion project of a family member when it is unlikely to ever be profitable. The beauty of being a family business is that the family can make unusual decisions – unconventional is the norm. However, we see that conflict almost invariably arises when a family is not open about why they are doing something. Too often, we see families convince themselves that they are making a decision for business reasons when it is really for family reasons. In these cases, they are setting themselves up to fail and, more often than not, for conflict.

In particular, family members assuming roles based on familial relationships rather than on qualifications or skills can be dangerous for a family business and can lead to experienced and qualified employees (or other perhaps more distant family members) feeling demotivated and resentful. Having said that, the opposite can also be true: we have a client where a family member was denied a job despite desperately wanting it and he is now incredibly resentful, and the decision has created quite a rift between the business and the family.

So, how can family businesses reduce the potential for disharmony and conflict when there are so many stumbling blocks along the way? Key to this is building a positive family business culture.

5. Building a positive family business culture

A positive culture within a family business promotes loyalty, boosts morale and enhances performance. Creating an environment where all stakeholders, whether family or not, feel a strong sense of belonging, feel valued and respected, should result in better commercial and financial outcomes. Ultimately, it should lay the foundation for the business's long-term success through the generations.

We would see the key components underpinning a positive family business culture as including:

- a clear purpose, shared vision and values;
- the use of fair process;
- clear roles and boundaries;
- a focus on continual improvement; and
- good communication.

5.1 A clear purpose, shared vision and values

Establishing a clear purpose and shared vision and values can align family members and guide decision making across the generations. Collective vision crafting is a key first step for any family in business considering the future. It should involve the family members coming together firstly to share their personal aspirations and secondly to consider together what they believe success would look like.

Having a shared purpose and being able to answer the question "Why do we have a family business and what are we trying to achieve?" can be a very powerful uniting force. Clear goals allow the family to focus on what is important rather than become distracted by unimportant issues which have the potential to derail and destabilise.

Exploring and defining the core values of the family and business as a guide for behaviour and decision making can also be a powerful exercise.

The purpose, vision and values, once established, can then be integrated into everyday business practices. We have seen family businesses build annual awards for their staff around their values, for example.

5.2 Fair process

Adopting the principle of fair process in a family business is crucial for maintaining harmony and trust, and long-term success. Given the unique dynamics of family businesses, fair process helps manage both business and familial relationships effectively and creates a positive family business culture.

Fair process refers to the concept that the processes and procedures used in decision making should be transparent, consistent and impartial. It ensures that all parties involved feel respected and treated equitably. The principles of fair process include the following:

- *Engagement:* Involving all family members in the decision-making process by seeking their input and considering their views. This fosters a sense of inclusion and respect.
- *Explanation:* Clearly communicating the reasoning behind decisions and the criteria used. This helps individuals understand the logic and fairness behind the outcomes.
- *Expectation clarity:* Setting clear expectations and standards before

decisions are made. This ensures that everyone knows the rules of the game and the potential consequences.

- *Consistency:* Applying procedures and rules uniformly across similar situations to avoid favouritism. Treating one family member differently than another invariably leads to perceptions of unfairness, which can snowball into conflict quite rapidly.
- *Impartiality:* Ensuring that decision makers are unbiased and do not have a personal stake in the outcomes. This helps maintain objectivity and fairness. The use of independent non-executive directors and advisers can assist here.

Fair process is particularly important in relation to employment decisions. In this context, we find that the use of independent non-executives in performance appraisals and decisions around promotions, salary and bonuses for family members along with clear appraisal systems and remuneration benchmarking, very helpful.

5.3 Clear roles and boundaries

Family businesses often start in a very informal manner. To ensure that as the business and family grow, a positive culture is maintained, it may well be desirable to hold on to this informality. However, it is critical that there are clear roles, reporting lines, authority limits and boundaries in place. Indeed, defining expectations within the family business context can be extremely important not only for professional success but also in personal relationships.

In particular, we would propose ensuring there is clarity on the following:

- *Roles:* Who does what? Roles, responsibilities and performance standard expectations should be clear for all, family or non-family.
- *Authority limits:* What sits within the mandate of the board versus what requires shareholder approval?
- *Reporting lines:* Who reports to whom?
- *Access to information:* Who should receive what information, in what form and with what frequency?
- *How decisions are made:* Who needs to be around the table and what is required for a decision to carry?

Agreeing how to agree and make decisions is critical. For any group – whether that be the board, family council or shareholders – clarity on how decisions are made is absolutely fundamental. Ideally, of course, consensus should be the starting point. If regular votes are being conducted, it probably indicates that insufficient effort is being put into working towards alignment. However, it is important that there is clarity around how a decision is taken and what would happen in the case of deadlock.

This is really all about good governance, and the gold standard for any family business is articulating a family charter or constitution which sets out how the family and the business will interact. Good governance underpins a positive culture.

5.4 Continual improvement and learning

We like to discuss the Japanese concept of *kaizen* with our family business clients. *Kaizen* refers to a business philosophy or system that involves all employees actively engaging in ongoing, incremental enhancements to improve efficiency, quality and overall performance.

The beauty of the concept is that it entails acknowledging that things can always be improved, and it means that criticism is only seen as constructive and helpful. When this is internalised, a family business culture tends to be open and dynamic. It depersonalises issues. We even know of one family where at each meeting someone is allocated the role of playing devil's advocate, the idea being that rigorous debate is likely to achieve a better outcome in any and every situation.

Encouraging this sort of outlook can be extremely valuable in terms of supporting a positive and open culture where family members trust each other and feel safe to contribute with their full selves.

Family businesses can also be somewhat insular, so we would always recommend that they should look to leverage the experience of networks outside of their business, including other successful families. Similarly, encouraging family members, whether they work in the business or not, to work on their own learning and development is key. We increasingly see budgets being put aside for an executive coaching or mentorship programme for next-generation family members to great effect. Investing in the family's talent and celebrating positive growth and personal achievements can be incredibly powerful in terms of contributing to a positive culture.

5.5 Good communication

Perhaps the most important aspect of a positive business culture is communication. In a family business scenario, we do not believe that it is possible to over-communicate. "Communicate, communicate, communicate" should be the family business mantra. In the following section, we explore how to ensure effective communication within the family business.

6. Effective communication

6.1 Open and honest communication

Without open and honest communication in a family business, family members can feel isolated, important issues can be missed and unhelpful assumptions can be made. When families are skilled communicators, we find that not only do they have more rewarding personal relationships with each other, they are also better able to make good business decisions.

However, our experience is that often transparency and communication can be lacking in a family business or at least information sharing is uneven, with some family members 'in the know' and others not. This tendency for opaqueness frequently starts with the founder, who may not feel the need to share information. It then becomes the norm to keep information close rather than share it, even though this is no longer suitable in a multi-faceted multi-generational family situation where the stakeholder group is more varied and complex.

Interestingly, it is also sometimes the closest families who actually have the most trouble communicating honestly because they are so keen to avoid difficult conversations which might put their relationships and family harmony at risk. Ironically, this can be their downfall. In a family business, avoiding the difficult questions is unlikely to lead to success in the long term.

In order to address this, we have seen that introducing a more formal approach to reporting, information sharing and communication coupled with a purposeful approach to increasing trust and understanding between family members, can be very successful.

6.2 Regular family meetings

To encourage open communication, regular family meetings are recommended.

Formal (or semi-formal) family meetings can create a structured environment for addressing issues in the business, for aligning goals and for clarifying roles and responsibilities.

We would typically suggest that families put aside two to four sessions each year, a half-day to a full day in length (separate to board meetings where non-family members may also participate) to discuss a broad strategic agenda, including their shared business interests, what is working, what is happening and what they would like for the future. These formal meetings should have clearly defined agendas, and minutes of meetings should be kept and circulated to ensure that decisions and action items are clearly documented and accessible to all. These may take the form of family council meetings, if such a body has been instituted.

Families should also consider the support of an independent facilitator to help ensure the interactions and communications are constructive. Just having an 'outsider' in the room can help a family behave in a more focused and professional manner. When there are tricky personal dynamics, the use of a facilitator can also help create the sense of family meetings being a 'safe space' in which important and personal issues can be explored.

While face-to-face meetings are important, for families who are not co-located or where they are juggling lots of other commitments, shorter, more frequent interactions can also be useful. Most of our clients use group messaging apps for quick ongoing updates and hold interim meetings using video conferencing facilities.

6.3 Reporting and information sharing

In addition to agreeing a regular structured meeting schedule outside of the day-to-day business operations and board meetings, we would also suggest that every family business should clarify what information should be shared with whom and when.

This should include establishing what those who work in the business should be informed about and what those who are shareholders should know.

In any case, we would always suggest following the 'no surprises principle'. We even have one family where their key reporting pack was centred around the three topics of 'the good, the bad and the ugly'. Keeping family members engaged and feeling informed is foundational both for building trust and enabling good decisions to be made over the long run.

6.4 Team building and mutual understanding

Building trust facilitates open and honest communication. We always advocate taking an intentional approach to nurturing relationships between family members within a family business as we see the positive impact this has on the dynamics and resultant decision making.

Examples we have seen families adopt include:

- holding sessions led by 'soft skills' experts on topics such as emotional intelligence and communication;
- carving out deliberate family time when business issues are not on the agenda, whether that be a weekend away, or a regular Sunday lunch;
- scheduling team-building sessions, for example, yoga, clay pigeon shooting and everything in between;
- holding sessions for family members to share personal aspirations and goals; and
- the use of psychometrics to encourage understanding of each other's preferences and values.

In essence, misunderstandings and incorrect or imperfect assumptions often on small perhaps unimportant matters, are where conflict can germinate, so by prioritising transparent communication and trust, family businesses can create a more harmonious and productive environment in which to grow.

In the following section, we consider how to manage conflict when it does arise in a family business context.

7. Conflict management

The management of conflict is a key skill in any organisation and especially so in a family business where personal relationships can dominate interactions. In our view, every family in business should have a clear mutual understanding of how they would deal with conflict if it were to arise.

7.1 Developing a conflict resolution protocol

Creating and maintaining a structured written conflict resolution protocol is helpful to ensure that conflicts are managed effectively. In accordance with the fair process principle, such a protocol should be developed by the family in an inclusive way so that everyone is part of the process. The idea being that since they were part of the design of the conflict resolution process, when it is actually applied in an instance of conflict and while they might not like the outcome, they should be happy that it was reached by fair process, and therefore should be able to accept that outcome.

The ideal position is to agree a conflict resolution protocol when everyone is harmonious so that it can be agreed in principle before being applied to a specific case. Typically, such a protocol includes a series of stages, each of which aims to resolve the conflict and all of which aim to resolve the matter without needing to resort to litigation. Generally, the ultimate step in such a process is the use of a formal mediator or arbitrator where the decision might even be binding.

7.2 Mediation and third-party involvement

When conflicts cannot be avoided or resolved internally, mediation or other third-party involvement may be necessary.

In some cases, however, there may not be a specific dispute to be resolved but there is simply a very poor dynamic at the family level. We frequently refer our family business clients in this situation to specialist therapists who can help them understand the root of the dynamic, overcome unhelpful patterns, and equip themselves with better communication skills and interaction techniques to improve their working relationship.

If the conflict is more severe and there is a specific matter to be resolved, an external arbitrator or mediator may be necessary. The benefits of resolving a conflict in this way include maintaining confidentiality and control. A family business dispute in the newspapers does little for its reputation. Avoiding litigation and the court room must be the goal.

8. Succession planning and change management

The process of transferring leadership from one generation to the next can be so complex and fraught with emotions and friction that we did not feel that we could complete this chapter without specifically addressing what we have seen work well across our portfolio of diverse family business clients.

8.1 Importance of early planning

By starting the succession planning process early, families can create a structured plan that includes timelines, development programmes and contingency strategies, and ensure that there is alignment between the different generations in terms of goals.

An extended time frame also allows the current generation to gradually step back to facilitate the next generation to build their credibility and gradually to take more responsibility. This should also help minimise disruption to the business operations and allow for more stress-free conversations within the family.

8.2 Preparing the next generation

Clearly, it is critical that the next generation of leaders have the skills and knowledge required to take the business forward. Planning a comprehensive programme of education, on-the-job training and hands-on experience in the years before the intended transition is hugely important. In our view, such preparation is required whether the family member in question has/or will have an executive role in the business or not. If a family member is to be a shareholder, understanding what it means to be an owner requires its own preparation.

8.3 Managing expectations and emotions

Succession planning in a family business is not only a strategic and operational challenge but also an emotional one, and the family dynamics can often complicate the process. Managing expectations throughout the entire process is essential. Clear and open communication from the current leaders at the outset around their vision and expectations for the future is crucial, but often overlooked. A forum for addressing the concerns of the next generation is also required.

It is important to remember that the transition of leadership can bring feelings of loss, anxiety and even resentment among family members. Acknowledging and addressing these feelings openly can help in mitigating any conflict. Providing platforms for family members to share their thoughts and concerns over the changes suggested and to have their voices heard is a critically important piece to the transition process, as is recognising contributions and acknowledging achievements and success. While always tricky, it is important to find the balance where business needs are met while respecting and valuing individual family members' feelings and contributions.

8.4 Retaining professional support

Engaging independent professionals – experts in family enterprise matters – in the transition planning and implementation process is beneficial. They can help by facilitating discussions, providing strategic advice tailored to the unique dynamics of the family and the specific family business involved. Creating a comprehensive succession plan that addresses the vision for the future along with answering the question "What does success look like?" from both a business and family perspective can be challenging without someone bringing an outside perspective.

External consultants can also share what other families find works well and should be able to provide valuable insights into best practices.

9. Conclusion

Family businesses are special, and the families that own them are often driven by a genuine desire to work together and make an important impact on the world. However, as enterprises, they are also vulnerable because of their unique dynamics where Dad is also the boss, Aunty is also the non-executive director, and your sister is your fellow shareholder.

The complexity at an emotional level cannot be overstated, so this chapter just serves as a taster and starting point for further reflection. Each family enterprise has its own special features and its own challenging dynamics – whether that be so much emphasis on family harmony that the hard topics are left undiscussed or perhaps intense unresolved sibling rivalry. The overlapping systems of 'family', 'business' and 'ownership', so elegantly illustrated by the Three-circle Model, guarantee complexity.

However, ultimately, it is our thesis that prevention is better than cure, and any family business with a goal of longevity should be encouraged to do what they can today to improve communication, nurture a positive culture and create a healthy family dynamic. Against this backdrop, family businesses can be a force to be reckoned with.

The family business – options for preventing and dealing with family disputes

Guy Abrahams
Nick Jacob
Daniel Ugur
Forsters LLP

1. What causes family disputes?

There are many reasons for family conflict. If we want to prevent family disputes, it is vital to break down the reasons why conflict arises. The difficulty with families is that emotion inevitably plays a part. Issues that create conflict include:

- the first generation's (G1) desire to retain control;
- the quest for control by future generations;
- competition for leadership; and
- merit entitlement (a feeling that meritorious work or conduct should give greater entitlement).

However, perhaps this all boils down to the perception of fairness. Fairness, like beauty, is in the eye of the beholder, so, it is crucial that everybody perceives they are being treated fairly. How should the family cake be divided? Can – or should – it take into account future growth and profit? How do we ensure that those working in the business feel sufficiently incentivised, while those not working in it feel they benefit sufficiently from their parents' efforts?

A lack of clarity over goals, and indeed incompatible goals and values, is another difficult area, as is ambiguity over roles. Sometimes we see a change in behaviour, particularly when family members feel disconnected, or are marginalised or ignored – the latter often being the case. Sometimes this is caused by sibling/cousin rivalry. Many families have difficulty identifying their values. Many are aspirational but not realistic. Every family wants their members to be humble, modest and considerate, but what do these actually mean and how are they satisfied? A family needs to identify the core values by which they have governed themselves and will need to operate in the future, and these need to be built into the legal arrangements.

So, what can we put in place to avoid all these problems? Can legal solutions take the emotion out of family dynamics?

Lawyers tend not to deal with emotion or psychology, but they need to. They must raise issues with all adult family members in an unemotional but empathetic manner which will be perceived as fair and constructive. They need to read body language and understand what people are really saying. They also need to facilitate good communication – something sadly lacking in many families. Only then can they launch into the legal solutions.

2. Is conflict necessarily bad?

Ideally, any areas of potential conflict will be resolved in advance through open and frank discussion with consultants or lawyers, with suggested solutions being proffered. However, often this does not happen and conflict arises. Good advisers, who perhaps have mediation skills, may be able to 'mediate' the conflict, and if it has not become too bitter, make the parties see that it is in their interest to find a path through the conflict and work to a common end for everybody's benefit. If this can be achieved, everybody wins because any initial resentment or jealousy is ventilated, acknowledged and forgiven, and ideally the family can then move on, even more united than before the conflict arose. The main obstacle is that it is very difficult for a family to move on from any resentment, so setting themselves specific tasks and targets is crucial to overcome hard feelings.

3. Do advisers help prevent disputes?

What is crucial is getting the right team of advisers in at the beginning. That requires the family to understand what they want to achieve, which very few families do at the outset. They should seek the counsel of recommended advisers – consultants, psychologists and lawyers – who specialise in these fields. The more specialist people they talk to, the clearer they are likely to be as to what they need to achieve, and who is beneficial for them. It may be that the directors of the family office (if there is one) can help to formulate what the family wants to achieve, but they should only facilitate and not be a substitute for the family engaging in the process.

It is important to identify the type of adviser and their skills. Family business consultants, for example, are trained to identify areas of potential disagreement, which may grow into major family disputes in the future. There is, however, a significant gap in relaying that information to lawyers who, ideally, need to know and understand what those areas are in order to factor them into legal arrangements. Far too frequently, the lawyers, who will be structuring experts, do not factor in potentially contentious areas into their structuring arrangements.

The experience of disputes lawyers is crucial to understanding where disputes might arise in the future, and the circumstances which give rise to them, in order to prevent them. It is well worth sense-checking situations with them to see where others have gone wrong to try to avoid that happening in any current case. Perhaps the most common question asked of family governance advisers is: "What do other families do in this situation?" It is best to appoint advisers who can draw on experience and give constructive solutions.

4. Are disputes inevitable once the family gets larger at the third or fourth generation?

There is rarely inevitability about a dispute. It is the job of the lawyer to try to ensure that disputes do not become inevitable by helping to identify issues that might develop into contentious areas, with the family being prepared to face up to the difficult issues with the help of advisers. Yet too rarely does that happen. At second generational level (G2), there will often be harmony – but not always. For example, in the case of the well-known Indian Ambani family, as father Dhirubhai died intestate, sons Mukesh and Anil vied for control, so it was evident that there was a failure to plan at both G1 and G2 level.

However, harmony is less common (and more difficult) as the family member numbers grow at G3 and G4 level, so it becomes even more important to find ways to prevent disagreement.

The problem commonly arises because planning has been carried out for G1 and G2 but does not take into account future growth of the family. Hence, regular reviews of the arrangements need to take place; these arrangements should not be made all at once and must definitively stand the test of time. They should be reviewed at least annually and evolve as future generations grow up and new generations become involved.

So, what can lawyers do to facilitate this? Firstly, they can help ensure they are aware of all the issues that a family business consultant has unearthed. Secondly, a meaningful family constitution or family charter makes clear why these reviews are necessary and sets out a mechanism for carrying them out. Thirdly, an annual review, ideally prior to the family's annual retreat/assembly, should address these issues as G3 family members are growing up. Opinions vary as to the age at which children should be introduced to the business, but it makes sense to gradually introduce G3 to the type of business(es) run by the family, identifying who does what, where the businesses operate and that there may be satisfying opportunities for G3 to contribute in the future.

Lawyers can also draw up a shareholder agreement which will show G3 that the future of the shareholding and the business has been well planned. Introducing them to the concept early is much more likely to achieve buy-in than foisting it upon them when they are forging their own careers.

It is wise to introduce younger members to any trust structure that holds shares, and the rationale for setting up the trust. That way the vehicle is far more likely to be accepted when they are older and understand, for example, that each generation is effectively the 'guardian' of the shares rather than the 'owner'.

When G1 or G2 has put together an effective succession plan, it is often a challenge to get potentially larger groups of family members at G3 and G4 level to buy in to those arrangements. It is all very well stipulating in the constitution or charter that they are obliged to adhere to it, that they are obliged to sign a deed of adherence to the shareholder agreement and that they are obliged not to challenge the trust holding the business shares – but how do you enforce that? The constitution or charter should never be legally binding, as you cannot oblige future family members to be bound by a legal arrangement to which they have never agreed.

This is where it is very dangerous to underestimate the importance of G2 bringing up their children to understand and accept the arrangements that have been put in place. Indeed, we would go so far as to say that this is a key rationale as to why having governance in place at an early stage helps this process. It is much more difficult for G1 and G2 to dictate what the governance arrangements should be to adult G3; minors or young adults at G3 level can be brought up to understand and more easily accept such arrangements.

5. What are the legal mechanics used to prevent and plan to avoid disputes?

Legal mechanisms and frameworks alone cannot prevent a family dispute from arising. In fact, poorly conceived legal structures can in themselves create a forum for dispute, especially where there is a lack of understanding or appreciation by future generations as to why the structures were put in place. However, a well-thought-out structure that is properly implemented, and which ensures the buy-in of G3 and G4, can prevent an emotional seed from taking root, blossoming into a full-blown dispute and prejudicing the integrity of the family business. It is important to note that there is no 'panacea' or 'one size fits all'. A family may use a combination of legal mechanisms or none at all. But in any event, it is critical for the lawyers who will be drawing up the documents to understand the family and its objectives before recommending legal solutions. The purpose of this section is to set out what legal mechanisms could be used.

5.1 Family constitutions or charters

Families will often use family constitutions or charters to help prevent and plan for dealing with disputes. The terms 'constitution' and 'charter' are interchangeable, and for the purposes of this section we will use 'constitution'.

A family constitution is generally a non-binding agreement between key family members setting out the main philosophies of the family. Although non-binding, a family constitution is still a key framework document for dealing with family disputes. The process itself of discussing in a structured manner, agreeing and signing a constitution is just as important as the document that is produced at the end of the process. Where there is a family business, the constitution could cover (among many other things):

- how family members become involved in the family business;
- whether there is an expectation that they should become involved in the family business;
- how family members involved in the business are rewarded;
- dispute resolution provisions (such as mediation) should a conflict arise; and
- exit provisions in the event that a conflict cannot be resolved.

Exit provisions are a potentially contentious topic, yet they are an important release valve for family tensions. A starting point for a family frequently concerns how to keep the family business together. If a conflict arises and cannot be resolved, it can be best to allow a family member to walk away, but at what economic cost? The disgruntled family member should not take shares in the family business and, therefore, liquidity arrangements need to be put in place to provide a cash payout. The payout value is often linked to the notional value of the shares with a discount, but the question arising is what percentage discount? The discount has to be low enough for even a disgruntled family member to accept, but it also needs to be high enough to disincentivise family members from voluntarily choosing to walk away and 'cashing out'. The discount typically ranges between 30% and 50%. The valuation mechanism must also be clearly and comprehensively set out.

The mechanics of payment need to be sufficiently flexible to be workable. One really useful mechanism is for the holding or operating company to be able to buy back its own shares, as the company will likely have at least some of the liquidity to do so. Otherwise, future profits are likely to be the best mechanism to pay, as loans can be expensive. Family trusts should also have the power to make appropriate payouts in such circumstances. A realistic payout period must also be agreed.

The fundamental point about exit routes is that they should be agreed when relationships are friendly and strong, so everybody knows and agrees what will happen. This is more difficult with younger generations, but much more acceptable if the provisions have been in place for senior generations.

Setting out the expectations around the family business seeks to get the buy-in from all family members to mitigate the risk of conflict in the future. Buy-in from every generation is critical if the governance structure is to be prevented from falling apart.

Although a family constitution is generally non-binding, family members would be expected to sign and confirm their intention to follow the principles set out within it. A constitution will not itself stop a family member disputing or litigating and, therefore, it is important to consider how to embed the key principles of the constitution in the governing legal documents.

It is also vital that the constitution is a 'living and breathing' document that has continued relevance and is not just words on a page. One useful mechanism is to review one aspect of the constitution at every annual retreat. It is also vital to ensure it is not too complex and to make clear in what circumstances it can be changed in the future and the mechanism for so doing.

5.2 Trusts

A legal solution regularly used to prevent, and plan for, conflict around a family business is to place the shares into trust (subject to tax considerations). Trusts are very useful arrangements as they allow a family to divest themselves of the legal ownership of the shares, while being able to continue to benefit economically. It is, however, important that there is a full understanding of the nature and working of a trust to ensure that everyone is comfortable with it. The risk of conflict increases as a family grows and the shares are spread across multiple family members and generations. With the shares held by trustees, the fractional ownership risk is removed. However, the concern is that if no family member has any identifiable shares, they may not feel adequately connected to the business. The concept of each generation being the 'guardian' (through the trust mechanism) rather than the 'owner' of the shares is a useful one to promulgate.

In respect of setting up a trust, the following aspects can be considered to better protect the family business.

- *Governing law of the trust:* Each trust jurisdiction has its own firewall legislation. By 'firewall legislation' we mean legislation that has been put in place to prevent claims in a different jurisdiction being brought against a trustee. Typical claims may include family provision or inheritance claims, community of property claims, trustee in bankruptcy claims, or forced heirship claims. It would be prudent to consider these if the family business is being held via a trust and conflict mitigation is key.
- *Choice of trustee:* The family could decide on using lay trustees, professional trustees or set up their own private trust company (PTC). If there is a concern about potential conflict and a risk the trustees will be brought into any litigation, then the choice of trustee becomes very important.

If using a PTC, it would be advisable to have a professional trust company providing administrative services – in some jurisdictions this will be a requirement. The structure of the PTC will be an important consideration. In respect of the PTC board, there is also consideration about which, if any, family members sit on the board, and whether there are additional independent directors, which would generally be wise. Great care should be taken in drafting the articles, as generally this will be a public document from which outsiders can see how the PTC is operating and succession to the board. Options to avoid this can be looked at.

Consider the following example. The patriarch or matriarch states that he or she wants to retain control of the family trusts. No independent trustee can be trusted. Rarely is the question asked whether a trust is really the right vehicle. So, the lawyers suggest a PTC with a majority of family members on the board, but do they anticipate to what issues this might give rise? Do they think about whether it will really be run as a trust company when the family have little, if any, such experience? If it is not, it is likely to be a nominee arrangement, losing all the protection that a trust gives. Do they anticipate that they are actually creating an additional vehicle for the family to argue about? What happens if uncle dislikes nephew and refuses to permit a distribution to nephew, but allows one to his own son? Is it right that the same person might be an enforcer of the purpose trust which might own the PTC shares, a director of the PTC, a beneficiary of the trust, a director of the holding company and a director of the operating company? Instead of the PTC helping to prevent disputes, it creates a vehicle that may encourage disagreement without anticipating the future effects other than the retention of control.

However, if all these issues are dealt with properly, it might be an extremely useful arrangement for the family. The point is that all too often these issues are not addressed.

- *Reserved powers/protector provisions:* If conflict prevention is a key consideration, the number of reserved powers (powers reserved to the settlor, such as the power to manage the investments) and protector provisions (protector being a third party whose consent may be required for trustees to make certain decisions) and who takes on these roles will be important. If the reserved powers or the protector provisions are too extensive and are held by a family member, there is a risk that these could be attacked by any creditor or family member seeking an increased share who might seek to undermine the trust. However, if well-structured and planned, they can be very useful tools.
- *Dispute resolution provisions:* As with constitutions, dispute resolution provisions – mediation and/or arbitration – should be considered. If the shares in the family business are held in trust, the dispute resolution provisions could be included within the trust deed. These provisions would be triggered should there be a dispute about any aspect of the trust. The idea behind these is to seek to resolve a dispute outside the court system and public eye.

- *No-contest clauses:* These could be included to mitigate the risk of a family member attacking the trust or its validity. It is not possible to prevent a beneficiary from bringing legitimate claims against a trust, but a no-contest clause could be used to stop vexatious litigation.
- *Prenuptial/postnuptial provisions:* A potential conflict can arise when a beneficiary divorces. This can result in the shares in the family business being brought into a divorce settlement and being split up. A trust offers a level of protection in a divorce scenario, but the trust fund could still be taken into account in a division of the assets. The best way to protect the trust assets is to ensure that the family members enter into prenuptial or postnuptial agreement that excludes the trust assets from any division. A provision could be included in the terms of the trust requiring all beneficiaries to enter into a prenuptial or postnuptial agreement, in the absence of which that beneficiary will be excluded. This is often useful on a 'reverse psychology' basis – the beneficiary's spouse will only be able to benefit from the beneficiary's distributions if the agreement is entered into; otherwise, the beneficiary will be excluded and the spouse will have nothing to share during the marriage. Dynastic trusts (trusts that benefit multiple future generations and not just the generation getting divorced) are also effective in the divorce scenario.

5.3 Foundations

An alternative to using a trust to hold the shares in the family business is to use a foundation. Foundations are less widely used than trusts in common law jurisdictions, but much more usual in civil law jurisdictions. From a common law point of view, a foundation is often considered more of a hybrid vehicle akin to a trust or a company. Many of the provisions relating to trusts would also apply to a foundation, although there is a foundation council rather than a trustee.

Each jurisdiction with foundation laws has slightly different provisions. However, a key advantage and difference between a foundation and a trust is that foundations are incorporated and have separate legal personality; therefore, the legal and beneficial interest in foundation property is held by the foundation. In such a scenario, no beneficiary of the foundation has an interest in the foundation property, which may reduce the risk of attack. Furthermore, the council may not owe any beneficiary a fiduciary duty, which means that it can hold riskier assets, which may include operating businesses.

5.4 Companies

Companies are extremely useful entities in the context of family governance, because they can be used to create mechanisms that govern how each member of the family participates in the business, and there is no limit to the subtlety and complexity of the mechanisms that can be introduced. For example, in some jurisdictions it is possible to have a 'hybrid' company, which is a combination of a company limited by shares and a company limited by guarantee. Different rights can be given to shareholders and guarantee members. As we have said, the scope for family discord to disrupt the workings of the family business is greatly reduced if there are clear, agreed and binding rules determining how decisions are made – companies can be structured to include such rules, possibly along with a shareholder agreement. Typically, a family business will already be incorporated, so when it comes to implementing governance structures the family can (subject to tax considerations) either reorganise the shares in the holding company, or create a new holding company with the desired share structure to hold the entire group.

Examples of typical provisions in the articles of a family company include the following:

(a) Restrictions on who can be a shareholder

The articles can provide that shares can be held only by someone who is, for example, a blood descendant of the patriarch or matriarch. The obvious purpose of such a restriction is to ensure that non-family members, typically spouses, can never be shareholders (including on a divorce). The class of permitted shareholders should be extended to include trustees of a family trust, although the term 'family trust' has to be carefully defined; typically, trustees would be permitted to be shareholders if the only people who could benefit from the relevant trust were members of the permitted class of shareholders.

(b) Division between control and benefit

Shares ordinarily carry the right to vote, but other shares can be issued which carry no rights to participate in decisions of the members but which, conversely, carry the right to the capital value of the shares and dividends. The voting shares can be reserved for the elder generation who want to retain control, for example, and the shares that carry economic rights only can be given to more junior members of the family or to a trust. In this way, it may be easier to persuade the senior generation to cede some control. In time, of course, it is possible that the voting shares are transferred from one generation to the next; the succession to them is vital. It is very often the case that, as the family grows, it becomes unworkable to have voting shares held by all family members, because either power is too concentrated in one branch of the family, or it is too fragmented, so frequently by the time G2 is receding, the voting control might be in the hands of trustees, or voting and economic shares are merged again.

(c) *Composition of the board*

In the context of governance, certain shares can carry the right to appoint a majority of the directors, meaning that the holder of that share can, if they feel that the management of the company has become unsatisfactory, change the composition of the board so as to populate it with directors who are of a similar view. The iterations are endless, and some further possibilities are best illustrated by an example. Suppose there is a family business, run by the originating family which has now developed so that there is a principal offshoot. That slightly smaller, but still important, branch of the family wants to stay involved in the management of the business, but it is acknowledged that the primary branch should retain ultimate control over certain matters. The articles may provide that business can be conducted only if there is an equal number of directors from the two branches, but also provide that, in the event of a stalemate (with one side voting for a proposal and the other voting against it), the chairperson has the casting vote, and in turn that the chairperson can be appointed by the holder of a particular share, which remains in the hands of the founding patriarch or matriarch.

The articles can also provide that each director sits on the board for a certain time – four years, for example – and at the end of that period must step down unless reappointed. Standard articles usually provide that the directors are responsible for appointing others to the board but, as illustrated above, there are other mechanisms that can be deployed so as to keep more control at shareholder level.

5.5 Shareholder agreements

In addition to the articles, an important constitutional document that is deployed in many cases is a shareholder agreement. While the articles can set out what rights attach to each share (ie, the rights between the company and the shareholders), a shareholder agreement is essential to introduce more subtle rules governing the proceedings as between holders of the same type of share (ie, the contract between the shareholders). It should also deal with permitted transferees of shares in the future, consistent with the articles, so there is clarity on this issue; that should need to be married up with beneficiaries in any trust set up to hold the shares. Also, it can be prudent to put more governance provisions into a shareholder agreement than the articles, because the latter are usually in the public domain, whereas shareholder agreements are private.

Shareholder agreements often include a list of 'reserved matters' – that is, matters which would ordinarily be decided by the board, but which are considered to be so important that the consent of the shareholders is required. For example, reserved matters might include the company taking out borrowing above a certain threshold, starting a new type of business or selling an existing one, or appointing directors of trading subsidiaries. As ever, introducing the concept of reserved matters is to ensure that ultimate control is preserved by a certain person or group. It should also deal with the basis of decision making.

The shareholder agreement might also include provisions concerned with appointing directors. Absent any special provisions in the articles or elsewhere, it is the directors who appoint others to the board, but a shareholder agreement could set out what sort of qualifications a person must have, or what qualities they must be able to demonstrate, before they can be considered for election to the board. For example, anyone wishing to be appointed to the board of the holding company of a group might be required to have served on the board of a subsidiary for a certain amount of time, and be able to demonstrate experience of having managed transactions of a particular type or magnitude. These sorts of provisions typically make their first appearance in a family constitution, but they can be given more 'teeth' if they also appear in a shareholder agreement, which will be legally binding. Generally, it is best not to have these sorts of provisions appearing in the articles, as they would be personal and entirely specific to the particular family, and thus indicative of their principles and dynamics.

Perhaps above all, a shareholder agreement demonstrates to the next generation that the governance arrangements are well thought out and well set out, making it a more attractive proposition for the younger generations to become involved. Contrast that with poorly structured, or unstructured, arrangements which will be a disincentive for them to become involved. They might justifiably also think that the business is run in such a way.

5.6 Wills

As illustrated by case of the Ambanis, we cannot overlook the importance of the wills of each member of the family. If all the shares in the business have been settled in trust, then the family's wills are not relevant, save for other assets (unless, which is rare, the trust instrument is drafted to enable a beneficiary to direct trust assets in his or her will). However, if there are shares in personal ownership, then wills can be very important. Without prompting from the lawyers, the family's wills are often overlooked, typically because family members are simply not willing to contemplate their own mortality. An untimely death can end up being not only a tragedy on a personal level for the surviving family members, but a trigger for years of dispute, all of which could have been pre-empted. A family constitution may be drawn up to require wills to be in place.

5.7 Lasting/enduring powers of attorney

There have been so many instances when senior members of a family running a business have become mentally incapacitated to the significant detriment of the business and the family if there is inadequate planning in place. Not only is it wise to have an appropriate power of attorney in place, but provisions should be incorporated in the family constitution and shareholder agreement pre-empting incapacity and ensuring all functions can be carried out effectively as and when incapacity arises.

5.8 Insurance solutions

There are many insurance solutions on the market, but perhaps the most important is some sort of 'key man' cover. This is particularly relevant during a period when there is no obvious successor to the principal. It will be essential to appoint someone suitable to take control of the reigns. Insurance may also be desirable if there is an intention for one family member or branch to be able to buy out another on death, or simply to provide liquidity at that time to pay taxes and other costs so the family business does not need to be broken up.

6. Conclusions

The key to making legal mechanisms as effective as possible is to ensure that the process of ascertaining the family issues, concerns, worries, wishes and aspirations is dealt with comprehensively. Going through this process ensures both that the right legal mechanisms are adopted, and that the detail of those mechanisms is geared towards family harmony in the long term, with effective business succession for the future. The remaining issue is to decide who can alter those mechanisms, and how and when ruling from the grave is less than ideal, as change in so many areas of our lives will be sure to mean that structures set up in the past will need to be reviewed regularly and critically.

Family businesses and divorce

Katie O'Callaghan
Boodle Hatfield LLP

This chapter examines the effects of marital breakdown on a family business as a whole, the individual shareholders and their families. The financial impact of divorce on family businesses is significant and should not be underestimated. Certainly, in the United Kingdom many of those involved do not appreciate the breadth and depth of the English Family Court's powers to make financial orders on divorce. The wide-ranging nature of its discretion means that it is crucial for family businesses to use proper protocols to protect assets and reduce the otherwise high levels of stress that can stem from a marriage breakdown within the family where multiple family members of different generations are tied together financially. Those who plan ahead are likely to reap significant benefits in the long term. Open discussions about these issues early on can lead to better outcomes. Prepared families can manage risks and focus on sustainable growth safe in the knowledge that they have put in place suitable measures to maximise the protection of the business.

This chapter has two main sections. Section 1 covers potential exposures to family businesses in the event that a shareholder spouse gets divorced. Section 2 addresses the protective practical and legal measures that family businesses ought to consider in advance to mitigate risk. These include the consideration of pre- and postnuptial agreements, family governance techniques, trusts and family investment companies (FICs).

The chapter addresses both heterosexual and same-sex married couples, civil partners and cohabiting couples. References to 'spouses' and 'divorce' should also be read as applying to civil partners and civil partnership dissolutions. All references to 'the court' are to the English Family Court, which is responsible for determining the financial outcome as a consequence of a divorce that has been issued in England and Wales. We appreciate that many reading this chapter will be outside the United Kingdom but hope that the example of the United Kingdom provides helpful input when discussing matrimonial risk with families. We also discuss the reach of the English courts, which is, of course, relevant for international families.

1. Exposure: risks to a business-owning family upon a marital breakdown

1.1 The court's powers: spouses vs cohabitees

It is first vital to understand the extreme difference in the law in England and Wales between spouses and cohabitees upon a relationship breakdown. Spouses have extensive rights to bring financial claims against their ex-spouse in the event of a divorce. For example, the court has the power to order:

- the payment of a lump sum or series of lump sums by one spouse to the other;
- the sale or transfer of properties owned by either spouse or in their joint names;
- the sale or transfer of shares or other assets;
- the sharing or transfer of pensions;
- the maintenance of a spouse for a defined term or on a lifelong basis (it is important to note that maintenance claims are capable of being capitalised into one lump sum payment in place of ongoing monthly sums); and
- child maintenance during minority or until completion of education, including tertiary education – this may include the cost of a nanny and school fees.

From a family business perspective, the court could make an order that a shareholder spouse's shares ought to be transferred to their ex-spouse or sold.

In contrast, common law marriage does not exist in this jurisdiction and there is no concept of the 'common law spouse'. As such, whether an unmarried couple have lived together for two years or two decades, a cohabitant does not have anything like the same financial rights as a spouse in the event of a relationship breakdown. If the cohabitees have no children together, any claims are strictly limited to those arising out of property law. The risk of being exposed to a financial claim against one cohabiting partner's shareholding in a family business upon separation – however long the relationship might have been – is therefore negligible.

If the unmarried couple have a child together, the court has more extensive powers but they are still far more restrictive than those that can be awarded on divorce and are limited only to claims on behalf of or for the benefit of the child. As a consequence, it is unlikely that such an award could ever include the transfer of a shareholding unless it is the only asset available. Even then, the court would most likely deal with the matter by ordering, for example, the purchase of a property by the shareholder for the benefit of their ex-partner and child on the basis that the shareholder could access funding via the company.

1.2 Approach of the court to the division of assets on divorce

The court has wide discretion when determining which orders it should make and how to divide up assets on divorce. This applies to worldwide wealth. The issues covered in this chapter therefore apply to family businesses globally as well as to those established in this country. The potential risks, together with the protections available, are no less important if the business is located abroad. Family business owners in particular need to be alive to the fact that this discretion extends not only to 'matrimonial' wealth built up by a couple during a marriage, but also to wealth brought into the marriage by one party or assets such as shares which are inherited or gifted by one party's family. Shares in a family business will be treated as a financial resource by the court. As such, they will be taken into account as part of any financial proceedings.

The court is renowned for granting generous awards to the financially weaker party on divorce. It is no coincidence that London is known as 'the divorce capital of the world'. The starting point where the assets are greater than both parties' 'needs' is a 50:50 division of the assets. Arguments can then be advanced to depart from equality on the basis that it would not be a fair outcome if, for example, some of the assets were acquired prior to the marriage or post-separation or are inherited, gifted or dynastic in nature.

When the court is considering the treatment of shares held in a family-owned business, the illiquid nature of the shares is likely to be highly relevant to outcome, as is the fact that the business is owned by multiple third parties. The court would seek to tamper as little as possible with the shareholding unless there is no other means of meeting the non-shareholder spouse's financial claim. If the remaining asset base is minimal and there is insufficient wealth within the matrimonial pot, the court would examine practical ways of meeting the departing spouse's needs. In doing so it will have regard to the following:

(a) Nature of the shareholding

A shareholding of a dynastic quality, particularly one inherited by one spouse, gifted from family or put in trust before a marriage, is more likely to be treated as 'non-matrimonial' property than, for example, a more recently acquired shareholding which perhaps built up during the marriage.

It is important to note that many financially weaker spouses have successfully advanced arguments through the courts that non-matrimonial assets (to include shares) have been 'matrimonialised' by virtue of being 'mingled' with marital assets or used as a primary resource for the maintenance of the family. The practical advice to family business owners is that keeping such assets strictly separate from the rest of the marital assets, even if they are received during the marriage, will assist in maximising the prospects of ring-fencing them on divorce as non-matrimonial.

If the court determines an asset is non-matrimonial, it may exclude it from the marital pot or depart from a 50/50 outcome as a consequence.

(b) Lifestyle during the marriage

The standard of living enjoyed by the spouses during their marriage is highly relevant in considering what is reasonable for each of their needs in the future.

Where the family's lifestyle has benefitted materially from the family business's success (eg, through regular dividends), this is likely to be a vital component of the case, particularly if it has been the family's primary source of income.

(c) Income stream

A court will be more hesitant to tamper with the underlying shareholding if the family is dependent upon the income stream that flows from it. It is seen as counterproductive given this is likely to be required to meet the needs of both parties post-divorce.

(d) Length of the marriage

The longer the marriage, the harder it is to justify a departure from a 50:50 outcome. Where there is a shareholding in a family business, the length of time within that marriage that the shareholding has been enjoyed by the shareholder and the departing spouse would also be relevant.

(e) Personal assets

The personal assets of each spouse that are held outside of the family business will be a key consideration in how the court treats a shareholding. If the court is able to meet the non-shareholder spouse's award from other assets, it would seek to do so. However, if the bulk of the wealth is held in the value of the shares, it may have no option. In such instances, the court is likely to consider lump sum payments by the shareholder spouse over a period of time based on the liquidity of the company; forecasts on future capital events; and/or likely future income from it. A transfer or sale of the shares would be a last resort.

(f) Liquidity

The court will want to establish whether value can be extracted from the business and if so, how easily and over what period of time. This is vital given the court will need to balance meeting the non-shareholder spouse's entitlement without damaging the company's financial position.

It is important to note that while the court has the ability to order a sale of a spouse's shares in a business, it does not have the power to order a sale of the company's underlying assets. Accordingly, when considering liquidity, the court cannot order the sale of an investment property, for example, which is owned by the business.

Liquidity issues are often addressed by ordering deferred lump sums to a departing spouse which are equal to a percentage share in the business, the trigger date being the next liquidity event of the business.

(g) *Clean break*

Where possible, the court will want to sever spouses' financial ties as quickly as possible to achieve a clean break.

For this reason, a transfer of shares by one spouse to the other in a private family business is not an appealing outcome, especially where one of them is heavily involved in the day-to-day running or management of that business. However, sometimes this is the only feasible option available to the court if it wants to avoid a sale of the shares (or indeed if a sale is extremely challenging) and there is not enough liquidity within the company or elsewhere to meet one spouse's entitlement. A court is more likely to be deterred from this sort of structure if there are multiple shareholders. Where the divorcing spouse is the only shareholder (even if they ultimately intend to pass those shares onto future generations), there is more risk of a transfer of shares in the absence of other wealth to meet the other's needs.

In such circumstances, the court will need to consider whether there should be future longstop dates by which one spouse should be bought out of the business so that they are not tied indefinitely. It will also need to put in place appropriate measures to ensure the business is run with both spouses' interests protected.

This may ring alarm bells to family business owners who could end up with a restrictive shareholders' agreement in place to protect the divorcing spouse's shareholding which dictates how the company ought to be run.

1.3 International businesses

An asset is not outside the reach of the court if it is based offshore. Provided one or both of the spouses are habitually resident or domiciled in England or Wales, divorce proceedings can be issued. The court has the power to make orders in relation to a spouse's worldwide wealth. Although many judges would favour making orders over assets based in this country rather than those which are offshore, international families with business interests need to consider carefully the exposure of its shareholders to this jurisdiction given that it is known to be far more generous to the financially weaker spouse than most others.

Foreign assets do, however, come with their own challenges given the court has less influence over whether or not that order is capable of being enforced in the foreign jurisdiction. As such, many judges favour making orders over assets based in this country to try to mitigate the risk of the financially weaker spouse having to spend months – possibly years – seeking to enforce any breach of an order. This is certainly something for family businesses to be aware of if its shares are the only asset of a shareholder spouse in this jurisdiction.

1.4 Disclosure and privacy considerations

There is an absolute duty on spouses to provide full, frank, clear and up-to-date disclosure as part of the financial process on divorce. Even if the asset was acquired before the marriage, kept entirely separate to marital wealth and/or was received during the marriage from family by way of gift or inheritance, the obligation remains to disclose fully.

In respect of business interests, this involves full details of the percentage shareholding, an estimate of value, full accounts and a breakdown of the level of income received – by way of earned remuneration and/or by way of dividend.

The duty of disclosure continues during the litigation: if a spouse's financial situation has changed since providing their original disclosure, they must inform the other party and the court at the earliest opportunity.

It is important to note that financial proceedings upon divorce are no longer invariably held in private. There is now a great deal of emphasis on transparency and allowing access to the press. There is an inherent risk that a case could be publicly reported if a financial settlement is not reached. While the court can impose reporting restrictions, it is unlikely to exclude the media entirely. The reputational risks associated with an acrimonious divorce can therefore be significant – not just for the individual shareholder spouse embroiled in it but also for the wider family and for the business as a whole.

There is an increasing trend towards alternative dispute resolution to resolve finances on divorce. This can take many forms and has the advantage of complete privacy and discretion. It is often quicker and more cost-efficient. Having said that, it requires both spouses to commit to the process, which can often be problematic. The potential for damage to a family business's brand in the long term is a serious consideration and the opposing spouse may well use this as leverage to exert pressure on the shareholder spouse to put a generous offer on the table to avoid adverse publicity.

1.5 Company valuations on divorce

Company valuations are often a contentious topic in divorce proceedings. Any private family business owner will know that seeking to attribute a value to the business carries with it a level of subjectivity, discretion and uncertainty. However, the court will expect a value to be established for any shareholding so that it can determine how that value should be accounted for in the distribution of the overall assets. Where a spouse brought the shareholding to the marriage, the court may wish to establish the value of those shares at the time of the marriage versus the value at the time of divorce so as to ascertain the growth during the marriage. This is particularly so if the shareholder spouse plays a significant role in the business, which is likely to have contributed to any increase in value in the shares as opposed to a passive shareholder.

The starting point, which is slightly artificial, is the price an arm's-length purchaser will pay for the shares. Accordingly, the valuation of private company shares can be complicated.

If it is not possible to agree a valuation, the court will usually appoint a single joint expert (SJE) to produce a report. It is by no means certain that an SJE valuation would be a prerequisite and the court must grant permission for an SJE to be instructed if it is not agreed by both spouses. The test applied by the court is whether the valuation is 'necessary'. That will depend on the facts of the case, for example, on the size and nature of the shareholding, the family's reliance on the income stream from that shareholding during the marriage and the remainder of the wealth outside of the shareholding. However, it is best to assume it will be required in the event that a shareholder gets divorced.

The valuation exercise of the shares of the individual shareholder will be informed by a number of factors such as their marketability, discounts for the size of shareholding and availability of purchasers.

The SJE will be asked to report on value and liquidity, to include the ability to extract funds, for example, via dividends or borrowing in order to meet the departing spouse's claim(s). The report may also include an opinion on the dividend policy and the entitlements that particular shareholder derives such as salary, bonus and benefits. This will inform the court's view as to the likely structure of any financial outcome, including not only the division of the capital but also the income provision for spousal maintenance, child maintenance and the payment of school fees etc.

The court is mindful that it is not appropriate to treat shares in a business and other assets, such as cash and property, as like for like – one is likely to be illiquid and potentially risky, whereas the other is often described as 'copper-bottomed'. This is a factor when determining the distribution of wealth between spouses as the court must balance risk. This can lead to the court determining that an unequal division of the total assets is appropriate to reflect the risk imbalance.

1.6 Employment considerations

It is not uncommon in family businesses for a shareholder's spouse to play a role, whether formal or informal, in the company. This can create complications on the breakdown of a marriage for obvious reasons. It is strongly advised from a matrimonial perspective that spouses do not become shareholders in the business, particularly if it is multi-generational and there is a desire to continue its legacy by passing it on to future generations.

As for being on the payroll, this could also create difficulties. Firstly, the spouse might argue that their efforts and role in the business have contributed to the generation or preservation of the family's wealth and secondly, they might argue that their earning potential is impacted if they are forced to give up their role. The former could lead to arguments that the increase in value of the shares during the marriage ought to be treated as 'marital' and divided 50/50 and the latter could lead to increased claims for spousal maintenance.

In an ideal world, the involvement of spouses would be avoided altogether, albeit this is often unrealistic and impractical. If they are involved, it is better that this is done formally with appropriate remuneration commensurate to their work in a bid to mitigate claims that the value of work undertaken during the marriage ought to be recouped through any financial settlement.

2. Protection: what can a business-owning family do to mitigate risk?

Raising the topic of legal mechanisms such as prenuptial agreements and offshore trusts are not the natural language of love and so introducing them as part of pre-wedding planning with a new fiancé(e) can be difficult. However, planning for the possibility of divorce is a vital component of prudent governance and succession planning for business-owning families.

The strong advice is to consider protective measures well in advance of them being needed. A proactive rather than a reactive approach is essential.

2.1 Family governance

A policy that sets out the expectations that apply to all shareholders (and future shareholders) in a family business can serve to depersonalise sensitive conversations around subjects like prenuptial agreements and inheritance. If and when any children or grandchildren of a family-owned business marry, they will be entering the marriage with a valuable, family-generated asset which may have been gifted to them prior to the marriage or which they may be due to receive during the marriage. In order to protect these interests for future generations, the family office and/or directors (in conjunction with the shareholders) should adopt and maintain a strategy which consistently emphasises the 'dynastic' nature of this asset.

The family office or the directors of a family business might wish to come up with a strategy for discussing with the shareholders the more sensitive issues outlined in this chapter in the context of an overall policy for any family business. For example, requiring all shareholders to enter into a form of prenuptial agreement in advance of marriage might form part of the family governance documentation.

This can create complexity if it seeks to bind a third party who is not a shareholder, but it can be included as a strong recommendation to the family, together with other important expectations such as keeping their wills up to date.

A general policy which is applicable to all shareholders and which is put in place at an early stage is likely to render the issue less personal and simply part of prudent forward planning for what is a dynastic family asset.

It is also important to ensure that there is a strategy established in advance for dealing with any sticking points or disputes which might arise from such policies given that some individual shareholders will not instinctively like the idea of some of the protective measures being asked of them. Ideally, any succession planning or governance documentation would demonstrate a willingness on behalf of the relevant generations to acknowledge the importance of such measures for the wider family and the business as a whole.

An additional question is whether a family policy ought to be established in relation to shareholders' spouses and civil partners and the extent of their involvement in, knowledge of and enjoyment of the family business and its successes.

The family office and/or directors need to be aware that if a shareholder is entirely reliant upon the distributions from the company to fund their lifestyle, this will raise the presumption in the eyes of the court that the asset is a resource and that the distribution could or should continue post-divorce. A court will not be persuaded that such benefit will suddenly cease or drastically diminish post-divorce (which is often asserted by the shareholder spouse in a bid to minimise exposure to claims for spousal maintenance).

Care should therefore be taken as to quantum and frequency of distributions to the next generation and how they are documented. The same can be said for loans from the business to a shareholder. This can, of course, be challenging in situations where the shareholder's sole source of wealth is the business. Protocols and policies relating to dividends and/or capital events should consider the matrimonial position and the attitude of the court.

For example, if dividends were to be declared on an *ad hoc* basis as and when individuals need funds, it would be open for their spouse to argue that it was always the case that their spouse had easy access to cash 'on demand' and that this should be considered when making a financial award in their favour. The court will not hesitate to make financial orders based on assumptions, for example, that the company will ensure a dividend is declared to a shareholder spouse in order to comply with the terms of that order if history evidences that the shareholder benefitted from the company as and when needed.

It would seem prudent (purely from a matrimonial perspective) for a family and corporate governance structure (ie, a board compact or family charter) to be established to set out the clear strategy and aims for the preservation of capital held within the family business, and a strict and consistent dividend policy could be agreed and recorded.

Although the court would always be reluctant to order a sale of shares in a family-owned business, ultimately it has the power to do so, and so consideration of these issues as part of a corporate governance review would be prudent to seek to ensure that, overall, the family business remains as minimally affected as possible.

As for the ownership of the underlying shares themselves, there can be very good tax reasons for wanting to pass shares to a spouse (eg, in the United Kingdom such transfers are exempt from inheritance tax). However, if the key focus is preserving the shareholding for future family members, shares in the company should not be transferred to new spouses. Family businesses therefore need to balance matrimonial protection against the potential tax benefits of involving spouses.

One way of potentially protecting the business for future generations might be to add restrictions in the articles of association/shareholders' agreement and/or family charter, which would prevent the transfer of shares to third parties who are not lineal family members. Any succession plan or governance policy that has been agreed will clearly impact on the drafting of those documents (and vice versa) and so it is vital that the principles have been established as part of any succession planning process and have been recorded clearly and accurately. Those who are affected need to be aware of such plans and policies and be content with them.

2.2 Prenuptial and postnuptial agreements (PNAs)

In most cases, the preparation of a PNA is not an attractive prospect. The idea of entering into such an agreement is often sprung on one party by the other in the lead-up to the wedding. They are asked to deal with the time-consuming requirements of agreeing the terms of a PNA while planning for their special day, which is far from ideal. However, if approached with care, consideration and careful planning, this form of agreement can be a highly effective way of mitigating risk to a family business in the event of a divorce.

(a) Status of PNAs

PNAs are increasingly common in this jurisdiction and are generally considered to afford people with the greatest protection in relation to assets held in their personal names.

PNAs do not have legally binding status in England and Wales. In essence, the current state of the law is that the court should give effect to a PNA that is freely entered into by each party with a full appreciation of its implications unless in the circumstances prevailing it would not be fair to hold the parties to their agreement.

The criteria to maximise the prospects of a PNA being respected and upheld on divorce are now well established. In short, it is best practice that the following points apply:

- Each party has independent advice from a family law specialist on the nature and effect of the PNA;

- The parties provide a summary of their finances at the time of entering the PNA;
- Neither party is put under pressure to enter the PNA; and
- The terms of the PNA are fair to the financially weaker spouse.

If PNAs are compliant with these requirements as set out by the courts in previous cases, they have a strong chance of being upheld.

If a PNA is under scrutiny by the court as to whether or not its terms should be upheld, the essential questions that the court is likely to consider are:

- Did both parties understand it?
- Were both parties properly advised as to its terms?
- Did either party put the other party under pressure to sign it?
- Was there disclosure?
- Did each party willingly sign the PNA?
- Did either party exploit a dominant position either financially or otherwise?
- Was the PNA entered into in the knowledge that there would be a child or children?
- Has any unforeseen circumstance arisen since the PNA was made that would make it unfair to hold the parties to it?
- What is the financial provision in the PNA and does it adequately meet the needs of the financially weaker spouse?
- Are there any grounds for concluding than an injustice would be done by holding each of the parties to the terms of the PNA?

It is important to note that even if a PNA is not upheld fully by the court on divorce, it can still act as a 'drag' on the financially weaker spouse's claims thereby ensuring that their entitlement is significantly discounted as a consequence of having entered into the PNA.

(b) Cohabitation rather than marriage

While perhaps obvious, it should be highlighted that PNAs deal with the division of assets on divorce only. Therefore, for cohabiting partners, thought might be given to 'living together' or 'cohabitation' agreements.

An interest in a family business is unlikely to be capable of being attacked upon separation even without one of these agreements but such documents have the advantage that:

- they legally regulate the arrangement between the cohabitees;
- they record intention at the outset and can provide for more certainty to avoid litigation on relationship breakdown;
- they protect assets, confidentiality and provide a mechanism for resolution of disputes on separation; and

- they commence the use of regulating personal relationships via legal documents at the outset of the relationship – they are a useful precursor to PNAs.

(c) ***Postnups vs prenups***

While postnuptial agreements are approached by the court in the same way as prenuptial agreements, it is generally considered to be more challenging to get a postnuptial agreement 'over the line' given there is less incentive on the financially weaker party to enter into it once the marriage has taken place and given it is likely to limit their entitlement on divorce in some way. Conversely, the focal date of an impending wedding tends to give parties the impetus to complete a prenuptial agreement. Having said that, there will be circumstances where it is simply not possible to put in place a prenuptial agreement in advance of a wedding and, in such instances, it would be wise to consider seriously the idea of entering a postnuptial agreement.

(d) ***Fairness***

To give a PNA the best chance of being upheld, it must be fair to the financially weaker party. Therefore, it would not be possible for the financially stronger spouse simply to ring-fence all of the assets in their own name and provide nothing to the financially weaker spouse on a divorce if the financially weaker spouse does not have sufficient assets of their own to meet their needs. This can create a challenge if the shareholder has little to nothing in the way of assets outside their shares in any family business. Equally challenging is a situation where a party has not yet inherited any shares but expects to do so in the future, but has little or no other wealth at the time of signing the PNA, which can be a common scenario for the next generation of any family business. An agreement which is manifestly unfair to the financially weaker party will not be upheld. It is important to understand that a PNA does not mean that there will be no financial provision on divorce. However, it is likely to assist in ensuring that any financial provision is less onerous than it would be if determined by a judge without such an agreement in place.

(e) ***Communication***

Communication between generations is vital. It is almost always easier for the person who is seeking the PNA to be able to present the concept to their fiancé(e) as a standard policy which applies across the family as a whole (or at least, across that generation). This removes the sting and limits the feeling that this is a personal affront against the other party. If they understand that the agreement is a standard family-wide protocol that was put in place by a family office, founding shareholder parents and/or trustees long before their relationship even began, it is often a far more palatable conversation to have.

(f) *Disclosure requirements, confidentiality and privacy*

One of the prerequisites for giving a PNA the maximum prospect of being upheld in the event of a divorce is the provision of full financial disclosure at the time of entering the agreement.

The concern with wealthy individuals and families is that disclosure is a large and complicated exercise which will involve significant work, yet this does not have to be the case. It is essential that both spouses are represented by solicitors who regularly deal with PNAs of this nature. Generally, the disclosure requirement is approached pragmatically and it does not result in a massive accounting exercise. Instead, the key is ensuring that the disclosure captures the salient aspects of the wealth and potential wealth.

It is best practice to include within this some narrative about future prospects, namely potential inheritance or gifts that a spouse may benefit from during the marriage. It is common for the financially stronger party entering the PNA to have some level of knowledge about the likelihood of acquiring shares in their family business. However, in many instances, that party does not have in-depth knowledge about their parents' intentions as to passing down wealth either during their lifetime or upon their death. While it is advisable to include as much information as possible – particularly if the protection of that future wealth is the very reason for entering the PNA – there is no obligation on the financially stronger party to push for detailed information about their inheritance prospects if that is not forthcoming from the older generation (and indeed, the older generation may not yet have clear intentions and/or those intentions may change over time). Ultimately, the disclosure can only be based on the current knowledge of the two parties entering into the PNA. As such, the financially stronger party is only obliged to include details in the PNA about what they know about their future prospects. It may, therefore, be that the most the party can say by way of disclosure is that they may benefit from the demise of a member of the family and/or from a trust but the extent of their potential benefit is presently unknown to them.

In other scenarios, the next generation does have relatively extensive knowledge about their likely prospects but either they or their parents are reluctant to include the full extent of this in their disclosure, perhaps because their future spouse is not fully aware of the family's financial position. Where a family adopt a low profile as to their wealth, they are understandably nervous about communicating details of that to a third party who is not a lineal member of the family. As mentioned above, if the purpose of the PNA is to seek to ring-fence future family wealth, it is beneficial to include as much information as possible about what the expectation is so that there is a clear record at the point of signing the agreement as to what the circumstances are envisaged to be in the future. In such cases, a pre-disclosure confidentiality agreement can form part of the process, which should safeguard the privacy of the information disclosed.

Even without having such an agreement, PNAs tend to include confidentiality provisions which oblige both parties to keep the content of the agreement, together with the disclosure attached to it, confidential.

PNAs also tend to incorporate confidentiality and privacy provisions including seeking, in the event of marriage breakdown, the exclusion of the media. This cannot be guaranteed to work but it is likely to be persuasive and ought to provide some comfort to family businesses. Moreover, many PNAs now include a commitment to resolve any disputes arising from the terms of the agreement by way of mediation, informal dispute resolution and/or arbitration rather than issuing proceedings via the court. This ought to assist in ensuring that any such disputes are dealt with out of the spotlight and in complete privacy.

(g) International considerations

For those couples who have connections to multiple countries either as a result of their asset base, their domicile, habitual residence or future plans to live abroad, advice may need to be sought from specialist lawyers in those jurisdictions when entering a PNA. While this does add an element of complexity, it is an important consideration given that the enforceability and validity of PNAs varies from country to country. It is therefore vital, particularly if one of the key assets is shares in a family business, that it is established in advance of any marriage how a foreign court would approach a PNA and the powers that court has to disregard it and make orders in relation to shares held in a business. By way of example, the law in relation to financial provision on divorce differs substantially in Scotland compared to England.

PNAs will ordinarily include a jurisdiction clause stating the parties' intention as to the jurisdiction in which any divorce should take place in order to seek to retain some control over where proceedings might be issued in the future and thereby ensuring that they take place in a jurisdiction where the PNA would be respected.

2.3 Trusts as a vehicle for holding company shares

Trusts can be useful to keep inherited assets such as a family business ring-fenced, particularly if they are set up as non-nuptial settlements long before a beneficiary has any intention of marrying. They can therefore offer another useful layer of protection for family businesses.

In the event of a divorce of a beneficiary, it is likely that the trustees will be asked questions about the trust and to provide documentation. It will be important for the trustees to take their own independent advice before replying to such enquiries.

Typically, trustees will wish to be as helpful as possible to the divorcing beneficiary given it is in the trustees' interest to maximise the protection of the trust. However, it is important for the court to see the trustees act – and be seen to act – impartially so they maintain their independence. It is essential not to conflate their knowledge about the strategy for the settlement with the beneficiary's knowledge, as the two may be very different and have implications not only for the beneficiary getting divorced but also the other beneficiaries.

When trusts are set up, there will often be a letter of wishes from the settlor setting out their overall intentions for the trust and how they wish the beneficiaries to benefit, and in what circumstances. Moreover, these letters of wishes can also be updated and ought to be where there are material events within the family or a changing attitude of the settlor.

The letter of wishes can usefully underline that the trust's assets are dynastic assets intended to benefit future generations of the family. Letters of wishes are not always made available as part of any disclosure within financial remedy proceedings on divorce. However, if they are beneficial in recording the underlying intention and dynastic quality of the trust, it may be beneficial to the beneficiary spouse if the letter of wishes is disclosed.

The court is accustomed to considering offshore trust structures. Using such structures will not provide complete protection to assets they contain, though it will add another layer to the ring-fencing of assets. Offshore enforcement is clearly more complicated and costly, so the court is likely to look to meet a spouse's claim from assets onshore, if possible, to offer them more security.

It is important to be aware that the way in which trustees manage the trust funds and the benefits that have flowed to beneficiaries at different times is likely to impact the outcome. The court will want to understand what has been happening on the ground, such as the extent of the distributions made to the beneficiary spouse during the latter years of the marriage and whether the family was entirely dependent upon these to meet the standard of living. This will be highly relevant to the court's consideration of a departing spouse's needs post-divorce.

2.4 Family investment companies

Like trusts, FICs can be set up to ring-fence family assets. Establishing a family investment company can also act as a useful trigger to ask spouses of family members to sign postnuptial agreements if that is deemed desirable at the time and prenuptial agreements are not in place. FICs are simply private limited companies used to hold family investments. They are often considered in circumstances where a family business has been sold in order to hold the proceeds of sale. These are then invested for the benefit of family members.

The articles of association of the company can be drafted to restrict non-lineal descendants from becoming shareholders. Different share classes, including redeemable, preference, or different classes of ordinary shares can be created to create flexibility. For example, some share classes may carry voting rights and others may not. Dividends will be paid by the board and so if the voting provisions are carefully structured, control over which family members receive dividends can be managed to avoid creating regular income streams. A regular dividend income can be treated as a resource and so for some family companies it has 'paid dividends not to pay dividends' from a matrimonial protection perspective.

3. Conclusion

The very nature of a family-run business – and the relationships rooted within it, which often span generations – is what sets it apart from the publicly owned corporate giants in our world. The consequence of a family-owned business failing to consider the impact of marital breakdown not only carries the risk of becoming embroiled in protracted and expensive litigation but also of materially destabilising the company and damaging relationships between family members. While a transfer or sale of shares is considered a last resort by the court, the other mechanisms used by the court to extract value in order to meet the financially weaker spouse's award can be extremely detrimental – or even ruinous – to the business as a whole and/or other shareholders.

Vigilance and forward planning from an early stage – and which is reviewed regularly – are critical to put in place clear strategies and suitable measures in a bid to mitigate these risks to enable such businesses to thrive for further generations.

Sophisticated reputation management for family companies

Lily Kennett
Victoria O'Byrne
Schillings

1. Introduction: time to rethink reputation management

When we consider an individual or corporate reputation, we are fundamentally making a series of complex value judgements. Reputation is often defined as a measure of trust, based on opinions as much as actions. The reputation of an individual or an organisation determines how others will view them, how they will be treated and whether they will be listened to. In short, a resilient reputation is something they earn over time as a result of the actions they take and keeping the promises they make.

'Reputation management' is too often used as a euphemism for crisis management or spin. The reality is quite different. Reputation management is the act of determining a client's positioning and proactively shaping their narrative, engaging with key stakeholders such as banks or strategic partners, to explain who they are, what they value and what they do. Managing reputation is not just something clients should consider after a damaging event or when under attack; it is strategically positioning themselves and their business to harness future opportunity.

Put simply, it is a form of investment. However, it differs from many investments as reputation is an *intangible* asset that yields *tangible* results. Just as a client may be recommended to diversify their stocks or buy shares in a growing business – aware that such short-term actions will lead to long-term benefits – time spent on reputation should be seen as an investment.

When reputation is well maintained and invested in over time, clients build resilience – or capital in the bank – which they can call upon to leverage key opportunities or manage critical moments. Organisations with good reputations can attract better people and business partners with whom to build more profitable, long-term relationships. They succeed at selling themselves and their businesses as 'premium' services and have more loyal customers. They have greater influence with their key stakeholders, such as policymakers, and are more likely to be given the benefit of the doubt by the media and others scrutinising their investments and activities such as regulators.

Investing in reputation therefore not only enhances a client's ability to create value and exploit opportunity, but also means that if their reputation is challenged by factors out of their control, they are better able to withstand them and return to business more quickly.

Investing in reputation allows clients to reach new audiences, gain new supporters, foster trust and build resilience. Proactive reputation management will ultimately set them apart from others, protecting their licence to operate and enabling business objectives to be pursued with less friction and distraction.

2. When reputation is at risk

There are any number of reasons why a client's reputation may be at risk; some predictable, others less so. A situation that is known which develops in an unexpected way, or a sudden unexpected event outside of their control can both have the potential to threaten their reputation. However, some fairly consistent triggers include:

- a perception of weak leadership;
- a lack of transparency, accountability or action;
- poor stakeholder relationships leading to failures in understanding;
- an unwillingness to speak or explain; or
- a high-profile issue affecting an entire industry.

These are all situations which invariably attract the attention of the media and social activists, and when a client's reputation bank is low on credit it can be an uphill battle to be heard and understood.

3. Why invest now?

Building a resilient reputation takes time and so the best time to invest in reputation and get on the front foot is yesterday. Our information climate is fast-paced, voracious and increasingly prone to disinformation. Only a solid reputational foundation and a capacity for organisational resilience can help protect from shocks.

Transparency, for both businesses and individuals, is now an expectation in many parts of the world. Demand for transparency continues to grow year on year, with a range of sophisticated investigative tools available to the media, non-governmental organisations and regulators. 'Big data' journalism is on the rise and disclosure requests, such as freedom of information requests, are common and well used by the media, investigators and private citizens to query the contacts, investments and actions of the wealthy and the powerful.

This trend towards transparency, fact-finding and analysis, when combined with our fast-moving digital information landscape, can lead to a rush to judge in the 'court of public opinion'. Add to this the potential for misinformation (simply wrong), disinformation (deliberately placed inaccuracies intended to do harm) and distortions caused by generative AI, the potential for reputational impact becomes hard to ignore. With these forces facing wealthy families as much as any other organisation, it is more important than ever that they prioritise their reputation and tell their own story to their priority audiences before someone else does it for them.

But there is another reason too. When something goes wrong, a client's ability to recover their reputation and rebuild trust will depend on behaviour; investors and stakeholders will use the situation as a chance to re-rate their ability to deal with the unexpected. What makes the difference? Strong leadership, quick decision making and clear, proactive and consistent communications. Get it right and the client will not just recover, they will have an opportunity to enhance their reputation.

4. Transparency, private data and public interest

Many wealthy families and their family offices (where relevant), have a marked preference for privacy, maintaining their business out of the spotlight and generally keeping below the radar as much as possible.

The rights and benefits of personal privacy are not in doubt and the desire to retain both confidentiality and anonymity are understandable. However, in the current climate, many wealthy families need to consider how the desire for privacy can be navigated harmoniously with an appropriate level of transparency. While this can seem daunting and requires thought and planning, such efforts will protect a business from the kind of intrusive and destabilising scrutiny that often accompanies a crisis. Advisers should reassure their clients that sharing the right information to build credibility and trust need not be at odds with privacy and discretion.

Both authorised and unauthorised sources are driving these demands for transparency. Firstly, bodies such as the Organisation for Economic Co-operation and Development, the European Union and governments worldwide are all driving for a more transparent corporate culture. Secondly, heightened media scrutiny of those with wealth as much as political power, is now a fact of life. Additionally, the rise in cyber attacks, mass data leaks and reports by whistleblowers will continue to be covered through extensive reporting. Information uncovered through such leaks and reports can remain accessible online via media archives and databases such as those maintained by the International Consortium of Investigative Journalists (ICIJ).

These movements are not entirely new, and the concept of public records has been around for centuries. In the United Kingdom, *The London Gazette* has been publishing insolvency notices since 1712, and we have been able to look at the electoral register or our neighbours' planning applications for decades. Since 1997, we have been able to search Companies House for documents and information regarding UK businesses – and the Freedom of Information Act in

2000 allowed people an insight into records held by UK public bodies. Similar repositories of public documents exist globally for listed and private companies, land ownership, planning approvals, litigation and others that may touch on the lives and business affairs of wealthy families.

The accessibility of such documents has been eased greatly by the digitalisation of records worldwide, and a broader movement towards greater corporate transparency and regulatory requirements has gained traction in recent years.

The trend towards transparency continues to evolve globally and is also leading to an increase in the sheer amount of information available for scrutiny. The recently initiated UK's Register of Overseas Entities, part of the Economic Crime and Corporate Transparency Act, requires information on beneficial owners and managing officers of UK land or properties. The register, which launched in August 2022, now contains almost 30,000 entities (according to the most recent figures shared by Companies House in September 2023). Law enforcement organisations, journalists and the general public can access this information freely: just a year after launching, there had already been over 500,000 searches of the data. Beyond the United Kingdom, registers of beneficial ownership have been established in 87 jurisdictions worldwide, with dozens more in various stages of implementation.[1]

In a world where information is at everybody's fingertips and opinion can be formed and shared in seconds, people have become less able to separate fact from fiction. The rise of citizen journalism over the last two decades has further increased the glare of public scrutiny, with decisions made by individuals and corporates alike watched and minutely assessed – and sometimes judged and criticised.

There is an even greater risk posed by the potential for information to be made public through a mass data leak, whether malicious or accidental. Being caught up in a data leak is undoubtedly a gruelling business. Even the fact of the leak can lead to long-lasting reputational damage, along with extensive media interest, the loss of key lenders, business partners, staff or customers, and reduced confidence in the organisation and its leaders. For the thousands of businesses that were implicated in the five major offshore data leaks – the most recent of which was the Pandora Papers in 2021, which leaked 11.9 million files – their data is now public.

The data from these leaks is held in the ICIJ's Offshore Leaks Database, which they describe on their own website as containing information on more than 810,000 offshore entities linking to people and companies in more than 200 countries and territories. These documents, many, if not most, of which would have previously been confidential – are now publicly accessible, searchable by name, organisation, country, city or address, allowing anyone to

1 Open Ownership, www.openownership.org/en/.

pore over the data and draw inferences and conclusions. Moreover, the data being processed online by the ICIJ can be fed into many compliance databases, resulting in red flags and resultant difficulties.

This mass availability of data and information (via legal or illegal means) has in some cases facilitated its misuse by bad actors in disinformation attacks and smear campaigns. It has also made it much easier for journalists and regulators to scrutinise individuals, businesses and their clients. This is unlikely to abate, and in fact is likely to continue to increase. It has therefore never been more important for clients to be as prepared as possible to deal with a level of scrutiny which can feel deeply uncomfortable, up to and including the unexpected disclosure of private and confidential information.

5. (Dis)information and the digital world

When true – but private – information is sought, scrutinised and perhaps even published, it is inarguably an unpleasant invasion of privacy. Far worse in many instances are cases where false information has been created and distributed at pace. Such misinformation may be accidental, resulting from haste, naivety, or simply poor research. However, sometimes – and with increasing frequency – deliberate disinformation is created and spread with malicious motivations.

Deliberate or not, the widespread use of social media to drive narratives and to act as a source for the media, together with the rise of generative AI for both images and text makes it much harder for any of us to spot the 'truth' and identify the falsehoods. A single social media post can be the trigger for a string of false allegations, or act as the origin of a fast-spreading, viral story, but it can be very hard to identify this retrospectively. The speed and volume of information flow (on social channels, in particular) and the divisive nature of online debate means that often there is no consensus as to what the truth might actually be.

Disinformation can cause extensive harm simply by muddling the picture for the mainstream. When inaccuracies spreading online contradict information being given on official channels, or are picked up as fact and published on those same channels, real and lasting harm can occur.

For example, a defamatory article drafted by a generative AI tool and maliciously published on a junk news site at a very low cost by someone with a grudge might be republished by a more credible news site thirsty for content and quickly end up cited on Wikipedia, or in compliance databases or due diligence reports. This could lead to a 'red flag' in a compliance report or due diligence summary that results in the refusal of a partnership or a loss of business. Unless the organisation has proactively invested in reputation management – including a review of what a business partner might be likely to find about them – the subject of the report would have little or no recourse. Indeed, they may never know why they were rejected or an anticipated business opportunity fell away.

Generative AI clearly has huge potential and many benefits – and advisers should stress this to their clients. Nevertheless, wherever tasks are done with maximum efficiency and without human judgement, there are likely to be increased risks to an organisation's or individual's reputation. As AI tools start to do more of the heavy lifting in information integrity, compliance vetting and topline data analysis, these risks are likely to grow and will be compounded by those 'black swan' AI risks that we are already aware of including deepfakes, impersonations and defamatory smear campaigns.

The existence of these challenges means that it will be increasingly important for organisations and individuals to tackle them proactively as well as in the moment.

Many clients assume that this sort of thing 'doesn't happen to me' or that reputation management is only necessary for a different sort of person or business – someone riskier, less private, more prone to pitfalls. However, these same people may not know and understand the foundations of good reputation management; how a reputation is built and maintained, and the way in which having a robust and resilient reputation benefits them – both in crisis and in the ordinary course of business.

Advisers and their clients benefit from a shared awareness of the client's digital footprint – what information about them is already in the public domain. Is it accurate? Are they on any databases that might be relied upon by banks, third-party due diligence providers and business partners as signifiers in respect of their reputation? Do they have any personal digital assets – such as websites or social media profiles – that they can employ to accurately represent their own business, track record and values? Are they doing this?

It is crucial, before any action can be taken for clients and their advisers, to fully understand what information exists about them in the public sphere – be it through leaks, public records, junk news sites, or social media. This is best achieved through a thorough, in-depth investigation. Only then can clients begin to tell their own story and build reputational resilience.

6. The increasing demand for scrutiny

While the transparency trend discussed above has *supplied* data and information, there is also a *demand* for more information about people and organisations.

Public attitudes in the last 10 years have shifted towards the right to scrutinise those in positions of power – be that political power, wealth, privilege or celebrity influence. While many wealthy families and family offices retain a preference for a discreet profile, it is likely that they will be scrutinised at some point. Advance preparation will pay off when the spotlight turns to a client.

Many wealthy families value their privacy and typically keep a low public profile, yet it is important that they do not operate in a 'communications vacuum'.

For a wealthy family or family office with no 'discoverability', a bad news story (true or false) will dominate a simple online search for them because there is simply no other content available to counter it. It is important to ensure that the assets and channels they own and control are populated, maintained and available to those scrutinising them, so that clients tell their own story before someone else does it for them. Taking control of their own narrative allows clients to be on the front foot, creating confidence. It also provides ready channels to counter speculation or correct misunderstandings quickly, while there is still time to influence external perceptions.

Today, the entire ecosystem of advisers around a company or individual are targeted, with the trusts, private bankers and law firms who advise their clients becoming part of the story. This trend is only intensifying with the proliferation of offshore leaks and information in the public domain linking advisers to their clients. Advisers should also consider their own reputational resilience in the case that their client is implicated in a bad news story, or caught in a leak.

Being discoverable is not the same as being famous or high-profile: it means being clear on who an individual's or business's target audiences are, and ensuring their strategic position and narrative is understood by this group. By shaping their profile and narrative proactively, a client's reputation can hold firm against any inaccurate, defamatory or otherwise challenging content that may materialise. Identifying a client's vulnerabilities and the issues they might face is a good place to start, but developing a communication strategy will safeguard their reputation and ultimately improve it.

7. How should wealthy families and family offices invest in their reputation?

Having reputation capital in the bank does not make an individual, business or wealthy family immune to a crisis. Wherever there is success, there will be attention, and, like bad weather, a crisis is likely to hit a client at some point. But being prepared means that that they are much more likely to weather the storm and avoid long-term damage.

Ensuring a client invests in their reputation today – and every day – will mean that they are better positioned to harness opportunities: be it reaching new audiences ahead of an expansion to a new market; communicating their values in preparation for an investment round; or getting key stakeholders and influential audiences on board with a new venture or family succession.

How can this be accomplished? Given the complexity of reputational challenges, a sophisticated toolkit is needed to get ahead of the curve. Whereas a lawyer may have sufficed twenty years ago, today's fast-moving threat landscape requires a rich combination of skills and experience.

How should advisers help their clients invest in their reputation now?

7.1 Understand their profile and how they are perceived

Clients should firstly find out what data and information currently exists about them in the public sphere through thorough detailed investigation. This discovery exercise should involve intelligence experts and may involve lawyers if they need to intervene on anything that is untrue.

7.2 Determine their strategic position and narrative

Once they have determined what is out there and their current digital profile, clients should work with communications experts to establish their most effective positioning for the audiences that matter most to their licence to operate.

7.3 Build and shape their profile

Clients should take steps with appropriate experts to monitor their online footprint and build a profile that is controlled by them rather than being determined by others, and supports their immediate and long-term goals.

8. Summary

The idea that clients only turn to reputation management professionals when a crisis hits is outdated and fundamentally represents a misunderstanding of how reputation is built and maintained. It is not about surviving under the radar, but thriving and having the freedom to operate and succeed in their chosen field.

Reputation management in today's world is proactive and pre-emptive. It is about accessing opportunities as well as managing threats and building reputational capital in the bank to create resilience. Investing in reputation is crucial for wealthy families and family offices to ensure they are continually able to achieve their objectives in a frictionless way.

A strategy for reputation management does not just mitigate risks, it should help a client to achieve tangible benefits as well: increased deal flow, profitable business partnerships, success on strategic hires. This investment in reputation can undoubtedly pay real dividends, as well as provide peace of mind, but only with a clear and consistent approach. The issues that need addressing are complex and the strategies necessary to address them must also be multifaceted, which can require teams that combine lawyers, investigators, communication experts and digital specialists to effectively manage this most valuable – and wholly irreplaceable – asset. In this way, clients will be better understood by the audiences that matter to them, enabling their family and their business to thrive.

9. Case studies

9.1 Smear campaign

The reputational consequences of a malicious smear campaign can be damaging and, in some cases, irreparable. In these situations, a team of multidisciplinary experts in investigations, law and communications can act quickly to avert the worst consequences of such an action and safeguard reputation for the future.

Our client, a business owner, was a victim of a widespread smear campaign likely instigated by a commercial rival. Our client was involved in international litigation proceedings brought against them by a former employee. These proceedings had been seized upon to a surprising degree and had become the hook for a series of false allegations, leading to misrepresentations about them in the media and elsewhere online.

Our client wanted to better understand where these allegations were coming from, who had planted them and how to deal with them. Our investigations team provided information to refute and contextualise the allegations for the benefit of media and other relevant third parties, and identified other information which might be of use in the proceedings.

This information and analysis helped to shape legal letters and allowed the client to push back on the false allegations. Working with our communications advisers, we were able to reframe the existing narratives and develop a coordinated strategy to promote the truth and rebuild our client's reputation.

Lessons learned: Understanding the context of the false allegations via thorough investigation meant legal arguments were strengthened and communications avenues were opened. This tripartite engagement allowed our client to quickly get back on the front foot with their litigation and other business opportunities.

9.2 Data breach

The media attention and negative press which can result from a crisis like a data breach has the potential to impact a business's reputation for years. The way in which such crises are dealt with can add fuel to the fire when not managed in a strategic way with advice from reputation experts.

Our client, a business with a global presence, suffered a data breach when thousands of confidential files and internal emails were stolen. This data was passed on to a group of investigative journalists. Reviewing the files, the journalists found draft documents linking our client to parties of interest.

The journalists contacted our client indicating that they planned to write a story detailing these alleged connections. Our client had never seen the documents, and had evidence to disprove the allegations, but the journalists intended to run the story anyway.

Our lawyers engaged with the publication to remove false allegations, and strongly reaffirmed our client's position. Our communications experts dealt with the journalists while our lawyers engaged the publication's legal team. They prepared a comprehensive contingency plan, laying out responses and actions to the most likely scenarios in the event the article is published, as well as activating a positive content strategy to rebuild the business's reputation.

Lessons learned: Leaks and breaches are almost inevitable given the amount of information companies retain today: knowing exactly what data you hold is the first step in preparedness – and having a crisis plan in place is essential. Here, legal and communications experts worked in tandem to not only counter the false allegations and prevent their publication but pre-empt further action.

9.3 Investment opportunity

Working with reputation management experts to harness opportunity and enhance reputation ahead of high-stakes moments – rather than turning to the professionals when something goes wrong – is how reputation should be approached. Our high-profile clients wanted to anticipate scrutiny and avoid public criticism of the launch of a new investment in a new region.

We knew it was important to develop a robust positioning and narrative to anchor all storytelling, as well as give the principals a compelling vision of the story tailored to their specific areas of expertise and interests. We also needed to identify and mitigate areas of reputational risk, proactively.

Firstly, our intelligence experts conducted a thorough landscape analysis and market review to gauge the climate and scan the horizon, while our digital resilience specialists undertook in-depth digital research into issues and principals to inform narrative development.

Our strategic communications advisers held Q&A sessions with the principals and their teams, drafted the narrative, tested and adjusted it based on stakeholder interviews, and aligned it with the simultaneous brand communications work.

We delivered a precise, innovative narrative that met the principals' goals and defined the fund and its leadership ahead of the long-term campaign roll-out, pre-empting any criticism and building resilience for the new venture and its principals.

Lessons learned: Having access to expert analysis on the digital, market and political context was key in establishing the fund's position and ensuring our messaging landed correctly. The data provided through technical digital investigation enabled our communications advisers to develop a narrative that would allow the fund and its principals to thrive – and their reputations to be protected – both on- and offline.

9.4 Reputation defence

Working proactively on your reputation means you are more likely to weather a storm if one does hit. Our client realised the value in getting ahead, investing in their reputation and shaping their narrative before someone else did it for them.

Our client, a prominent family, had fallen victim to a spate of reputation threats from anonymous social media accounts and asked us to ensure they saw the next one coming: we knew precisely how to create an early warning system.

Using the evidence of previous attacks, our intelligence and digital forensics teams analysed the behavioural patterns common to the online tactics the perpetrator used. Then, using social media, we compiled a forecast of trends and events that were likely to impact our client.

Armed with this information, our strategic communications experts advised the family on how to conduct their affairs to avoid the spotlight. In addition, our legal team contacted the media outlets who had disseminated false information previously and ensured a more balanced code of conduct.

By applying preventative measures, we put the family back in control of their true narrative. Not only do they now attract fewer threats, but they can spot them coming and act before the online rumour mill takes hold.

Lessons learned: Insight is foresight. Our investigation team's analysis of past events allowed us to develop a bespoke toolkit of advice tailored to the types of attacks the client was vulnerable to. This coordinated, data-led approach meant our client was in the best position to weather any future storms – and allowed them to shape their narrative.

Understanding the wealth holder spectrum

Matthew Braithwaite
Wedlake Bell LLP
Gina Pereira
Dāna Stewardship Advisory

1. Back to basics

What do we mean by a 'wealth holder spectrum', and how do we define 'wealth'? A good starting point is to go back to basics and look at the dictionary definitions of some of these words. According to the Collins dictionary, the word 'spectrum' means "a range of a particular type of thing". Tellingly, the word 'wealth' has two distinct meanings; on the one hand, it can mean "a large amount of money or valuable possessions", and on the other, "a large amount of something good". It is the second meaning which is much harder to articulate: what is something good? As we are about to explore, the answer is a subjective one – it is commonly accepted that one person's idea of being wealthy will differ from another's.

By implication, it would be natural to assume that a range of wealth defined by reference to money or valuable possessions would pit someone who is 'poor' (the converse of rich or wealthy – we explore the subtle difference below) at one end of the wealth spectrum and Elon Musk, being (at the time of writing) the richest person in the world (with a net worth in excess of US$410 billion[1]) at the other end.

2. Rich or wealthy, or both? What is the difference?

Note that the terms 'rich' and 'wealthy', although used interchangeably (indeed, the Collins dictionary definition of 'rich' is 'wealthy'), refer to different concepts. To be considered rich does not necessarily mean someone is wealthy. The term wealthy describes the long-term preservation of wealth for generations, with a person's spending and investing habits reflective of this objective. True wealth is, therefore, sustained wealth, the ability to invest money to produce income for years or generations to come. Someone can be fleetingly rich, but this wealth can be lost if not managed correctly. To be wealthy, therefore, is to exhibit different behaviours, which create longevity in the wealth created. This is an important distinction which we will revisit throughout this chapter.

1 *Forbes*, "The World's Real-Time Billionaires", www.forbes.com/real-time-billionaires/#395211aa3d78.

3. For richer or poorer

The Collins dictionary defines 'poor' as "having little money and few possessions", but it is entirely possible to be financially poor but possess a large amount of 'something' that is good. That something could be, for example, a loving family, close friends or a desire to do good through charitable causes. A person could be financially poor but 'life wealthy' psychologically (see further discussion on this below). Conversely, a financially wealthy person could, for example, be alone, have few friends and be generally unhappy ('life poor'). Poverty, by definition, means the state of being extremely poor. As the adage goes, money cannot buy happiness, but can it?

The emotional and psychological relationship with money cannot be ignored. Since the early 1980s, academics have investigated the psychology of money and its impact on behaviours, demonstrating the complex psychological and emotional connections with financial wealth and socio-demographics. Such research has led to the creation of money attitude scales, which have been used to identify spending behaviours, personal values and money management.[2]

A study led by Dr Paul Bain and Dr Renata Bongiorno, psychologists at the universities of Bath, Bath Spa and Exeter[3] challenged the truism that people have "unlimited wants" in life; they contend that the idea that people have such wants has rarely been challenged and that this may be related to exposure to high-profile media examples of ultra-wealthy people. They point to examples of other research within their study, which suggests that income beyond a moderate level has less impact on a person's well-being, with some finding a decreasing rate of positive impact, no increase or even a decline in well-being at very high incomes. While greater wealth increases consumption choices, more choice does not always increase satisfaction. They add that these findings suggest that having greater wealth may not necessarily be seen positively; our status compared to others, or happiness, is derived more from relative measures rather than by absolute measures.

The study involved nearly 8,000 participants from 33 countries spanning six continents that were surveyed to determine how much money people wanted in order to achieve their "absolutely ideal life". The study calculated that in 86% of countries, most people thought they could achieve their absolutely ideal life with US$10 million or less, and in some countries, with US$1 million or less. These sums in absolute terms are not insignificant, but in relative terms, by Western standards, they are not extravagantly wealthy. As noted above, Elon

---

2 Giulia Sesini and Edoardo Lozza, "Understanding Individual Attitude to Money: A Systematic Scoping Review and Research Agenda", *Collabra Psychology* (2023) 9 (1): 77305, https://doi.org/10.1525/collabra.77305.

3 Paul G Bain and Renata Bongiorno, "Evidence From 33 Countries Challenges the Assumption of Unlimited Wants", *Nature Sustainability*, Vol 5, August 2022, pp663–673, https://researchportal.bath.ac.uk/en/publications/evidence-from-33-countries-challenges-the-assumption-of-unlimited.

Musk's wealth would be enough, based on this study, for more than 400,000 people to achieve their absolutely ideal lives.

4. The financial wealth spectrum

A spectrum of wealth can just be a measure of financial wealth, from the very poorest in society to the wealthiest. This is but a 'snapshot' approach and ignores whether the wealthiest are 'wealthy' or just 'rich'. We contend that this is best described as a 'financial wealth spectrum'. A financial wealth spectrum is hard to define or standardise because wealth is relative, and its parameters will depend on each person's perception of being financially wealthy (or rich) at one end of the spectrum and poor at the other.

Media examples of financial wealth spectrums include the *Forbes* World's Billionaires ('the Forbes List') and *The Sunday Times* annual Rich List ('the Rich List'), albeit neither charts the poorest in society. The Forbes List is the annual ranking of billionaires and was first published in 1987. The 38th annual Forbes List contained a record 2,781 billionaires with a total net wealth of US$14.2 trillion. According to *Forbes*:[4]

> *There are now more billionaires than ever: 2,781 in all, 141 more than last year and 26 more than the record set in 2021. They're richer than ever, worth $14.2 trillion in aggregate, up by $2 trillion from 2023 and $1.1 trillion above the previous record, also set in 2021.*

Forbes conclude that two-thirds of the list's members are worth more than a year ago including Facebook founder Mark Zuckerberg, whose net worth increased by US$112.6 billion. The Rich List ranks the 1,000 'wealthiest' families who are resident in the United Kingdom by their net (material) wealth – so by their richness (as it were).

What is the purpose of these lists and what do they achieve? In modern society they are a reflection of late 20th-century capitalism and arguably only serve to widen the divide between those who have (plenty in both cases) and those who do not. However, in an increasingly less tolerant society of large amounts of wealth, these wealth holders have to consider their reputations and justify what their wealth is doing beyond its accumulation for personal gain. More and more, families have to exhibit their philanthropic credentials and demonstrate that they are paying their fair share of tax.

5. The evolution of capitalism

Capitalism has fuelled industrial and technological revolutions, reshaped the natural world, transferred the role of the state in relation to society, lifted innumerable people out of poverty over the last two centuries, significantly increased standards of living, and resulted in innovations that have radically

4 *Forbes*, "World's Billionaires List: The Richest in 2024", www.forbes.com/billionaires/.

improved human well-being. However, since the late 20th century, decreased investment in public services, including public infrastructure, improving education and mitigating health risks, is likely to have contributed to the gap between the richest and poorest in society. According to UBS's World Wealth Report 2024, the percentage of adults globally whose wealth exceeds US$1 million has tripled since the beginning of the millennium to 1.5% of the population, with the wealth held by this group amounting to nearly half of all global wealth. The disparity in wealth is evident in the United States, where, as well as being home to 44% of the highest 1% of global wealth (together with Canada), income inequality between the richer and poorer increased by approximately 20% between 1980 and 2016, based on data published by the US Congressional Budget Office.[5] As political unrest and polarisation around the world over recent years has shown, there are growing signs of discontent with the *status quo*.

6. The societal shift in the perception of wealth

As a consequence of rising inequality, people have less trust in institutions and experience a sense of injustice.[6] The financial crisis of 2008 hit the working classes the hardest, and resulting bank bailouts led to societal resentment and caused people to lose faith in financial institutions. The publication of the Panama Papers in 2016 and then the Paradise Papers in close succession in 2017, led to a blurring of the boundaries between legitimate tax planning and tax evasion, which only further incited a sense of distrust and the gulf between rich and poor. It has fuelled the rise in polarised politics, which has caused civil unrest in many liberal democracies, including France and the United States.

The move to transparency of material wealth in relation to taxation has progressed over recent decades, driven by tax evasion practices exposed in the global media and widely reported on social media. The demand for transparency has recently evolved from the requirement to disclose to government authorities to disclosure in the public realm, evidenced by the United Kingdom and European Union's political push to introduce public access to beneficial ownership registers.

These developments also contribute to a much wider anti-wealth sentiment across United Kingdom, the European Union and North America,[7] eroding human rights to privacy, and underscoring the importance of managing the

---

5 Juliana Menasce Horowitz, Ruth Igielnik and Rakesh Kochhar, "Trends in income and wealth inequality", Pew Research Center, 9 January 2020, www.pewresearch.org/social-trends/2020/01/09/trends-in-income-and-wealth-inequality/.

6 Edelman, "Edelman Trust Barometer 2020", www.edelman.com/sites/g/files/aatuss191/files/2020-01/2020%20Edelman%20Trust%20Barometer%20Global%20Report.pdf.

7 Andrew Daniller, "Americans' views about billionaires have grown somewhat more negative since 2020", Pew Research Center, 28 July 2020, www.pewresearch.org/short-reads/2021/07/28/americans-views-about-billionaires-have-grown-somewhat-more-negative-since-2020/.

reputation of families with significant financial means. It is no coincidence that *The Sunday Times* in the United Kingdom started to publish the annual Tax List in 2019, listing the top tax contributors among wealthy families and the *Forbes* list of the biggest financial donors,[8] and it is in these lists that – from a reputational standpoint at least – the wealthy now wish to feature.

The COVID-19 pandemic saw a swell of humanity and innovation becoming a uniting force within families and across generations. The economic effects of the pandemic have been most greatly felt at the lower end of the wealth spectrum where the loss of jobs has been concentrated. It is this end of the wealth spectrum which contains the frontline workers who were revered as the heroes and heroines of the pandemic. Against this backdrop is the perception that the wealthy weathered the storm much better financially. Consequently, the wealthy, or often the rising generation within wealthy families, feel a moral weight of expectation that they are seen to give back to bridge this societal gulf between rich and poor.

Transparency and accountability driven by technological innovation and regulation influence attitudes toward wealth. In a world where information is swiftly disseminated via social media, differences in attitudes towards wealth have become increasingly evident, mirroring greater awareness of the complex challenges and opportunities that confront both society and the global ecosystem. Prominent among these influences, beyond the perceptible disparities in wealth, are the looming threats of biodiversity loss and the escalating anxiety surrounding climate change. Some 196 parties adopted the highly profiled and publicised Paris Agreement at COP 21 in 2015. It became a game changer for the global climate agenda, where governments agreed on concrete actions and time frames to reduce carbon emissions and adapt to the impacts of climate change. Stemming from the Paris Agreement was the introduction of a range of financial policies and regulations, including mandated climate-related financial disclosures that aim to direct investments towards a sustainable economy.[9] These obligations are extended extraterritorially, creating a *de facto* global standard where companies situated outside of regulated markets are incentivised to adopt similar standards to continue to operate in and maintain access to regulated markets.[10] However,

---

8 Billionaire media mogul and philanthropist, Ted Turner, was critical of *Forbes* magazine's publication of a list of the rich and sought to motivate his fellow billionaires to give more by urging the creation of a list of the biggest philanthropic donors, which *Forbes* now publishes annually.

9 The European Commission's Action Plan: Financing Sustainable Growth (https://eur-lex.europa.eu/legal-content/EN/TXT/?uri=CELEX%3A52018DC0097) introduces regulatory changes specifically focusing on financial institutions, including the Alternative Investment Fund Managers Directive (AIFMD) and the Sustainable Finance Disclosure Regulation (SFDR) and Taxonomy Regulation. Beyond the European Union, jurisdictions including the United Kingdom, Australia, Canada and Singapore are introducing sustainability regulations in financial services.

10 Paola Fonseca and Roberto Randazzo, "Embracing Global Sustainable Corporate Governance", 19 March 2024, https://gailnet.org/embracing-global-sustainable-corporate-governance/.

President Trump's executive order directing US withdrawal from the Paris Agreement heralding the beginning of his second term in office will inevitably have a material impact on the global effort to combat climate change.[11]

In recent years, against this backdrop, businesses have increasingly needed to measure their success through more varied metrics than just profit and growth, and significantly wealthy families are no different. By some estimates, family-owned businesses account for more than 70% of the global GDP and 60% of global employment.[12] They outperform their non-family-owned counterparts due in part to strategic actions combined with a mindset that focuses on purpose beyond profits, long-term perspective and emphasis on reinvesting in the business, financial conservatism and efficient decision making.[13]

The Five Capitals economic model[14] calls for the integration of five pillars of human capital – natural, human, social, manufactured and financial – into existing economic models. An example of this is the B Corporation movement, which upholds the principle that companies must do more than deliver profits to shareholders; they must invest in their employees and contribute to improving human, natural and social elements of capital rather than solely focus on financial capital. It is through this lens that the wealthy are now also being viewed. Bain and Bongiorno, in their "absolutely ideal lives" study, conclude that if the wants of people to achieve their absolutely ideal lives are relatively modest, then it is hoped that this can make it socially easier for people to behave in ways that are more aligned with what makes them genuinely happy and support stronger policies to help safeguard the planet, and by implication satisfy the Five Capitals economic model.

7. The origins of wealth

How one acquires material wealth can also inform attitudes and influence how it is managed. Wealth generators may have started from nothing and built a fortune that formed an entirely different life for their family. The transition from poverty to abundance comes with a unique psychology, feelings of vulnerability versus safety and self-reliance that can inform how they approach wealth planning. Conversely, wealth inheritors report experiencing internal

---

11 Nate Perez and Rachel Waldholz, "Trump is withdrawing from the Paris Agreement (again), reversing U.S. climate policy", npr, 21 January 2025, www.npr.org/2025/01/21/nx-s1-5266207/trump-paris-agreement-biden-climate-change.

12 United Nations Conference on Trade and Development, "Empowering Family Businesses to Fast-Track Sustainable Development", 13 April 2021, https://unctad.org/news/empowering-family-businesses-fast-track-sustainable-development.

13 McKinsey & Company, "The Secrets of Outperforming Family-Owned Businesses: How They Create Value – And How You Can Become One", 28 November 2023, www.mckinsey.com/industries/private-capital/our-insights/the-secrets-of-outperforming-family-owned-businesses-how-they-create-value-and-how-you-can-become-one.

14 Articulated by Jonathon Porritt, author of *Capitalism As If The World Matters*.

conflicts regarding their fortunes, fuelled by questions of financial origins, provision of ongoing financial support and perceptions that money may be a source of familial discord.[15]

Younger generations, in particular, grapple with finding purpose when faced with the financial wealth they did not help to create. Ambivalent feelings can lead to disengagement, particularly without meaningful involvement in family estate planning, business operations, family governance, family office governance, or philanthropic endeavours. It is no coincidence that the rising generation is at the forefront of championing higher wealth and inheritance taxes as part of this quest to find purpose in their wealth.[16]

When family members experience disparate psychological and emotional relationships with money, the risk of conflict escalates in the absence of healthy communication and conflict resolution tools. The modern family can complicate matters further, including divorces leading to second (or third) marriages, step-parents and step-siblings, and spouses who are accused of having ulterior financial motives. Such families are often high on the financial wealth spectrum but in life, also high on the 'poverty' spectrum.

8. The psychological wealth spectrum

The examples above illustrate the broad scope of micro and macro factors that can influence wealth holders' experiences with money and inform their attitudes towards it. So, on balance, a financial wealth spectrum has limited value by ignoring the psychological overlay. An alternative approach is to define a wealth spectrum by referencing these psychological factors, including the thoughts, feelings and emotions towards wealth. This is perhaps best described as a 'psychological wealth spectrum'. Such a spectrum is harder to define, and the results can turn perceptions of what it means to be 'wealthy' on their head.

Morgan Housel, author of *The Psychology of Money* and podcast presenter, mapped out an emotional wealth spectrum in an episode of his podcast.[17] In summary, Housel categorises those at one end of his spectrum as in 'poverty' – not in the sense of not having material wealth but instead constrained by their own thoughts and feelings towards their wealth and by the attitudes of those around them. Examples of such poverty include: (i) those who are overwhelmed by feelings of envy and inadequacy towards those who earn more; (ii) those whose wealth has been gained in a way which brings an active disdain from those they want to like them; (iii) those whose wealth leads to boredom at best

---

15 Campden Wealth and BNY Mellon, *The Next Generation of Wealth Holders in the United States 2022*, www.campdenwealth.com/report/next-generation-wealth-holders-united-states-2022.

16 See Patriotic Millionaires (https://patrioticmillionaires.uk) and Millionaires for Humanity (https://millionairesforhumanity.org) by way of example.

17 The Morgan Housel Podcast, "The Spectrum of Wealth", 29 June 2023.

and self-destruction at worst; and (iv) those with a large income and wealth made in jobs which derail their social and family life, which Housel terms as "psychological deep poverty".

At the other end of Housel's spectrum are the categories of wealth where materiality and emotion are not assimilated; 'psychologically positive wealth'. Examples of this wealth construct include: (i) those who can go to bed and wake up when they want – they have time to eat well and exercise and can do what they want, when they want; (ii) those who can and want to help and care for others, and who are not seeking recognition for it; and (iii) those who are respected and admired, regardless of their financial circumstances. Housel assimilates those in this last category of wealth to psychologically being on the Forbes List.

Bain and Bongiorno in their "absolutely ideal lives" study drew on further research, which showed that higher incomes typically involve trade-offs with responsibilities, risks, time or ethicality, which is likely to lead people to report a lower ideal wealth as they consider the costs, and which pulls them into the realms of psychological poverty, as articulated by Housel. Wealth through philanthropy or inheritance may come with implicit expectations from the giver; however, a growing movement of 'trust-based philanthropy' aims to be more collaborative than controlling of grantees. Bain and Bongiorno, in the context of explaining the rationale for their study, say that such issues can be minimised if people could obtain wealth purely by chance, such as through a lottery win, as for most people a lottery is the most psychologically feasible route to significant wealth and one which is more likely to avoid these emotional trade-offs, even if the risk that the wealth is more fleeting is much higher.

How is such a wealth spectrum helpful to advisers? Does it inform the advice advisers provide when it comes to structuring wealth, for example, for future generations? Someone who has a healthy relationship with their wealth may have less of an attachment to material wealth, which may inform their approach to wealth structuring, whereas someone who has a problematic relationship with wealth may be more controlling of their wealth, which determines what they can and cannot do with it. Understanding where a person lies on this spectrum may aid them in understanding whether behavioural change is needed for them to become wealthy, whether in terms of fostering longer-term sustainable wealth or seeking out other positive wealth traits beyond financial metrics.

Differing attitudes to wealth management have come to the fore in recent years chiefly as a consequence of the much talked about 'Great Wealth Transfer', which is predicted to see in the region of US$83 trillion of wealth transfer to be passed on in the next two decades.[18] This has catalysed the desire for wealth

18 UBS, "Global Wealth Report 2024: Growth returns to 4.2% offsetting 2022 slump", 10 July 2024, www.ubs.com/global/en/media/display-page-ndp/en-20240710-gwr-2024.html.

holders, like businesses, to be more responsible with their wealth management and adopt responsible stewardship principles to fulfil the five pillars of capital and ensure future longevity of their wealth. According to one study, over 80% of millennial financial wealth owners (broadly defined as those born between 1981 and 1996) emphasised aligning their investments with their values and that environmental, social and governance (ESG) metrics are an integral part of their investment strategy.[19] The growth in demand for sustainable investment products substantiates these reports. According to the Global Impact Investing Network, in 2024, the estimated size of the worldwide impact investing market exceeded US$1.5 trillion.[20]

9. The behavioural wealth management spectrum

An organisation which has sought to arrange differing behaviours and attitudes towards wealth management in an evolving spectrum is the Good Ancestor Movement (GAM).[21] GAM's Wealth Spectrum[22] (as it appeared when writing this chapter) maps different financial disciplines against four categories within a spectrum of wealth stewardship practices. Like the psychological wealth spectrum explored above, it is not determined by the extent of financial wealth, but by how a wealth holder's attitudes can translate into wealth management or distribution practices. By way of example, a person can be categorised as exhibiting 'extractive' behaviour (as discussed further below) yet have very little material wealth; conversely someone who demonstrates 'regenerative' behaviours may have substantial wealth. GAM describes the Wealth Spectrum as an emergent "thinking and reflection tool" and that "wealth holders and wealth advisers will find themselves engaged in a wide range of boxes across the spectrum".[23]

Referring to the GAM Wealth Spectrum could be helpful in the exploratory phase of the wealth planning process to assist the adviser community and clients in understanding where one sits and where one would like to be, as it is this positioning that can help the client determine investment objectives, taxation and state benefit strategies, business ownership practices, estate and succession planning, and the responsibility to help repair the impact of wealth creation on society and the environment.

---

19 RBC Wealth Management, "The Millennial Mindset: Insights into the Next Generation's Needs, Wants, Preferences, and Their Relationship with Money Management", 2022, www.rbcclearingandcustody.com/en-us/wp-content/uploads/cc/the-millennial-mindset.pdf.

20 Dean Hand, Maddie Ulanow, Hongyu Pan and Kelly Xiao, "Sizing the Impact Investing Market 2024", GIIN, 23 October 2024, https://thegiin.org/publication/research/sizing-the-impact-investing-market-2024/.

21 www.goodancestormovement.com/.

22 Good Ancestor Movement, "Wealth Spectrum", https://static1.squarespace.com/static/6127ff51b5a0390e46a10c17/t/668e5be82c7117321926e626/1720605673201/Wealth+Spectrum+2024.pdf.

23 Based on the 2023 version of the GAM Wealth Spectrum, available at: www.goodancestormovement.com/resources.

At the far left of the GAM spectrum, in a category entitled 'extractive', behaviours prioritise wealth accumulation over generations without constraints or regard for broader impact. Short-term financial returns are maximised, attempts at unionisation may be blocked, and efforts may be made to keep family control of operating businesses. Actions are taken by the wealth holder to minimise taxes using all available tools and maximise state benefits, but no reparative action is taken on their part.

Next on the spectrum, entitled 'individualistic', describes behaviours aimed at minimising taxes using socially defensible practices and maximising wealth accumulation over generations, using philanthropy and investment strategy to invest in maintaining social order for their own benefit. Here, the objective is to maximise financial returns through investments, integrate ESG factors and exercise shareholder engagement to profit from extractive companies. There is no action to repair. Within operating businesses, the aim is to maximise financial return for shareholders while investing in sustainability for long-term profit.

The next set of behaviours reflects 'engaged' attitudes. The objective is to generate a wealth plan based on need and redistribute or donate excess wealth. The investment strategy is the same as the 'individualistic' category, plus experimenting with impact-led investments that seek financial return. Tax-driven structuring is rejected, and tax is paid at the intended rates, using tax reliefs and deductions and opting out of state benefits. Certain responsible business ownership practices are adopted, and there is an exploration of repair through donor-controlled philanthropy.

At the far right of GAM's spectrum is the 'regenerative' profile. Here the world's maximum 'inequality quotient' is defined, reducing spending and redistributing excess capital. The objective is to invest in creating wealth within communities, acting as risk absorbers, and seeking to maximise impact while generating low or negative financial returns to reduce excess. Proactive steps are taken to pay a 'fair share' of taxes, with no engagement in fiscal minimisation strategies or state benefits. Responsible business ownership practices are adopted, deprioritising shareholders as stakeholders, and introducing community or worker-ownership models. The commitment to repair is the most robust along the spectrum, with active guarantees not to repeat and to undo any ongoing harm caused by financial wealth.

While the GAM Wealth Spectrum can serve as a helpful discovery aid to flag different attitudes and values that inform the wealth planning process, individuals may not fit neatly into one of the four categories. They can sit within different spots across the spectrum or beyond it. The difference in approach may reflect a divergent view of where responsibility lies, namely with the state or private citizens, as such perceptions often stem from socio-economic history. As Bain and Bongiorno's study concludes, though, in a world of limited wants, the appetite for wealth holders to embrace more regenerative wealth management practices should be strong.

10. A holistic approach to wealth planning

The psychological relationship with wealth is complex; many external and internal factors inform priorities impacting the wealth planning process. Given the multi-dimensional nature of wealth, is an approach that concentrates on the technical aspects of planning sufficient to address a more nuanced and complex reality? What if individual or family values go against the perceived norm? A recent application to the Jersey Royal Court exemplifies a family which is values driven. The judgment, *In the Matter of the May Trust*,[24] followed the trustees of a private family trust's application to the court for its blessing to make a distribution to the primary beneficiary of roughly one half of the trust fund, which would then be gifted to a charity which was also a beneficiary under the trust. The intention was that the primary beneficiary would not claim all the eligible gift aid, resulting in an avoidable tax charge had the trust made a direct distribution to the charity beneficiary. Ethics drove the underlying motivation behind the distribution request. The family members had agreed that, following their values, they had a moral obligation to pay taxes to generate revenue for the government to provide a broader social benefit. The court gave its blessing to the distribution, construing that 'benefit' involves an objective and subjective analysis comprising the views of beneficiaries, which in this case included discharging such a moral obligation. Although this scenario may be less typical, it highlights the wider breadth of values and objectives that wealthy families may possess.

A myopic focus in planning or assumptions about a client's priorities may have unintended consequences. Even sophisticated clients can be led by advisers, not knowing what questions to ask. This approach will inevitably miss divergent perspectives, values and attitudes which can set up a family for failure. Similarly, focusing only on the family leader can cause significant dynamics and issues to be overlooked. While an individual has the prerogative to determine how their wealth should be managed and shared, if the planning objective is to provide a functioning solution which will serve the family over the long term across generations, identifying and considering the broader family views, values and interests, is critical to gain stakeholder buy-in and mitigate risks of future conflict. Despite being labelled as 'soft', the psychological and emotional dimensions of wealth across the family unit are equally crucial to the technical elements of planning. They can pose significant risks or present an opportunity to strengthen the fortitude of succession planning structures that are put in place, and either appease or create tensions within a family tied to them for a lifetime and beyond.

---

24 [2021] JRC 137.

A deeper and expansive exploratory phase in the planning process can reveal significant details that inform solutions holistically. It may not be possible to address all objectives, and compromises may be required depending on priorities. However, without a broader perspective, advisers risk overlooking factors that can support the success or failure of any solution. The challenge is that many traditional wealth planning advisers are not equipped to probe into wealth's psychological or emotional aspects or may encounter commercial cost constraints that impede the process. Fortunately, increasingly, tools are being developed to help advisers and service providers discover significant individual and collective attitudes towards wealth and understand individual and collective family members' views, values and aspirations.

Understanding the multifaceted nature of wealth, encompassing financial, emotional and psychological dimensions, is essential for effective wealth planning. By acknowledging the intricate dynamics between these elements, advisers can adopt a holistic approach that addresses both individual and collective needs. This comprehensive strategy not only enhances best practices but also ensures that solutions are truly reflective of the diverse aspects of wealth, thereby fostering long-term stability and meaningful outcomes for future generations.

Providing advice on philanthropy: why, when and how to raise giving with family clients

Emma Beeston
Philanthropy adviser
Beth Breeze
Centre for Philanthropy, University of Kent

1. Introduction

Philanthropy might seem at first glance to be the 'odd topic out' in this book – where does giving money away fit into a world that is focused on holding and growing wealth? In this chapter, we review the evidence that family clients increasingly want and expect philanthropy to be raised by their advisers, and explain how to do that with confidence.

Family philanthropy is not new. Some of the largest foundations in the world, such as the Gates Foundation or the Wellcome Trust, have their roots in family giving, and families of every size and wealth level provide funding to causes from homelessness to heritage, climate activism to medical research. New forms of giving vehicle such as donor-advised funds and collective giving models have extended the ways in which families engage in philanthropy. The increased emphasis on living with meaning and purpose means philanthropy is more relevant than ever. For example, one survey found that 87% of affluent investors want to make a meaningful impact through charitable activities.[1]

Philanthropy advice involves the provision of skilled support to help families navigate the myriad choices they face when starting or scaling up their private giving. Philanthropy advice is not an add-on but a valuable part of an integrated advice offer that can support families to realise their ambitions. There are opportunities for advisers working with wealthy families to raise the topic, provide initial advice, develop an in-house service, or establish connections with specialist philanthropy advisers. In this chapter, we look at each of these in turn.

1 CEG Insights, "Addressing the Gap Between Investors' Expectations and Advisor Services" (2023), https://go.cegworldwide.com/fa-play-to-win-report-wealth-divide.

2. Why talk about philanthropy?

There are three good reasons for family advisers to raise the topic of philanthropy and support families with their giving: philanthropic funds are needed to tackle the world's problems; it brings benefits to the family itself; and families want to work with advisers who can help them with their giving.

2.1 Philanthropy advice is good for the world

The first reason is the end result: the public good that private funds can achieve in the world. Philanthropic funds are needed in this time of global polycrisis involving diverse and complex social, environmental and technological challenges. Philanthropy has a role to play in achieving the UN's Sustainable Development Goals, alongside the private and public sectors. Philanthropy is well-placed to take risks and support innovation, respond quickly in a crisis, take a long-term view or fund those on the margins. Doing good, whether in their local community or at a global level, is what motivates philanthropic families, and it is also rewarding for advisers to help encourage, facilitate and sustain this effort. Good advice has the potential to increase the amount of funds moving to good causes as research shows that wealthy donors who had taken some form of philanthropy advice gave nearly twice as much compared to the average annual donation level.[2]

2.2 Philanthropy advice is good for families

Families have a dual impact through their giving: they make a positive difference in the world and they create benefits for the family itself. Philanthropy is a powerful mechanism for connecting generations by working together to create and express shared values. Making a meaningful contribution to society can provide an identity for the family and enhance their reputation. Philanthropy provides a legacy for the family as the new generations learn and understand the family's history and values and seek to continue these.

Philanthropy is also used as an educational tool in preparation for running the family business while raising good citizens.[3] Involvement in the family's philanthropy teaches skills such as investing, governance, strategising and assessing impact as well as conveying family principles such as compassion, leadership and innovation. A survey of families, family offices and foundations found that 83% believed that involving the next generation in philanthropy prepares them to take on greater family responsibility.[4] Wider than this,

---

2 Charities Aid Foundation, "The Art of Adaptation: Why Talking Philanthropy Transforms the Adviser-Client Relationship" (2015), www.cafonline.org/docs/default-source/about-us-publications/the-art-of-adaptation.pdf.

3 See Peter Winneke, *Give While You Live: A Practical Guide to More & Better Giving in Australia* (2023), chapter 14.

4 Campden Wealth Limited, "Investing for Global Impact: A Power for Good 2022" (2023), www.campdenwealth.com/report/investing-global-impact-power-good-2022.

philanthropy is also seen as a way for wealthy parents to avoid burdening their children with harmful inheritances. Parents worry about the corrupting effect of wealth on their children because of its potential to isolate people and remove the motivation to find purpose through working. Parents use involvement with family philanthropy as a means for their children to learn about money, understand their privilege and have a meaningful life.

2.3 Philanthropy advice is good business for those working with business families

Adding advice on philanthropy to the core competencies when working with families also makes good business sense. Families' engagement with philanthropy is set to grow[5] and the younger generations are seeking advice on their charitable giving.[6] The business opportunity in responding to this need has been identified in both practice and in the research. For example, US businesses that offer charitable planning have significantly greater assets, organic growth and more new money per investor, compared to firms that do not offer this service.[7] One reason for this outcome is encapsulated in a report produced by the Canadian Association of Gift Planners:

> *Anything that attracts clients to your practice equates to an added revenue stream. Anything that binds clients to you and your firm, and not just individual clients but also their children and sometimes even their grandchildren – this is indeed a 'magical' glue that creates a 'sticky business'.*[8]

There is also a business opportunity in being an early adopter: where others do not offer philanthropy advice, doing so can attract new clients. Having meaningful conversations about clients' values, passions, relationship to their wealth and thoughts on their legacy strengthens relationships and supports the move to being a trusted adviser. Providing philanthropy advice helps retain clients and their extended family. This is particularly important given the higher chance of younger generations changing adviser.[9]

---

5 Ocorian, "Increasing Wealth Drives Family Office Focus on Philanthropy and Succession Plans" (2 May 2023), www.ocorian.com/press-release/increasing-wealth-drives-family-office-focus-philanthropy-and-succession-plans.

6 Charities Aid Foundation, "Advising the Giving Generation" (2023), https://view.professionaladviser.com/caf-advising-the-giving-generation/p/1.

7 Fidelity Charitable, "On the Leading Edge: Accelerating Firm Growth With Charitable Planning", www.fidelitycharitable.org/content/dam/fc-public/docs/insights/on-the-leading-edge-report.pdf.

8 Canadian Association of Gift Planners "Doing Good for Business: The inclusion of Philanthropy in the Canadian Professional Advisor's Business Practice" (2018), p4, www.cagp-acpdp.org/sites/default/files/media/Resources/BusinessCaseStudy2018/doing_good_for_business.pdf.

9 Schroders, "A Practical Guide to Intergenerational Wealth Transfer for Financial Advisers" https://mybrand.schroders.com/m/1f1c6f6447e8e961/original/Adviser_Home_Schroders_Intergenerational-Guide_Feb_2021_FINAL.pdf; and Cerulli Associates, "Cerulli Finds Just 19% of Investors Use Their Parents' Advisor" (14 November 2023), www.cerulli.com/press-releases/cerulli-finds-just-19-of-investors-use-their-parents-advisor.

3. What help do families want?

Philanthropy is so full of choices that it is hard to do well. Perhaps the most well-known quote on this topic is from the Scottish-American tycoon and philanthropist, Andrew Carnegie. Carnegie went from dire poverty to become one of the world's first multi-millionaires, but claimed: "It is more difficult to give money away intelligently than to earn it in the first place."[10] The difficulty that Carnegie refers to is not about the structural issues like tax and legal vehicles, rather it is about the complexity of identifying shared values and translating these into a robust plan that both reflects the family's passions and also meets community needs. Research shows that the main thing donors want from their advisers is a personalised discussion of their philanthropic interests along with tailored solutions on how their giving might be structured.[11] The same research also shows that advisers have an important role in providing connections and resources to clients (see Table 1).

The entry point to this personalised discussion involves skilled advice to navigate questions such as whether donors want to respond to immediate needs or address the root causes of problems. Do they want to give in their local community or globally? How will they identify and select causes and organisations to support? How will they think through what evidence they need to judge the effectiveness of their philanthropy and how best to work with the organisations they fund? These are difficult questions for any donor and even harder for a family trying to reach consensus across multiple generations and a range of views. This is why the philanthropy adviser needs to assist with the internal dynamics and process as well as the external goals of the family's giving. Advisers therefore commonly help with 'cultivating family capital' such as family governance, next-generation preparation and succession planning.[12]

4. When to raise the subject of philanthropy?

The research is clear that donors want their advisers to raise the topic of philanthropy and as early as possible.[13] This means that the 72% of advisers who do not include philanthropy as part of the initial fact-finding conversations and checklists when they onboard a new client[14] are missing an opportunity to respond to that demand and connect with their clients at a deeper level.

---

10 These words are widely attributed to Andrew Carnegie, although their origin is not confirmed.

11 Beth Breeze and Theresa Lloyd, *Richer Lives: Why Rich People Give*, (DSC, 2013), p178.

12 Daylight Advisors, "U.S. Philanthropic Advisors 2024: Professional Development, Practice, and Knowledge Gaps" (2024), www.daylightadvisors.com/research-philanthropyadvisors.

13 U.S. Trust, "The U.S. Trust Study of the Philanthropic Conversation: Understanding Advisor Approaches & Client Expectations" (2018), https://tpi.org/resource/2018-tpiu-s-trust-study-of-the-philanthropic-conversation-full-report/.

14 Charities Aid Foundation, "Advising the Giving Generation" (2023), https://view.professionaladviser.com/caf-advising-the-giving-generation/p/3.

Table 1: Types of philanthropy advice requested

Type of advice requested	Respondents who were asked for this service
Personalised discussion of their philanthropic interests, with tailored solutions on how their giving might be structured	75%
Signposting to materials produced by other organisations, such as Philanthropy Impact, New Philanthropy Capital or the Association of Charitable Foundations	67%
Introductions to other donors who share their interests	67%
Management of clients' philanthropy, including relationships with beneficiaries, project visits, assessment of feedback reports, etc.	58%
Recommendations of books and articles	50%
The provision of training on strategic planning	42%
Introductions to external philanthropy specialists	33%
Suggestions as to which charities they might support within their area of interest	25%
Introductions to potential beneficiaries	25%

Source: Beth Breeze and Theresa Lloyd, Richer Lives: Why Rich People Give *(DSC, 2013) p178.*

Raising the subject at an early stage can be as simple as asking questions such as the following:

- I'd like to discuss philanthropy (charitable giving) with you as part of our overall conversation. Is that something you'd be open to?
- My clients are increasingly including philanthropy as part of their estate plan. Is that something you would be interested in discussing?
- Is philanthropy important to you right now, or is it something you'd like to discuss in the future?[15]

15 Kris Putnam-Walkerly, "13 Questions to Ask Your Clients About Philanthropy" (7 June 2022), www.thinkadvisor.com/2022/06/07/13-questions-to-ask-your-clients-about-philanthropy/.

Raising these questions at the start of the client engagement enables advisers to return to philanthropy in later meetings as a natural – indeed expected – part of their role, which sits within an ecosystem of support for families, as shown in Figure 1, from The Ultra High Net Worth Institute.

Figure 1: Ten domains of family wealth[16]

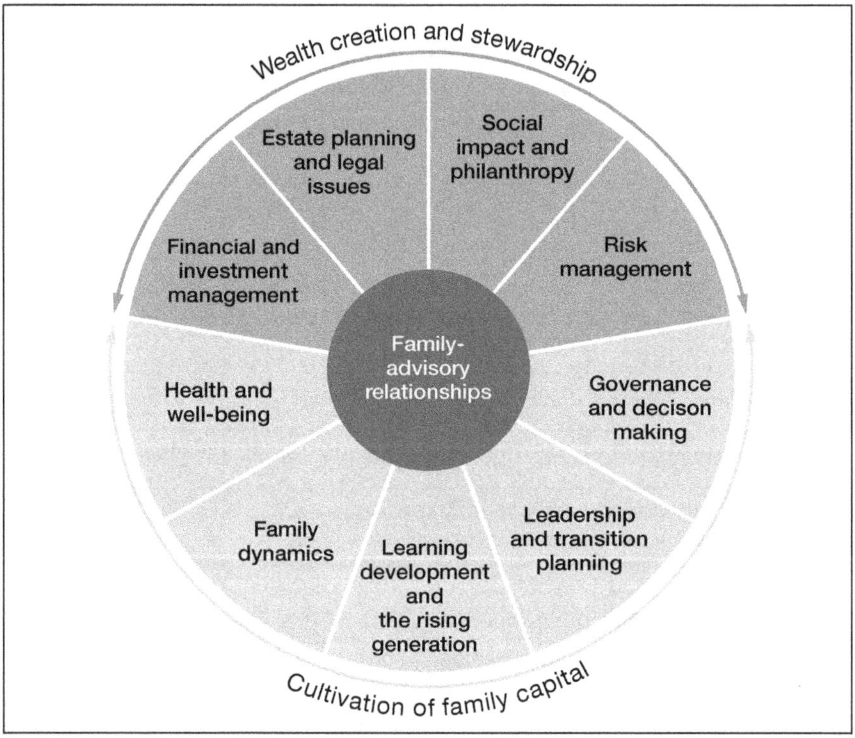

Some advisers may feel uncomfortable raising the topic of philanthropy and see it as a taboo subject. Yet philanthropy is integral to many of the conversations that are already taking place with wealthy families, whether that is about managing reputation or aligning the family's giving with their business. Other key moments to raise the topic of philanthropy include during conversations about the following:

- Starting enterprises – corporate giving options such as pledging a percentage of profits, payroll giving, skills-based volunteering, can be part of businesses from the start.
- Liquidity events – the sale of a business or an inheritance can include

16 The UHNW Institute, Ten Domains of Family Wealth, www.uhnwinstitute.org/our-thinking/. Used with permission. ©2024, The UHNW Institute. All rights reserved. The figure has been adapted for the purposes of reproduction.

philanthropy in the discussions on how best to allocate these new resources.

- Succession – philanthropy is an educational tool for younger generations and can be part of a successful transition from one generation to the next.
- Investments – philanthropy is part of the spectrum of capital and so one tool in the family's portfolio, especially where they are interested in ESG and impact investing.

5. What philanthropy advice covers

At its simplest, advisers offering philanthropy advice bring their technical knowledge and interpersonal skills to guide donors through the many options that giving presents. Table 2 on the next page sets out eight areas of interaction between the donor and adviser.

Every stage and interaction is full of options that need careful consideration and balancing. For example, when thinking about family involvement, who counts as family? Is this about involving children and at what age? Are partners included? What happens when there is a divorce? What level of involvement is expected? What if family members do not want to be involved? What happens if they change their mind later? This is also an iterative process, for example, the dominant values and the issues and causes that are the focus at any one time will depend on which members of the family are involved at different times. Importantly, the adviser cannot use off-the-peg solutions because every family will have their own unique circumstances and aspirations and – as emphasised earlier – they are looking for a personalised approach and tailored guidance.

For those advisers whose prime function is not philanthropy, the minimum requirement is to be comfortable in raising the topic of giving and to have a system in place to refer clients on to the appropriate expertise, for example, to dedicated philanthropy advisers working in community foundations, banks, advisory firms and as independent consultants. Some will be generalists and others will specialise, including in the following ways:

- in working with a particular group of donors such as women or young inheritors;
- through a particular approach such as strategic philanthropy addressing system change or participatory approaches where the communities most affected decide how funds are best allocated; and
- by focusing on a particular cause area, for example, the arts, climate philanthropy or social justice.

Some financial advisers will choose to refer on to specialist advisers while others will want to develop their expertise further and equip themselves to support a family in the initial steps such as exploring their philanthropic values

Table 2: The eight areas of interaction between adviser and donor[17]

Area of interaction	Key questions for donors to ask themselves
1. Financial assessment	Do I have the financial resources to be philanthropic?
2. Values clarification	What deeply held values guide my philanthropic desires?
3. Family involvement	How and to what extent should my other family members be involved, and how are they likely to be impacted by my philanthropy?
4. Structure	What philanthropic instruments fit my tax, financial and legal circumstances (as well as my values), and how will the instruments I choose be created?
5. Actions	What grants will be made or other actions taken to fulfil my plans?
6. Learning and peer networking	What opportunities are there for me to learn more about philanthropy, either from direct experience or from interaction with peers?
7. Collaboration	What opportunities are there for me to collaborate with other donors, and what are the advantages/disadvantages of doing so?
8. Evaluation	How do I define and measure the success of my philanthropic activities?

and interests and developing a giving plan. Some firms will develop an in-house function that offers all aspects of philanthropy advice including establishing a giving structure and managing grant making. The next sections of this chapter are for those looking to develop their advising practice beyond an initial discussion.

6. Philanthropy advice training

As of summer 2024, philanthropy advising is not yet a regulated, established profession with agreed ethical standards and measures of quality and accountability, leading some to call for a more unified, codified profession.[18]

17 Table 2 is the creation of the authors based on data from Thomas E Backer and Lilli Friedland, "Donor Advisors and Philanthropic Strategy" (Human Interaction Research Institute, 2008), www.csun.edu/sites/default/files/finalrep155.pdf, pp1–2.

18 As part of family wealth advising, see James Grubman, Dennis T Jaffe and Kristin Keffeler, *Wealth: 3.0 The Future of Family Wealth Advising* (Family Wealth Consulting, 2023), chapter 7.

The philanthropy advice market and profession is developing, and in the United Kingdom there are appeals to make philanthropy training mandatory for all financial advisers. Globally, there are some training programmes (eg, Chartered Advisor in Philanthropy®) and networks (eg, P150), but it is currently up to individual practitioners and firms to develop their own knowledge and agree their own approach, standards and code of conduct.

Advisers can start to equip themselves for this work through the following:

- Listening – to the communities, experts and change-makers.
- Learning – from the research, articles, reports and podcasts. Our book *Advising Philanthropists: Principles and Practice*[19] contains a rare research-based overview.
- Experience – volunteering their skills to a non-profit, becoming a trustee, joining a giving circle or starting a company giving scheme.

This is in addition to taking up the training that does exist and calling for the training they need.

7. Philanthropy advice tools

There are a range of different tools for advisers to use.[20] Frameworks can help convey to the donor that philanthropy is a journey, and can also break that journey and process into manageable chunks. Figure 2 on the next page sets out the various activities involved and also helps to show that philanthropy advice sits within a wider ecosystem of wealth managers, accountants and lawyers.

The main tool that advisers use is skilled active listening and asking revelatory questions – whether in guided conversations or when facilitating family workshops. These might be used in initial exploratory conversations such as asking the following questions:

- What changes would you like to see in the world?
- What have you given your time and money to in the past, and why?
- What kind of philanthropic family do you want to become?

Some questions can help the conversation to go deeper, for example to identify any particular passion or area of focus:

- Have you encountered a pressing social or environmental issue in your business?
- Has someone inspired you to create a lasting legacy?

---

19 Emma Beeston and Beth Breeze, *Advising Philanthropists: Principles and Practice* (DSC, 2023), www.dsc.org.uk/publication/advising-philanthropists-principles-and-practice.

20 *Ibid*, pp80–89.

Figure 2: Multiple advisers act in different parts of the advice chain

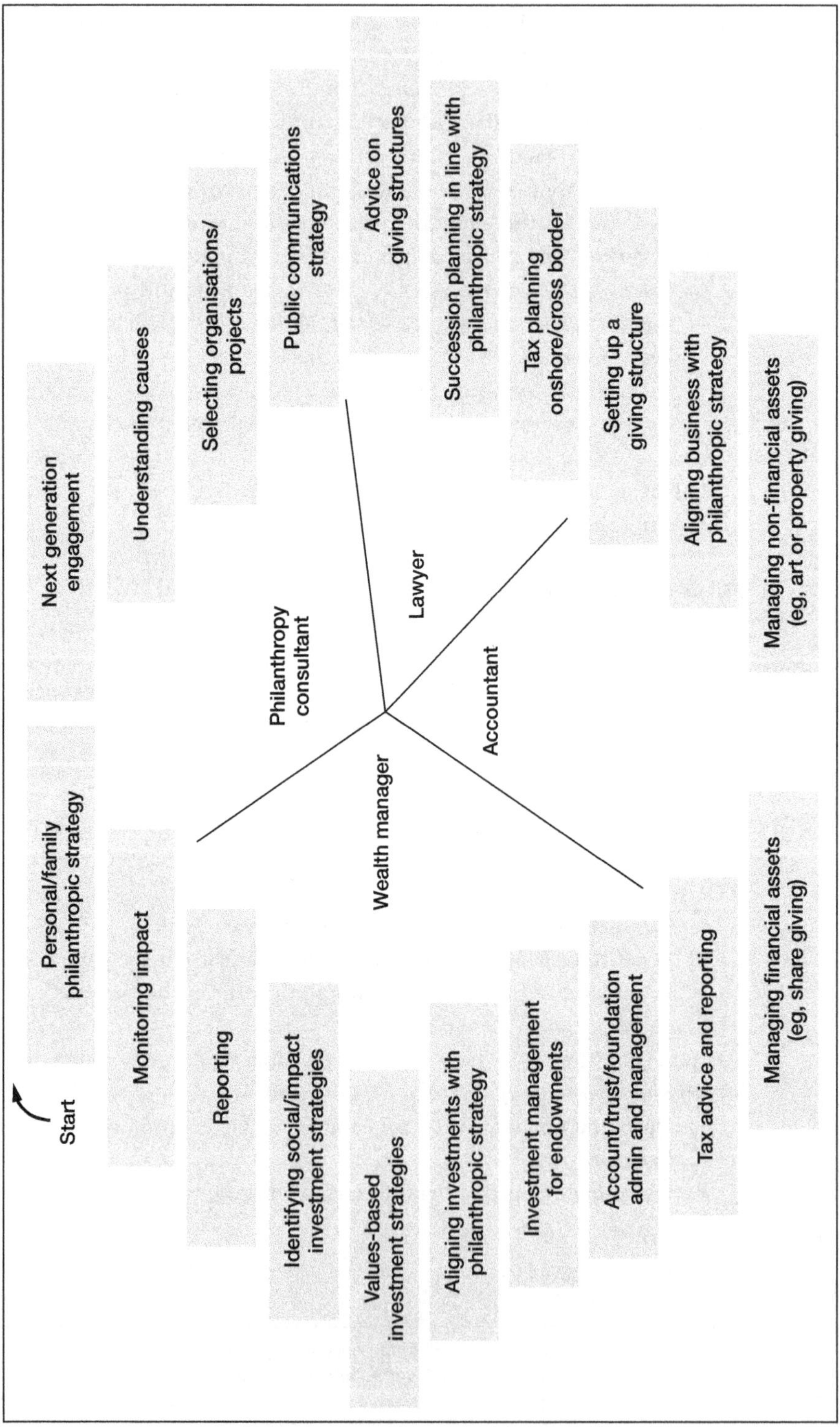

Source: Philanthropy Impact.[21]

Other questions can help to determine parameters, for example:

- What resources can you contribute to your philanthropic endeavours, such as cash, real estate, art, goods, or time?[22]

Another common tool to help identify what kind of philanthropist people wish to become is to use trade-offs to stimulate family discussions. *The Family Philanthropy Navigator* details 32 trade-offs for a family to explore and answer together such as the following:

- Local versus global – does the family want to support its local community or to give abroad where needs are greater?
- Immediate results versus long-term/sustainable results – does the family want to respond to disasters and short-term needs or does it want to pursue lasting change in the long term?
- Perpetual versus draw down – does the family want to allocate the interest earned on an endowment or distribute the entire sum to charitable causes over a set time period?[23]

8. Giving plans

The end result of all these conversations and exercises is to create a giving plan or a roadmap which captures and guides the family's giving intentions. The level of detail will depend on the funds available, the timeline, the family's needs and preferences and where they are on their philanthropic journey. Some plans will simply state how much the family will give and to which causes. Others are complex strategies that will include governance and staffing arrangements, or plans for developing new philanthropic initiatives and succession. Giving plans typically include some or all of the following areas:

- Motivations for giving: why the family wants to give. The values and beliefs that underpin their giving.
- A cause, focus or goal: what is important to the family. What they want their money to achieve – both in the world and for the family itself.
- How the family will give: the approaches that are important to the family such as tackling root causes or supporting new ideas.
- A budget: the amount the family plan to give. For example, a percentage

---

21 Philanthropy Impact, https://23impact.org/.

22 Example questions drawn and adapted from Gayle Jennings-O'Byrne, "Can We Talk? Philanthropic Passions and Motivations", *Investments and Wealth Monitor*, January/February 2016, p48; Kris Putnam-Walkerly, "13 Questions to Ask Your Clients About Philanthropy" (7 June 2022), www.thinkadvisor.com/2022/06/07/13-questions-to-ask-your-clients-about-philanthropy/; "UBS Philanthropy Compass: Shaping Great Wealth" (UBS, 2017), https://advisors.ubs.com/rottenstein/mediahandler/media/323414/ubs-philanthropy-compass.pdf, p22; "Barclays Private Bank Guide to Giving" (Barclays Private Bank, 2024), https://privatebank.barclays.com/content/dam/privatebank-barclays-com/en-gb/private-bank/images/insights/2024/february/guide-to-giving/Barclays%20Private%20Bank_Guide%20to%20Giving%202024.pdf, p11.

23 Peter Vogel, Etienne Eichenberger and Malgorzata Kurak, *Family Philanthropy Navigator: The Inspirational Guide for Philanthropic Families on their Giving Journey* (IMD, 2020).

of business profits or an amount to be given over a number of years, and how they want to allocate this over different categories.

- What the family will give: whether cash or other assets (such as art, cryptocurrencies or shares) and what they will contribute alongside their financial support (eg, time, skills or contacts). This also covers the size, nature and frequency of the giving.
- A time frame: one-year giving plans are common and coincide with financial and tax planning, but a plan can be for any period, and there are increased calls to provide non-profits with multi-year funding.[24] Agreeing a time frame results in acknowledging the need for exit strategies (when and how the family will stop supporting an organisation) right from the start.
- A giving vehicle: the mechanism the family will use to hold and distribute charitable funds, including whether they will give directly or through an intermediary. They may use more than one, such as a foundation for shared giving and separate donor-advised funds for giving by individual members.
- Level of engagement: how involved the family will be in implementing the plan and what relationship they want to have with the organisations they support.
- Others involved: whether the family will collaborate with other funders and which members of the family will be part of the giving plan.
- A review point: plans usually include a date for reflecting on the plan. This is a time to learn from the progress made and any challenges in implementing the plan and to make adjustments for future giving.

The choices involved in creating a giving plan are not easy and always, as indicated above, involve trade-offs. For example, narrowing their philanthropic focus to one or a few causes means the family can develop their understanding and expertise in that area, and maximise their impact by concentrating their resources. A focus provides clarity and cohesion for the family, anchoring their discussions and decisions, and avoids a scattergun approach, where lots of small donations are made to many causes, which dissipates effectiveness and reduces satisfaction. A study of family foundations found that those with a clear mission performed better and that having a clear mission increases the likelihood of a family foundation lasting because it is linked to increased collaboration, enthusiasm and positive dynamics.[25]

---

24 Chris Mills, Liz Firth and Ben Cairns, "Time to End the Dominance of Short-term Grants: The Evidence for Multi-Year Funding (Institute for Voluntary Action Research, 2023), www.ivar.org.uk/wp-content/uploads/2024/02/Time-to-end-the-dominance-of-short-term-grants-the-evidence-for-multi-year-funding-February-2024.pdf.

25 Kelin E Gersick, *Generations of Giving: Leadership and Continuity in Family Foundations* (National Center for Family Philanthropy, 2004), pp187–188.

However, new philanthropists can struggle if they narrow their focus too soon. If a family pins down its mission too early, it can be a constraint if it wants to switch to support other issues and causes. Another downside of deciding on a narrow focus is that it can suggest the idea that the world is divided into separate issues – housing, human rights, environment, health, poverty – when in reality these issues are all interrelated.

Philanthropy advisers need to help their family clients strike the right balance between having a focus that provides a clear steer for funding decisions while still allowing sufficient flexibility to respond to complex and emerging issues, as well as developments in family interests and concerns.

9. Philanthropy advice is multifaceted and about more than giving money

Philanthropy advice is more than taking a family through a set of questions and logical steps to create and implement a plan. There is an art to this work because advisers need to use their judgement to ask the right questions in the right order, manage the pace and depth of the process, and know when to share knowledge and examples. The role varies over time as trust builds and the family gains greater insight. For example, at the start the adviser may encourage the family to 'learn through doing' rather than delay starting until a perfect plan is in place, and then add more rigour over time as the family's experience and confidence grows. As explored below, the adviser's role also encompasses more than the giving of money because people can also provide non-financial support to the causes they care about. Advisers also need to be prepared to have conversations about personal beliefs and values, and to be able to provide donor education and challenge when needed.

9.1 The five Ts of philanthropy

While there is a long-standing focus on the giving of money, or 'treasure', philanthropy involves four other Ts:

- Time – volunteering, including serving on a non-profit board;
- Talent – contributing expertise such as knowledge of HR or budgetary processes;
- Ties – using your connections to make useful introductions to potential supporters; and
- Testimonials – adding your voice to raise awareness or endorse a cause.

Advisers therefore need to help the family identify and think through how to use all their relevant assets. For example, can they provide a non-profit with *pro bono* business skills or office space? Are they comfortable using their name and profile to add weight to a cause? Can they utilise their network to fundraise for the organisations they support?

9.2 Philanthropy is personal

Philanthropy is personal and often emotional – the family may come into wealth through the loss of loved ones; there may be conflict in the family about how much to give away; the family may be passionate about so many things that they are unable to reach a consensus; or they may have some unrealistic expectations about what is possible. So, the philanthropy adviser needs to combine technical knowledge with emotional intelligence and facilitation skills.

There is also a wider context for this work. The decisions of where and how to give are taking place in a world of growing concerns about wealth inequality so philanthropy is under increasing scrutiny. The adviser may need to facilitate discussions around the source of the family's wealth, how they feel about having money, attitudes to inheritance, and the donor's role in society. Useful questions that can help families reflect on the four core principles of accountability, equity, learning and relationships include the following:

- Who are we accountable to and what are we accountable for?
- How are we overcoming the barriers created by our wealth and privilege to listen to, and be guided by, the people closest to the issues?
- What is the origin of our wealth as a family philanthropy? Was any part of the wealth acquired by exploiting people and/or natural resources, or perpetuating or benefitting from inequities?
- How do we actively engage in learning that challenges our preconceived notions and invites a diversity of perspectives?
- How are we attending to family dynamics and are we willing to have empathetic approaches to hard conversations?[26]

9.3 Philanthropy goes beyond the family

In the course of this work, the adviser will likely become involved in relationships beyond the family that is their client. For example, the broader philanthropy ecosystem includes the non-profit organisations that are funded and the communities where that funding has an impact. Advisers can add value through widening the conversation from the family's own motivations and interests to encompass broader social needs. Advisers can source relevant evidence and knowledge on a topic and act as a bridge connecting the wealthy family to those working for social and environmental change, including those with first-hand experience, so that they become more informed givers.

Donor education is often an aspect of the philanthropy adviser role, especially where the family has had little prior contact with non-profit organisations. It is common for donors to have preconceptions about the efficiency and efficacy of non-profits, so the adviser needs to explain how non-

---

26 National Center for Family Philanthropy, "The NCFP Guide for Effective Family Philanthropy" (2023), www.ncfp.org/wp-content/uploads/2023/06/NCFP-Guide-for-Effective-Family-Philanthropy-2023.pdf.

profit organisations work, the challenges they face, and the value of funding to cover core costs such as salaries. The adviser can also introduce different approaches to conducting philanthropy such as trust-based, community-led, collective, prize, reparative, that have had less attention than strategic philanthropy.[27] Advisers often also link families to their peers for mutual support, and to other sources for training and information.

Philanthropy advisers need to decide how much they seek to influence or even challenge the families they work with and on what basis. Advisers can draw on their knowledge to challenge the donor's ideas and provide a reality check, for example, to encourage collaboration with existing efforts rather than founding an unnecessary new charity, or to promote good practice in grant-making.

Advisers need to be upfront about their approach and clear on their motivations. This will determine when they inform the donor of different options and practices, and how much they will challenge the family's assumptions and priorities as part of the process. For example, some advisers may believe in prioritising certain causes over others and encourage clients to support efforts to tackle global poverty and climate change over other issues. Other advisers may take a cause-neutral view and see their role as helping the client to give to things they care about, whatever those are.

10. Challenges specific to family philanthropy

As noted earlier, philanthropy brings benefits to the family: developing skills and relationships, building an identity, supporting family cohesion and creating a legacy. Ambitious claims are made for what family philanthropy can achieve, such as:

> *There is a classic dream of family philanthropy ... Relatives bring their best selves into a room to work together. They listen, express their opinions, make reasoned arguments and find compromises, honour their parents and provide extraordinary models for their children ... Cousins get to know one another. Grandchildren and great-grandchildren hear about their ancestors and learn what their family stands for. And the community sees that this is a family of quality, not just wealthy but generous, and unified in fulfilling its responsibilities.*[28]

---

27 Trust-based philanthropy is an approach that seeks to mitigate power imbalances between funders and fund-seekers, and acknowledges the expertise and trustworthiness of those working to deliver change in their communities. Community-led philanthropy is driven by local people's knowledge, relationships and assets, and may also shift decision making on identifying priorities and resource allocation to them. Collective philanthropy brings a variety of individuals and institutions together to maximise their impact through pooling funds and sharing resources. Prize philanthropy uses large prizes and competition to incentivise innovation by rewarding funds to the best solutions to a problem. Reparative philanthropy acknowledges that wealth comes from extraction and seeks to repair harm through redistributing resources to those who were oppressed in the creation of this wealth. Strategic philanthropy could mean any form of giving that uses a plan to achieve the intended result but is usually used to mean approaches that are evidence-based and impact-driven.

28 Kelin E Gersick, *Generations of Giving: Leadership and Continuity in Family Foundations* (National Center for Family Philanthropy, 2004), pp93–94.

However, working with families brings particular challenges for advisers. Some of these are practical such as – who is the client? For example, the adviser may be engaged by one member of the family and then find out that the key decision maker is someone else, or learn that their appointment was not agreed by a consensus. There are safeguarding issues to be aware of when working with children and young people as well as legal considerations where older members of the family are losing their capacities. Other challenges, explored below, have the potential to undermine the family's giving, making it fall short of the ideal set out in the quote above, if not identified and resolved.

10.1 Family dynamics

It is important to keep in mind that family philanthropy cannot act as a salve for existing family problems and unhealthy dynamics such as sibling rivalries, internal alliances and resentments. If these exist, they will also play out in the family's giving. Areas of conflict include:

- old family squabbles – where previous disagreements fester and lead to unresolved conflicts and frustrations being acted out;
- control issues – for example, where subsequent generations are expected to defer to the founding generation's wishes;[29] and
- poor communication about roles and responsibilities – this can be a source of tension where a family member is not meeting expectations.[30]

Rather than assuming that philanthropy will heal rifts and settle arguments, there is an important role for advisers to act as skilled facilitators to help the family talk about tensions and work together to create shared goals and agreed policies.

10.2 Reduced effectiveness

Keeping involvement within the family can mean a lack of expertise and limited diversity, which may result in suboptimal decisions about their philanthropy. There is sometimes a concern – however unfair – that family members take on philanthropic roles because they are underperforming in the business. This prompts the question whether being a family member is qualification enough, and whether additional non-family expertise needs to be sought.

Where the family wishes to retain full control, criteria can be set for their involvement, such as gaining relevant experience as a volunteer with other

---

29 Jennifer Wegbreit, Deborah Dauber and Ali Sirkus Brody, "Mitigating Challenges in Multigenerational Giving", *Stanford Social Innovation Review* (27 April 2018), https://ssir.org/articles/entry/mitigating_challenges_in_multigenerational_giving#.

30 Caroline W Hodkinson, Jaclyn G Feffer and Donna E Trammell, "Family Dynamics and Philanthropy", Bessemer Trust, www.bessemertrust.com/insights/a-closer-look-family-dynamics-and-philanthropy.

non-profits, before having a say in family philanthropy meetings. An adviser can also provide learning programmes for family members, ensure decisions are informed by wider viewpoints and expertise, and support the family to appoint experienced staff or consultants.

10.3 Multi-generational differences

A key issue for all families is successfully managing the differences across generations. In many families, the older generation has different priorities and outlooks than younger members. For example, younger generations may be more focused on impact and more likely to engage in advocacy for the causes they support. Successful approaches to involving the next generations include ensuring that younger generations have the ability to make decisions and not making children's involvement mandatory.[31] The work of the adviser extends beyond bringing the next generation into the family's existing giving because younger members may be asking the family to embrace new ideas about risk, impact, justice and the purpose of wealth. A successful transition therefore involves the older generation creating space for them to have their views heard and to bring their new ideas and perspectives to shape the family's future giving.

A philanthropy adviser supports families to tackle all these issues so that family members have the expertise they need, develop healthy ways of working together and successfully engage the next generation.

11. Conclusion

Families want to have a positive impact on society and to leave a lasting legacy, so they need advice on their giving. A good adviser brings knowledge of philanthropy and of societal needs, as well as relevant experience, connections and skills to support the family to work together to develop a shared plan for their giving and to ensure it is successfully implemented.

Good philanthropy advice ought to result in more and better giving. There is considerable debate about what counts as 'better', but the role of the adviser can support the family to:

- be more informed and thoughtful givers;
- give effectively and ethically;
- adopt good practice in supporting funded partners;
- understand and listen to the needs of the community;
- collaborate with peers and others who have shared goals; and
- consider issues of social and environmental justice, reparations and equity.

---

31 Fidelity Charitable, "What Works and What Doesn't: Eight Tips for Successful Family Philanthropy", www.fidelitycharitable.org/guidance/family-philanthropy/8-tips-for-successful-family-philanthropy.html.

A philanthropy adviser also has a role in bringing positive benefits to the family such as supporting them to work together across generations and ensuring there are opportunities to learn and develop skills. This is because philanthropy is:

an important mechanism to reinforce a family's identity and values across generations. It has an important role to play in closing the generational divide and helping the next generation to learn about the world they will inherit both inside and outside the family ... philanthropy is a way to bring families together, to emphasise their values and change the world for the better.[32]

Those focused on advising families on matters such as tax or the family business may not have much time to dedicate to philanthropy. However, all those advising the family should understand its value, initiate and engage in conversations about philanthropy, and be able to refer on to a specialist with confidence. For those advisers who get more involved, there are gains for their personal development and job satisfaction as a result of supporting those working to achieve positive social and environmental change, as well as contributing to their business success, and meeting the broader – and arguably more meaningful – goals of the families they advise.

32 Susan U Raymond, Bruce Love and Josh Moore, BNP Paribas/Campden Research Global Family Philanthropy Report *Giving Through the Generations: Demanding Impact, Building Unity, Securing Legacy* (Campden Media, 2009), pp11–12.

About the authors

Guy Abrahams
Partner, Forsters LLP
guy.abrahams@forsters.co.uk

Guy Abrahams is a solicitor practising in the United Kingdom. He advises individuals and families on how to structure the ownership of their assets and businesses to mitigate capital taxes and to ensure orderly succession from one generation to the next. That often involves orchestrating a formal governance process, culminating in changes to the existing ownership structure and constitutional documents of a family's business, whether it be an international trading empire or a landed estate.

Patricia M Annino
Partner, Rimon Law
patricia.annino@rimonlaw.com

Patricia M Annino is a partner at the Boston office of global law firm Rimon. She has been voted by her peers as one of the 'best lawyers in America' (trust and estates), a 'super lawyer', a top 50 Massachusetts female lawyer, Boston Estate Planning Council's 'estate planner of the year' and the initial recipient of EuroMoney/Legal Media's Best in Wealth Management – USA award. She is a former member of the Family Firm Institute (FFI) board of directors and a founding member of the FFI 2086 Society. She is a frequent presenter at FFI conferences, contributor to the *FFI Practitioner* and recipient of FFI's Richard Beckhard Award.

Patricia is a graduate of Newton Country Day School of the Sacred Heart, Smith College (AB), Suffolk University School of Law (JD) and Boston University School of Law (LLM in taxation). She is a fellow of the American College of Trust and Estates Council and a fellow of FFI.

Yannick Archambault
Partner, national leader – family office,
KPMG Canada
yarchambault@kpmg.ca

Yannick Archambault leads KPMG's family office practice in Canada. He and his team collaborate with KPMG's tax, law, audit and advisory professionals across Canada and globally. They deliver independent, objective and multidisciplinary advice and services to business owners, enterprising families, ultra-high-net-worth individuals (UHNWIs) and established family offices.

Yannick brings over 30 years' experience supporting and establishing trusted relationships with UHNWIs and their families. He has held numerous leadership roles within the financial services and private wealth sectors, which includes building single-family offices and multi-family offices, as well as leading as chief operating officer and head of the private wealth and investment management businesses at two of Canada's largest banks, servicing clients in Canada, the United States and Asia. Yannick holds an MBA, and

Chartered Financial Analyst and Family Enterprise Advisor designations. He is also a member of the Family Office Exchange MFO Council, UHNW Institute Leaders Council and Purposeful Planning Institute.

Nic Arnold
UK head, JTC Private Office
nic.arnold@jtcgroup.com

Nic Arnold heads up JTC Group's Private Office based in London. Her team is responsible for supporting a number of families with their international lives, across a range of independent consulting, project management and administrative services.

Nic specialises in family governance consulting, advising high-net-worth clients on the strategic direction of family wealth, operational integrity of their family offices and succession planning for the next generation. In addition, Nic works closely with her wider network to support clients with long-term asset protection and management tools such as trusts and family investment companies.

Nic has significant experience advising clients on luxury assets such as superyachts, private jets and art portfolios, and ensures that they are appropriately guided on ownership and operational matters with these sensitive and complex assets.

Nic is a chartered accountant and chartered tax adviser. Her 25-year career has spanned Anderson, Deloitte and PwC, where she focused on international private clients and headed up the firm's Luxury Asset practice. She is a regular international speaker on the topic of bringing order and resilience to client's lives and has received a number of awards in the private client field.

Hayden Bailey
Partner and head of private client and tax, Boodle Hatfield LLP
hbailey@boodlehatfield.com

Hayden Bailey is the head of private client and tax at leading London law firm, Boodle Hatfield. He has extensive experience in advising family business owners, entrepreneurs and city executives on their wealth and succession planning and UK capital taxation strategy. He also has expertise in advising these clients on partnerships, shareholder issues and corporate governance.

Hayden's notable projects include advising family-run property investment businesses on their family and corporate governance; acting as the long-term strategic adviser for large landed estates on their complex succession planning and structuring of business assets; advising majority shareholders in advance of a company's initial public offering; and safeguarding tax reliefs through transfers into appropriate family trust structures.

Hayden's expertise is widely recognised by the leading legal directories and he is regularly asked to contribute to industry and national press. In 2024 he was announced as one of eprivateclient's 50 most influential – a listing identifying the leading practitioners of the private client professions.

Emma Beeston
Philanthropy adviser
emma@emmabeeston.co.uk

Emma Beeston is an independent philanthropy adviser based in the United Kingdom. She supports families to identify their giving intentions and guides them on how best to contribute their resources in ways that respect those working for social and environmental change. She has over 30 years' experience of the non-profit sector and is an experienced grant-maker and co-founder of a giving circle.

Emma is a member of the P150 philanthropy adviser network, the National Network of Consultants to Grantmakers and a 21/64 certified adviser trained in facilitating multi-generational giving. She co-authored (with Professor Beth Breeze) the first book about philanthropy advising, *Advising Philanthropists: Principles and Practice* (Directory of Social Change, 2023) and teaches on master's programmes at the University of Kent and Bayes Business School. Emma delivers training in philanthropy advising for family offices and financial services professionals.

Victoria Blackburn
Director, JTC Private Office
victoria.blackburn@jtcgroup.com

Victoria Blackburn is a director in the multi-jurisdictional Private Office team at JTC Group. She has worked with UHNWIs and both large and small family offices for two decades while based in the United Kingdom, Jersey and Luxembourg.

She is known as a true 'facilitator' due to her ability get things done and find a solution even in the most challenging of circumstances. Victoria's network is diverse and her ability to see the potential in what can often at first seem the 'intangible' makes her a true visionary. Clients see her as a trusted 'go to' for guidance on all kinds of matters.

Victoria is responsible for JTC Private Office's next-gen education sector, which takes a holistic view, working with the older and the next gen to help build a successful bridge to succession. The approach focuses on four sectors: the two functional sections of business management and financial management, which are interposed with the symbiotic sectors of well-being and crisis management. She is also an expert in the luxury assets sector, with a focus particularly on the marine and aviation space. Victoria often manages large projects such as acquisitions and disposals of these high-value assets as well as helping clients understand the many facets and intricacies involved in running them.

She is an associate of the Chartered Governance Institute, has a master's degree in political science from the University of Nottingham and a BSc in politics from the University of Bristol.

Matthew Braithwaite
Partner, Wedlake Bell LLP
mbraithwaite@wedlakebell.com

Matthew Braithwaite advises UK and international clients, including individuals, families, trustees, beneficiaries and family offices, and in particular acts for high-net-worth individuals and family business owners, professional executives and entrepreneurs. Matthew advises on the establishment and use of trusts and other wealth-holding structures, and on the succession of family trusts and businesses, and governance issues. Matthew also advises on wills and wider estate and succession planning. He is a full-time member of STEP and a member of STEP's Responsible Stewardship of Wealth Thought Leadership Group.

Beth Breeze
Professor of philanthropic studies, Centre for Philanthropy, University of Kent
b.breeze@kent.ac.uk

Beth Breeze is professor of philanthropic studies and director of the Centre for Philanthropy at the University of Kent in the United Kingdom, where she teaches courses to practitioners including philanthropy advisers, grant-makers, charity leaders and fundraisers.

Her research and writing include the annual *Coutts Million Pound Donors Report* (2008–2017);

The Philanthropy Reader (2016, co-edited with Michael Moody); *The New Fundraisers* (2017); *In Defence of Philanthropy* (2021); *Advising Philanthropists: Principles and Practice* (2023, co-authored with Emma Beeston); and *Rich Expectations: Why Rich People Give* (2025, co-authored with Rhodri Davies and Theresa Lloyd).

She shares knowledge and evidence-based insights with the global philanthropy community through keynote speeches, media comment and meetings with policymakers. In recognition of her services to philanthropic research and fundraising, Beth was awarded the OBE in 2022.

Tony Cohen
Partner, Kinestra Partners LLP
tony@kinestrapartners.com

Tony Cohen has been an adviser and confidante to wealthy families for almost 30 years. Leveraging and combining his skills as a proven business leader and coach, he helps his clients enhance their organisational and family prosperity through mentoring, counselling and challenging the *status quo*.

Until 2017, Tony was vice chairman at Deloitte and the firm's global head of private clients, leading a team across the world, dedicated to working with successful entrepreneurs, multi-generational family businesses and family offices.

Tony is a founding partner of Kinestra Partners through which his primary focus now is on consulting to private families, specifically developing their plans and frameworks for the future to support them through change in complex family and business circumstances. In addition to his consultancy work, he is also special adviser to a multi-family office based in London.

Clients praise him for his down-to-earth and practical approach and his relaxed and effective communication style coupled with his continual pursuit of excellence.

Bryony Cove
Partner, private client, Farrer & Co LLP
bryony.cove@farrer.co.uk

Bryony Cove is an experienced private client lawyer working with a broad range of UK and international clients, from individuals and families, to trust companies and family businesses. At the core of her practice is helping clients and their families put in place the most effective strategies to manage the long-term stability and integrity of their estates. Bryony is herself a trustee for a substantial UHNW UK family in business, giving her a unique insight into the challenges clients face from their side of the table.

Justin B Craig
Distinguished professor, Tecnológico de Monterrey; Adjunct professor, Kellogg School of Management; Adjunct professor, Bond University
jcraig@bond.edu.au

Justin B Craig holds multiple academic positions including as a distinguished professor of family enterprise at Tecnológico de Monterrey in Mexico, an adjunct professor at the Kellogg School of Management at Northwestern University in the United States, and adjunct professor of Entrepreneurship and Family Enterprise at Bond University in Australia. His research, primarily focusing on the challenges and opportunities of business-owning families, has been published widely.

Toby Crooks
Partner, trust and wealth services, Rawlinson & Hunter LLP
toby.crooks@rawlinson-hunter.com

Toby Crooks specialises in the field of private client tax as part of the trust and wealth services department. He enjoys working closely with clients, legal advisers and family offices to understand their particular requirements and has a wide breadth of experience, having advised both UK and non-domiciled clients.

Toby is a chartered accountant, chartered tax adviser and a member of STEP. He is the holder of an advanced diploma in international trust management and is a member of PAIAM (Professional Advisers in the Art Market). He was previously the representative for the City of London on the Worldwide Council of STEP and is a member of the public policy committee.

Toby holds a diploma in organisational leadership from the Said School of Business at the University of Oxford.

Dominic Epton
Managing director, Rothschild & Co Wealth Management
dominic.epton@rothschildandco.com

Dominic Epton is a managing director with over 20 years' experience in wealth management and investment banking at Rothschild & Co.

Prior to joining the Wealth Management team in 2011, he worked for five years in Rothschild & Co Global Advisory. He started his career as a lawyer, spending seven years at a global law firm in London. Dom has been recognised by Spear's as one of the industry's leading ultra-high-net-worth advisers. He is a member of the Chartered Institute for Securities and Investments and holds the Private Client Investment Advice and Management certificate.

Matthew Fleming
Partner and head of family governance and succession, Stonehage Fleming
matthew.fleming@stonehagefleming.com

Matthew Fleming is a partner in the Stonehage Fleming group, responsible for helping clients develop and implement their intergenerational strategies. He and his team also support families as they identify and mitigate the risks associated with those strategies, from intragenerational dynamics to effective family communication.

A former army officer, Matthew served in the Royal Green Jackets. As a professional cricketer, he played for Kent County Cricket Club for 13 years and represented England 11 times. He was the fifth generation to work in the family firm when he joined in 2005 and has held various positions within the business, including managing partner of Fleming Media and a director of Ian Fleming Publications and James Bond Enterprises. He was commissioned into the Royal Green Jackets in 1985. Matthew has also had a number of external non-executive appointments, including chairman of AGL Comms, a director of the Norfolk and Norwich Hospital and 10 years as a director of the England and Wales Cricket Board.

Dan Frosh
Board of directors, Family Firm Institute Inc.
dfrosh08@gmail.com

Dan Frosh is a family enterprise adviser who works with enterprising families to help empower them to navigate the complexities of wealth and family dynamics to achieve enduring multi-generational success. Leveraging over a decade of experience as an attorney and family business adviser, Dan guides families to develop successful governance practices, strengthen family unity, plan for leadership and ownership succession, and to align around a collective vision for their future.

Dan formerly served as a senior adviser at Cambridge Family Enterprise Group where he advised leading families from around the world on strategies for the successful continuity of their enterprises.

Dan writes and speaks internationally on topics

relating to family enterprises and wealth and has served as a facilitator in the Future Family Enterprise programme at the MIT Sloan School of Management. He is a fellow of the Family Firm Institute (FFI) where he also serves as the vice chair of the FFI board of directors and is the consulting editor of *FFI Practitioner*, a weekly publication that provides analysis, trends and research that support advisers to family enterprises.

Judy Green
President, Family Firm Institute Inc.
judy@ffi.org

Judy Green is president of the Family Firm Institute and managing partner of Green Associates LLC. She holds degrees from Lawrence University, University of Minnesota, and a PhD from Marquette University as well as a Graduate Certificate in Business and Management from Harvard University Extension School. A frequent author and commentator on topics related to family enterprise, she has received the Barbara Hollander Award and International Award from the Family Firm Institute. Recently she was named one of the top 50 family enterprise advisers by Family Capitol as an "advisor to advisors". Judy is also the editor of a digital magazine, *Olive: A journal devoted to ambiguity.*

Catherine Grum
Director, Catherine Grum Consultancy Ltd
catherine@catherinegrum.com

Catherine Grum advises families and family offices around family office establishment, strategy, family governance and succession. She believes that when families understand their values and the purpose of their wealth, they can build on much stronger foundations. By then aligning their structures and activities with this, she helps them create sustainable long-term solutions.

For more than 20 years, Catherine has helped enterprising families with their needs. She acquired her distinctive insight from her positions as a private client lawyer at A&O, a wealth adviser at Barclays, a leader of a private office and a board member of its international trust companies at Salamanca Group, and a founder of family office advisory practices at BDO and KPMG.

Catherine now runs her own independent consulting business, working with clients from across the United Kingdom and the Middle East. She has an MA in jurisprudence from Oxford University.

Katharine Haggie
Partner, private client and family office services, Rawlinson & Hunter LLP
katharine.haggie@rawlinson-hunter.com

Katharine Haggie advises families and their businesses on a broad range of aspects covering succession, structuring and practical matters, with UK taxation being at the centre of her expertise. She has a broad range of clients across the United Kingdom and internationally, resulting in experience dealing with cross-border and domestic issues.

She enjoys working collaboratively with her clients and their advisers. Her experience extends to valuation work, family office operational and structuring reviews and advising shareholders and companies in transactions.

Katharine is an associate of the Chartered Institute of Taxation, a fellow of the Institute of Chartered Accountants in England and Wales, and a member of the Society of Trust and Estate Practitioners.

Andrew P Hier
Senior adviser and partner, Cambridge Family Enterprise Group
ahier@cfeg.com

Andrew P Hier is a senior adviser and partner at Cambridge Family Enterprise Group and a fellow at Cambridge Institute for Family Enterprise. He is an internationally recognised expert and trusted adviser to multi-generational family enterprises, with particular expertise in the ownership dimension of family enterprises. Since 2003, he has advised family-owned businesses around the world on strategies for growing and passing their enterprises to the next generation.

Andrew has authored important works on the unique ownership challenges of family enterprises, family unity and key diagnostic parameters of family enterprise functionality. In 2020, he received the Family Firm Institute (FFI) Interdisciplinary Achievement Award for outstanding achievement in the advancement of interdisciplinary services to business families.

For over a decade, Andrew has co-taught the advanced family business advisory programme at FFI. He frequently teaches around the world at conferences, education programmes and private family meetings. For several years, he served as a facilitator and guest lecturer at Harvard Business School's Families in Business programme, and now at MIT. Earlier in his career, Andrew was CEO of an international apparel company. Prior to this, he practised law for 15 years, after earning his JD from Harvard Law School and AB from Harvard College.

Nick Jacob
Partner, Forsters LLP
nick.jacob@forsters.co.uk

A partner in the private client team with over 40 years' experience, Nick Jacob is a world renowned specialist in family governance and succession planning. Working with multi-generational business families, Nick makes it a priority to understand the psychology of the family, in order to uncover the issues and deal with these head on. Only then can Nick put in place the necessary legal structures to ensure the successful transition of wealth from one generation to the next.

Nick advises a number of globally significant families, trustees and family offices with assets and family members based in multiple jurisdictions. He specialises in all aspects of cross-border estate planning, especially trusts holding family businesses, that protect against family disputes, including divorce.

With "a phenomenal reputation in Asia", (*Chambers*, 2024), Nick has a particular focus on advising families in East Asia and understands the evolving cultural dynamics facing different generations in this region. This is demonstrated by Nick's recognition as a foreign expert in Singapore in the latest *Chambers HNW Guide*; one of only three individuals named for this expertise. He has also been cast as "The Godfather of Asian family governance".

Nick also specialises in UK taxation for individuals and trusts, cross-border taxation coordination, and advises banks and trust companies on technical issues. Nick is a STEP Emeritus Member and was named "Trusted Advisor of the Year" at the STEP Private Client Awards 2024. He was also Who's Who Global Private Client Practitioner of the Year 2023. Ranked in *The Legal 500*'s Hall of Fame and Band 1 in *Chambers HNW Guide*, Nick is recognised as "a leader in his field" for his "sophisticated private wealth planning advice", and a first class lawyer.

Catharina C Jecklin
Lecturer and researcher, Bond University
cjecklin@bond.edu.au

Catharina C Jecklin is a lecturer and researcher at the Centre for Entrepreneurship and Family Enterprise at Bond University, where she earned her PhD in 2023. Her research examines trust-control dynamics in organisations and their impact on innovation and workplace well-being. With a particular interest in family-owned businesses, Catharina explores how family firms build and leverage trust for long-term success.

Prior to entering academia, Catharina held various management and executive roles in business development and market research, communications and web design, as well as in business consulting. Navigating complex organisational challenges inspired her to translate real-world business issues into rigorous research with practical relevance.

As an educator by training, Catharina is an advocate for teaching cases and has published several Ivey Case Studies related to organisational transformation, trust and control and employee well-being.

Hiral Kanzaria
Partner, business tax, Rawlinson & Hunter LLP
hiral.kanzaria@rawlinson-hunter.com

Hiral Kanzaria is a business tax specialist who advises businesses across a range of industries. He focuses on providing pragmatic and commercially led tax advice, working closely with businesses, shareholders and other stakeholders to provide holistic advice that takes into account both tax-related and wider objectives.

Hiral advises on a range of corporate tax areas, including corporate structuring and restructuring, employee share schemes and international taxation. In addition, he is an M&A tax specialist, having advised on a number of buy and sell side transactions. This has included undertaking tax due diligence, transaction structuring and shareholder tax advice.

Hiral joined Rawlinson & Hunter in 2010. He is a chartered accountant and chartered tax adviser. In addition, he read law at the University of Liverpool.

Lily Kennett
Partner, intelligence and investigations, Schillings
lily.kennett@schillingspartners.com

Lily Kennett is a partner at Schillings and co-founder of the firm's Intelligence and Investigations practice. She is a highly respected adviser to business leaders, family offices and prominent individuals, working on strategy during high-stakes situations and providing counsel on long-term approaches to reputation.

Lily works in collaboration with lawyers, communications professionals, security experts and diplomacy advisers to support clients across the globe. Her work draws on a rich background that spans investigative journalism, international relations and over a decade in corporate intelligence and investigations. Lily spearheads Schillings's *pro bono* programme, which supports a range of non-governmental organisations and individuals working to counter online abuse as well as misinformation and disinformation campaigns online.

Nick Mayhew
Founder and managing director, Alembic Strategy
nick.mayhew@alembicstrategy.com

Nick Mayhew is a facilitator and coach for families who work together or who run an office to manage their wealth. He is a fellow of the Institute of Chartered Accountants, has had a 20-year career leading a major professional firm and has an MSc in the psychology and neuroscience of mental health. He was brought up in a Buddhist community by a psychotherapist. Alembic is a family business, which Nick runs together with his wife Sarah, a physiotherapist and generative coach.

In founding Alembic, Nick embarked fully on a lifelong passion to help people, linking his upbringing in meditation and Tai Chi with his career in company and M&A advisory work. Bringing these two things together means a focus on supporting ambitious business leaders with lots of problems to solve. His specialism is solving family rifts and helping families talk through the difficult things well.

Ken McCracken
Family business consultant, MFBC Limited
ken@m-fbc.com

Ken McCracken is a family business consultant. His work includes succession planning for family enterprises, including creating effective governance; helping clients implement their succession and governance plans, including serving on various family or owners' councils; and education and training for enterprising families and for their advisers.

Ken is co-author of the STEP Advanced Certificate in Advising the Family Business and the Advanced Certificate in Family Business Governance, both of which are provided online to an international audience. He also created and teaches the family business module in the STEP Professional Postgraduate Diploma in Private Wealth Advising. His other published works include *Creating the Trusted Team of Advisers for a Family Business* (Special Report, Globe Law and Business, 2018) and *The Alternative Family Business Dictionary*. Ken is a fellow of the Family Firm Institute.

Victoria O'Byrne
Partner, Schillings
victoria.obyrne@schillingspartners.com

Victoria O'Byrne is a founding partner of Schillings Communications LLP, the firm's recently formed strategic communications business. She draws on 25 years' experience in senior positions across UK business and government, having previously worked for the British royal family and Sir Richard Branson as group director of corporate affairs at Virgin. She was also formerly special adviser to a UK cabinet minister and director of communications for the legacy of the London Olympic and Paralympic Games in 2012.

A highly respected leader in strategic communications, Victoria specialises in working with high-profile and highly scrutinised individuals, organisations and campaigns to build their reputations, grow their coalitions of support and harness opportunity in high-stakes situations.

Katie O'Callaghan
Partner, Boodle Hatfield LLP
kocallaghan@boodlehatfield.com

Katie O'Callaghan is a partner in the family and divorce team at Boodle Hatfield, a private wealth law firm in London. Katie's practice encompasses all aspects of family law with a particular emphasis on complex wealth structures both in the United Kingdom and abroad. Katie offers expert guidance to clients where the majority of the wealth is tied up in family business. This raises issues on divorce not only about the value of the company but also the ways in which funds can be extracted from it to meet any potential entitlement of the other spouse.

She regularly advises clients on potential strategies to minimise the risk of family business assets being attacked on divorce, particularly where a business is owned by family members of various generations.

Katie is also a qualified mediator, helping people who have decided to separate, to end a civil partnership or divorce, or who are trying to deal with changes in family relationships to talk things through. Katie is trained to help clients focus on what really matters to them and their family and to help clients to discuss and agree the best arrangements for the future, whether that be in relation to their children, their money or the practicalities of how life will work in the future.

Gina Pereira
Founder and principal, Dāna Stewardship Advisory
gina@danastewardship.com

Gina Pereira is a wealth steward who helps families build resilience across generations through education, purpose and values. With over 20 years of experience as a lawyer, trustee and philanthropy adviser, Gina offers integrative support to wealth-owning families, including designing education and well-being frameworks that prepare the rising generation for wealth transition and integrating shared values into family governance frameworks, trust structures, philanthropy and other wealth-planning solutions by positioning purpose as the north star.

Gina is leading industry-driven trust and company law reform initiatives and policy developments designed to facilitate responsible stewardship of wealth. She is committed to advancing industry best practices through her various leadership roles, including as chair of STEP's Thought Leadership Steering Committee on the Responsible Stewardship of Wealth, as a board member of the Global Alliance of Impact Lawyers and co-chair of the Bermuda Business Development Agency's High Net Worth Steering Committee. She has proudly led two of her prior firms to receive the esteemed STEP Private Client Award.

Kaajal Prasad
Former partner, family office and private clients, KPMG Australia

Kaajal Prasad has over 16 years' experience advising private clients in all matters related to commercial and business advice, accounting and tax matters, structuring, consolidation and governance. She specialises in working with active family enterprises and family offices to guide them through the challenges of ownership and control, continuity, leadership succession, generational change, structuring, sustainability, governance mechanisms and developing the next generation. Kaajal serves as independent adviser to a number of family enterprise and not-for-profit boards, where she is able to apply her deep commercial expertise for the benefit of her clients.

She particularly enjoys working with family enterprises and their owners because they bring out her empathetic nature as well as her commercial expertise. Kaajal is a chartered accountant, registered tax agent and accredited family business adviser in Australia.

Russell Prior
Managing director, regional head of family governance, family office advisory and philanthropy, EMEA, HSBC Global Private Banking
russell.prior@hsbcpb.com

Russell Prior leads the services providing family governance, family office advisory and philanthropy advice to clients across HSBC Private Banking EMEA. This involves working with family businesses and families on the issues surrounding ownership and wealth transition. Before joining HSBC, Russell was executive director at Charities Aid Foundation and worked for Barclays PLC in large corporate banking and wealth management.

He is chair of the London Community

Foundation, and until recently had been chair of the Bell Foundation for eight years. He has been a trustee of a numerous charitable foundations, ran the 'philanthropy offices' for a number of major philanthropists and held a number of non-executive director positions.

Russell has written numerous articles and spoken at over 200 events on family governance and enterprise succession. He is the author of *Family Governance and Surplus Wealth: Sustaining Family Fortunes* (Globe Law and Business, 2021).

Jennifer Ridgway
Partner, Farrer & Co LLP
jennifer.ridgway@farrer.co.uk

Jennifer Ridgway acts for a wide range of international and UK-based families, individuals and trustees, advising on estate planning, wealth structuring and trust issues. She is committed to working with families, and those that advise them and their often complex structures, to achieve good succession between generations.

A significant part of Jennifer's practice is advising UK and offshore trustees on their duties and decision making, and providing UK tax advice in connection with trust structures. This work has also included advising beneficiaries on what they can expect from their trustees in terms of information and communication, and assisting families (both UK and non-UK families) during the evolution of their structures after a generational shift.

Her experience of trust matters and advice to trustees and families means she is frequently involved in aspects of UK and offshore trust litigation and non-contentious applications to court, and works closely with the firm's contentious trusts and estates team.

Aside from her extensive trust work, Jennifer has particular experience of acting for business-owning families, individuals involved in the arts, and active landed estates.

Jennifer is used to engaging with family offices and dealing with families who may have multiple branches or individuals with different needs. She is particularly used to assisting with managing confidentiality between branches, family members and the family office, and has assisted families with frameworks and protocols to manage communication and disclosure in this context.

Clients look to Jennifer as a trusted adviser and appreciate her sensitive and thoughtful approach to complex family matters, including difficult issues such as capacity, family breakdown and reputation concerns, as well as her technical expertise.

Alexandra Sharpe
Partner, Kinestra Partners LLP
alex@kinestrapartners.com

Alexandra Sharpe has spent over 15 years dedicated to working with family businesses, family offices and wealthy families, supporting them through generational change. As a specialist consultant, mentor and facilitator, her background as a chartered accountant, coupled with her master's degree in organisational and social psychology from the London School of Economics, enables her to navigate both the commercial and personal priorities that are important to her family clients.

Previously, Alex was a partner in a boutique family enterprise consulting firm, which was acquired by Deloitte in 2014. As a partner in Deloitte, she became national head of the firm's family enterprise consulting practice, where she led and oversaw projects ranging in focus from family succession planning, next-generation development and education to the creation of new family office structures.

Through Kinestra Partners, which she founded in 2018, Alex is now focused on personally working with a select group of significant family clients. Alongside her busy consulting practice, she also has a number of governance roles within family and family business structures. She is the non-family chairwoman for three different family councils, each with their own complexities, and has previously chaired various other family decision-making entities including the protector committee for a global family structure. Alex also has experience of remuneration committee membership and currently serves as member of a group board remuneration committee, representing the family's voice in this decision-making process.

Clare Stirzaker
Partner, Boodle Hatfield LLP
cstirzaker@boodlehatfield.com

Clare Stirzaker specialises in succession planning and related legal and tax matters for multi-generational families and their family offices. She works alongside some of the world's leading private businesses, and her practice focuses on helping individuals develop their succession planning strategy and design bespoke asset holding and wealth management structures including private trust companies, limited partnership structures and foundations.

Clare has particular experience of advising and supporting families on implementing family and corporate governance frameworks to support successful wealth transition. She also supports clients in developing their philanthropic strategy to enable greater and more effective wealth distribution. She is recognised for her work having won multiple awards from the leading private wealth award bodies.

Prior to joining the firm, Clare was a partner at PwC and also worked at Barclays Wealth, providing her with a real breadth of experience and commercial insight across the private client sector.

Katharine Taylor
Client adviser, Rothschild & Co Wealth Management
katharine.taylor@rothschildandco.com

Katharine Taylor is a client adviser at Rothschild & Co Wealth Management UK, having joined the firm in early 2016. Prior to Rothschild & Co, she worked for HSBC Private Bank and before that Barclays Wealth with a focus on clients working within the media and entertainment industries.

She has more than 20 years' experience working with high-net-worth individuals, families and charity clients. After obtaining a geography degree from Oxford University, she began her career in 1998 by training with PwC as a tax consultant and is a qualified accountant. When not juggling family life, she enjoys being involved with The Access Project mentoring and tutoring students from less privileged backgrounds, being a school governor and sitting on one of the balance and inclusion committees at work.

Daniel Ugur
Partner, Forsters LLP
daniel.ugur@forsters.co.uk

Daniel Ugur advises international individuals, families, trustees, beneficiaries, family offices and private banks on succession planning, personal taxation and trust law. One of Daniel's particular areas of focus is on the succession of family businesses, where he works with the family to set up family governance measures to help succession planning run smoothly. He also specialises in advising families who are either based in Asia or looking to move to or from the region. As such, he is a regular visitor to Asia on business to service his clients there.

Maria Villax
Head of family governance and strategy, Bedrock Group
maria.villax@bedrockgroup.com

Maria Villax advises families on the development and implementation of solid family governance structures to prepare for sustainable generational transitions. From family businesses to family offices, she helps families manage the complexity of family ownership to promote long-term unity. She also creates next-generation development programmes, designed to help the next generation become responsible owners for the future.

Maria started her career as a lawyer in Lisbon, specialising in criminal litigation and intellectual property. She then moved to London to study an MBA at Hult International Business School, focusing on leadership and communication. After a brief stint in the fashion industry, she then started consulting for family businesses and family offices around the world on governance best practices. As a third generation of a family business herself, helping families prepare for the long term is a purpose that deeply calls to her.

About Globe Law and Business

Globe Law and Business was established in 2005. From the very beginning, we set out to create legal books that are sufficiently high level to be of real use to the experienced professional, yet still accessible and easy to navigate. Most of our authors are drawn from Magic Circle and other top commercial firms, both in the United Kingdom and internationally.

Our titles are carefully produced, with the utmost attention paid to editorial, design and production processes. We hope this results in high-quality publications that are easy to read and a pleasure to own.

In 2021, we were very pleased to announce the start of a new chapter for Globe Law and Business following the acquisition of law books under the imprint Ark Publishing. Our law firm management list is now significantly expanded with many well-known and loved Ark Publishing titles.

We have also launched an online content platform, Globe Law Online, which allows for easy access across firms. Details of all titles included can be found at www.globelawonline.com. Email glo@globelawandbusiness.com for further details and to arrange a free trial for you or your firm.

We'd very much like to hear from you with your thoughts and ideas for improving what we offer. Please do feel free to email me on sian@globelawandbusiness.com. Happy reading and thank you for your time.

Sian O'Neill
Managing director
Globe Law and Business
www.globelawandbusiness.com